MW00884712

MEDFLY

Also by, Jerry Scribner

Chapter 19, State Government's Role, "A Guidebook to California Agriculture,"
By Faculty and Staff of the University of California, (Edited by Ann Foley Scheuring)

UNIVERSITY OF CALIFORNIA PRESS Ltd. London England 1983, pp 347-366
Chapter 6, Public Policy Considerations: The Medfly Case History, "Eradication of Exotic Pests, Analysis with Case Histories," Donald L. Dahlsten, Richard Garcia Editors, Hilary Lorraine, Associate Editor
Yale University Press, New Haven and London 1989, pp 74-86

MEDFLY

The
Untold Story of California's
Battle Against the
Mediterranean Fruit Fly

Jerry Scribner

For my wife, Penny Scribner, who supported my two-year absence on the Medfly Project, 60+ years of living with me and helping me finish this story.

And

For the dedicated men and women who worked tirelessly to save California and the nation from this truly frightening pest

CONTENTS

Preface

PREFACE

On June 5th,1980, a single Mediterranean fruit fly was trapped in Los Angeles. The discovery of the world's most destructive pest of more than one hundred species of fruits and vegetables grown in California led to an all-out attack to prevent it from spreading and ruining the state's largest industry—Agriculture. Then, on the same day, 300 miles away in San Jose in Northern California, where it was believed the flies could not survive, two more wild flies were trapped. As more flies were trapped in both locations, Federal and State agricultural officials released millions of sterile medflies to breed with the foreign flies. This innovative and hopeful strategy, known as the Sterile Insect Technique (SIT), quickly overwhelmed the invasion in Los Angeles. By December, the foreign flies in the South had been eliminated.

However, in the North, the SIT strategy proved to be too little too late. The foreign flies continued to breed, and by December, at least 100 square miles of suburbia were infested. The State project manager resigned. Federal and State agricultural officials announced that they planned to aerially spray the entire infested area with the pesticide Malathion mixed with fly bait. This method had saved agriculture in Florida and Texas from earlier medfly invasions there. Outraged residents immediately opposed the aerial pesticide plan, successfully blocking its implementation. On Monday, December 15th, the spraying was postponed until the end of January. The Chairman of the Legislature's Agriculture Committee then demanded a high-level agricultural official take over the project. Two days later, I learned I would be that official and that I needed to find an acceptable alternative to aerial spraying by the following Monday, five days away from when a legislative hearing had been scheduled in San Jose to hear the new plan.

Over the next two years, the California Medfly eradication program became the largest, longest, and most controversial eradication project in the history of the United States. The issue reached the California Supreme Court, the U.S. Supreme Court, and

President Reagan. Both the State Senate and Assembly voted to force aerial spraying of Malathion. California Governor Jerry Brown was threatened with impeachment. Japan and other countries banned exports of medfly host fruit from California.

As in all wars, mistakes were made. The men, women, and children trapped in the path of our eradication effort—could not escape the consequences of the decisions we made. Thousands of automobiles were damaged. Lawsuits claiming damage and personal injuries related to the spraying were filed and litigated for years after.

Until now, no one has written a contemporaneous account of this important chapter in the history of California. It is a story worth telling and one that illustrates the difficulty of responding to a biological emergency in a pluralistic democracy. Who decides when governmental action is required? Which government—should decide, local, state, or national? If human health is at risk, what rights does each citizen retain? These questions divided the country during Covid 19. They will again when the next biological threat arises. Growing food without destroying our natural environment and our health remains as important as ever.

My hope is that this personal history of California's battle with the medfly will help us understand the challenges inherent in reacting to similar environmental and health crises in the future.

BOOK

ONE

1911-1980

Chapter 1. (The Medfly and Malathion)

Ceratitis Capitata, the Mediterranean fruit fly, is only one of more than 500 species of fruit flies. Yet, it has long been recognized as the most important. A native of Africa, it spread around the Mediterranean and then around the world in the 1800s until reaching Hawaii by 1906. Medflies are now present across the globe, with more than 60 countries infested from the Mediterranean to South America, Central America, the Caribbean, and Australia. They reached Hawaii in the early 1900s. However, the continental United States has remained medfly-free by spending millions of dollars annually to prevent arrivals and, failing that, eradicating those medfly invasions that threatened to become permanent.

The medfly's unparalleled destructiveness is due to its phenomenal reproductive capacity and ability to place its egg-producing maggots in hundreds of species of fruits and vegetables. Adult medflies are elusive. The best available insect traps often only catch one out of 2,000 nearby. The most likely carriers of new foreign pests are people. In the case of the medfly, a piece of fruit from an infested country or Hawaii would likely contain eggs or maggots of both sexes and thus can be thought of as a biological ark or timebomb. Discarded in the garbage or almost anywhere outdoors just one piece of fruit is all that is needed to start a medfly infestation. By the time adult medflies are detected, thousands of female medflies may be roaming like bees through backyards, fields, or orchards. Each mated female "has the capacity to produce over 1,000 eggs in her lifetime." The females use the ovipositor on their rear end to puncture the skin of any available fruits and vegetables and place a few eggs in each. Pathogens enter through the puncture to promote rot. Meanwhile, in one or two days, the eggs become larvae (maggots) tunneling and fattening on the pulp as they mature through several life stages called instars. In less than a week, the host has turned into rotting, inedible and unmarketable mush. At this point, the maggots drop to the ground with or without what's left of the ruined fruit. There, they pupate into new adults. The entire life cycle from egg to new adult takes as little as three and a half to four weeks with each generation exponentially larger than the last. In addition, it has no known natural enemies in California or other tropical and

Mediterranean climates that can reduce its numbers more than marginally. Thus, the only way to grow host crops once medflies become an established endemic pest is by continuously spraying pesticides weekly or every ten days. Even then, much of the crop may be damaged and often, the fruit cannot be exported as many countries not already infested will reject imports from infested countries unless they are first fumigated to kill any eggs or larvae inside.

More than 100 crops grown commercially in California are subject to medfly devastation. The list includes oranges, lemons, grapefruit, limes, tangerines, peaches, nectarines, plums, apricots, persimmons, cherries, apples, avocados, pears, grapes, tomatoes, peppers, olives, figs, kumquats, walnuts, berries of all kinds and dozens of others. In addition, the fruit trees and gardens of millions of homeowners are equally subject to ruin by the medflies' voracious maggots.

In 1898, ships carrying fruit spread the medfly to Australia, devastating its fruit crops. Hawaii was officially declared infested in 1910. The following year, dock workers spotted medfly maggots crawling out of fruit being unloaded in San Francisco. California's fruit growers demanded Governor Hiram Johnson find a way to keep the flies from entering and ruining California as they had so many other countries. Johnson promptly dispatched entomologist A.C. Carnes of the State's Insectary to Hawaii with instructions to assess the danger and recommend steps to protect California. Carnes booked passage on the first ship available, and as soon as it docked in Honolulu, he raced off the ship and cut open three mangoes purchased at a nearby local fruit stand. All three were crawling with maggots. Next, he bought and cut open oranges, peaches, figs, and grapes and found maggots in each. Upon returning, he reported, "The Med fruit fly will be on the islands as long as they are above water."

Carnes's report spurred Governor Johnson to call the California Legislature into a Special Session on Christmas Eve at the end of 1911. Two-thirds of the members were already set to leave that day on the 3:30 train. An Urgency bill was passed unanimously after only forty minutes of debate. It created a new state quarantine law allowing inspectors to refuse entry to any fruit or plant host of the medfly as well as other members of the Tephritidae family of fruit flies, such as the Oriental fruit fly and the Melon fly. Johnson promptly signed the bill, making it effective immediately. Less than two weeks later, in early 1912, sixty-eight cases of pears arriving on the Steamer Tahiti were found infested with Mediterranean fruit flies. O.E. Bremmer, the chief quarantine inspector in San Francisco, ordered them destroyed. The San Francisco Examiner reported that the consignee of the fruit intended to contact the Governor and sue as the shipment was worth $1,700. Unfazed, Bremmer said, in effect, go ahead noting that:

> The district from which this fruit was shipped is now
> practically without a citrus tree as a result of the
> Mediterranean fruit flies work. [Furthermore] It makes
> little difference what Marcuse & Co. think about this
> matter. By the terms of the bill just signed by the
> Governor, we have the authority to confiscate and destroy
> any fruit entering this port found to be infested with the
> fruit fly.

In 1912, California successfully sought similar legislation at the federal level. Fruit and vegetable production soared as California built the largest and most stringent pest exclusion and detection system in the nation. In the 1920s, the state added vehicle inspection stations straddling major highways entering California, while federal quarantine inspectors guarded international points of entry, such as airports and harbors. Exclusion efforts for the medfly and other pests were backstopped by agricultural commissioners in each county trained to detect foreign plant and animal pests that managed to get by the first line of defense. The commissioners maintained and monitored an extensive system of thousands of insect traps. They also relied on reports from veterinarians, nurseries, farmers, and residents. They were supported by California's control and eradication staff at the California Department of Food and Agriculture (CDFA) in Sacramento, mirrored by similar staff at the U.S. Department of Agriculture (USDA) in Washington D.C. and later Hyattsville, Maryland. They operated like a pest-fighting fire department with personnel capable of being mobilized to conduct specific pest and eradication and control programs at a moment's notice. This pro-active pest exclusion, detection, control, and eradication system, combined with a Mediterranean climate and water, turned California's valleys, especially the Central Valley, into a veritable Garden of Eden supporting hundreds of different crops.

For the next six decades, California's natural barriers of mountains in the north and east, deserts to the south, and the Pacific Ocean on the west enabled it to exclude the medfly and other foreign pests. If there were occasional undetected medfly arrivals between 1912 and 1975, none survived to become a breeding population. Florida and Texas were not as lucky. Medflies invaded Florida in 1929, 1956, 1962, and 1963, and Texas in 1966. In 1929, only a massive, brutal two-year battle that included uprooting and burning thousands of infected trees, roadblocks, and spraying arsenic-based pesticides saved Florida's citrus industry. The National Guard was called out, and the combined federal-state campaign cost millions of pre-depression dollars. Until California's 1980-82 battle, the 1929 Florida fight held the record for the most expensive eradication program in U.S. history.

Medflies invaded Florida again in 1956. A Florida homeowner in Miami was the first to report maggots in a backyard grapefruit tree. Overnight, the rapidly multiplying medflies spread through South Florida citrus, tomato, and winter vegetable fields. As had happened in 1929, the medflies quickly occupied a huge swath of the state. USDA and Florida's agriculture department initially mobilized hundreds of workers to fight the flies using jeep-mounted sprayers applying the pesticide malathion mixed with a protein-based fly bait. However, the ground attack proved no match for the medflies' explosive reproduction and rapid spread. The jeeps were replaced by a fleet of multi-engine WWII heavy bombers and assorted smaller planes, each outfitted to spray the bait faster and farther. The malathion bait papered everything below with tiny droplets of the poison bait. The millions of hungry new flies emerging daily were attracted to the bait and died upon ingesting it, and this eliminated the infestation over a period of months. No human health problems were reported from the use of malathion. The low-level

12

flights by the multi-engine bombers, including a B-17, rattled the nerves and dishes of urban residents, and thousands of automobiles speckled with the bait suffered minor paint damage. One of the malathion-laden two-engine CV-82 bombers under contract to USDA crashed, killing the five-member crew. Fortunately, the crash did not occur over occupied dwellings but instead at an airport while attempting to land. The two-year battle covered 28 counties from Orlando to Key West and cost a reported eleven million dollars. Medflies returned to Florida again in 1962 and 1963. Each time, smaller numbers were quickly eradicated using the aerial malathion bait technique.

In 1966, Texas' citrus was invaded. As had happened in Miami, the first report came from a homeowner in the city of Brownsville, Texas, in the Rio Grande Valley, who complained her backyard grapefruits were full of worms. Inspectors identified them as medfly maggots, and once again state and federal officials aerially sprayed malathion bait. The low-level flights over the city of Brownsville and nearby commercial groves of ruby red grapefruit damaged automobile paint, but there were no reported human health problems. The pesticide malathion continued to be a popular and widely used over-the-counter pest control for gardeners, but public tolerance of aerial spraying malathion and other pesticides over cities for medflies and mosquito control began dropping even before the spraying in Texas.

In 1962, Rachel Carson's carefully researched and beautifully written *Silent Spring* profoundly changed awareness of the fragility of our environment, especially with respect to the use of pesticides and other chemicals. In response to *Silent Spring*, the Environmental Protection Agency (EPA) was created to regulate chemicals and pesticides nationwide. Further legislation mandated clean water, and Congress passed the Clean Air Act. In *Silent Spring*, Rachel Carson criticized malathion, noting that it was an organo-phosphate and that organic phosphates are among the most poisonous chemicals in the world." She wrote:

> The origin of these chemicals has a certain ironic
> significance. Although some of the chemicals

themselves—organic esters of phosphoric acid--- had been known for many years, their insecticidal properties remained to be discovered by a German chemist, Gerhard Schrader, in the late 1930s. Almost immediately the German government recognized the value of these chemicals as new and devastating weapons in man's war against his own kind, and work on them was declared secret. Some became nerve gases. Others became insecticides.

In addition to the veiled reference to the Nazi holocaust, she questioned the human health safety of malathion, including its use in medfly eradication Programs.

Malathion, another of the organic phosphates is almost as familiar to the public as DDT, being widely used in gardening, in household insecticides, in mosquito spraying, and in such blanket attacks on insects as the spraying of nearly a million acres of Florida communities for the Mediterranean fruit fly. It is considered the least toxic of the organic phosphates, and many people assume that they may use it freely and without fear of harm. Commercial advertising encourages this comfortable attitude.

Most significant to the aerial spraying debate about human health, however, was her speculation that some people, due to individual characteristics, such as the absence of a needed enzyme, might face a substantially higher health risk from malathion than the average person and might suffer severe health consequences or even die. She wrote:

The alleged "safety' of malathion rests on rather precarious ground, although—as often happens—this was not discovered until the chemical had been in use for several years. Malathion is "safe" only because the Mammalian liver, an organ with extraordinary protective powers, renders it relatively harmless. The detoxification is accomplished by one of the enzymes of the liver. If,

14

> however, something destroys this enzyme or interferes
> with its action, the person exposed to malathion receives
> the full force of the poison. (Emphasis mine)

The quotes above drove the public controversy in California over spraying the pesticide Malathion over an urban population. Managing the depredations of insects that destroy the food we need for human survival was not the issue. Medflies and mosquitoes have few friends. However, no matter how thoroughly Malathion had been studied and widely used, in the past. By 1975, When medflies appeared in California in Los Angeles, the public trust in pesticides had declined markedly. Fortunately, a new eradication strategy had been developed and tested by USDA. This new approach—releasing sterile medflies, mostly avoided the use of pesticides.

It would be another five years before I heard anything about medflies or how to eradicate them. I did, though, know Malathion killed stable flies. My wife and I lived with our horses on two and a half acres in Carmichael, a suburb of California, one block from the new unoccupied Governor's mansion built for Governor Ronald Reagan, whose term ended in December 1974.

On January 6, 1975, all 120 members of the California Legislature crowded into the Capital's ornate Assembly chamber to witness the inauguration of the youngest governor to be elected in more than a hundred years, Edmund G. (Jerry) Brown. After the eight-year conservative reign of Ronald Reagan, frustrated Democrats eagerly anticipated a new era of bold ideas and a return to the pro-growth policies of Brown's father, former Governor Edmund G. (Pat) Brown. That didn't happen. The younger Brown, a former Jesuit seminarian, openly questioned whether the government could or should solve every problem. Frugal, both personally and fiscally, he advocated sustainability, not growth, as the proper goal. He wanted to hold the line on taxes and live within the current revenue. In addition to fiscal responsibility, Brown called for curbing the power of lobbyists, protecting California's environment, and improving the rights and protections of farm workers. As a former legal aid attorney and now a liberal legislative staffer, I found Brown's inaugural speech a welcome change from Reagan's expansive pro-growth, top-down platitudes, and anti-government philosophy.

Jerry Brown and I were not acquainted in 1975. However, our paths paralleled each other as we began careers in law and politics that would soon intersect. Jerry Brown graduated from UC Berkeley two years ahead of me. Like others in our generation, we shared a commitment to civil rights and the environment. In the summer of 1963, as a Yale law student, Brown had briefly gone to Mississippi to support the work of the Student Non-Violent Coordinating Committee (SNCC) to end discrimination there. A year later, as a first-year student at Berkeley's law school, I marched with thousands of students protesting the University's efforts to restrict SNCC from collecting voluntary donations as students entered the campus. Later, I risked expulsion by sitting-in around a police car immobilized in front of the Chancellor's offices. I also met personally with Mario Savio, the leader of the protest known as the Free Speech Movement, to propose a peaceful solution. Brown reportedly talked with Savio by telephone, trying to broker a truce before 700 students invaded and occupied the campus administration building. After the mass arrests, I and other law students helped the defense attorneys.

During my last two years of law school, I worked part-time as a law clerk for the Legal Aid Society in West Oakland. In April 1967, both Jerry Brown and I, although we didn't know each other then, joined a small candlelight vigil protesting capital punishment outside the gates of San Quentin prison across the Bay from Berkeley. That night, Aaron Mitchell, a young Black man from Sacramento, became the only person executed during Ronald Reagan's eight years as Governor. No one would be executed in California during any of Brown's four terms as Governor of California.

In 1968, I became one of 100 young lawyers nationwide awarded a paid fellowship by Lyndon Johnson's Office of Economic Opportunity. After training in Philadelphia, I served as a poverty lawyer with the Sacramento County Legal Aid Society. Three years later, in December

1971, believing I could do more for the poor by working to change the laws that disadvantaged them, I took a pay cut to move to a legislative assistant position with the California State Senate. My new boss, State Senator Anthony Beilenson, a Harvard-educated lawyer widely admired for his intelligence, collegiality, and effectiveness, warned me I would be disappointed at how little we could accomplish.

I was not disappointed. Over the next three and a half years, I drafted dozens of bills on consumer issues related to auto repair, abusive loan and collection practices, and other laws oppressing the poor. Beilenson chaired the Senate Health Committee, so I also drafted health bills, including a bill that allowed minors to receive birth control without parental permission. Because Governor Reagan had earlier vetoed this proposed Beilenson legislation, I suggested the new bill insert the words "or the prevention of" in front of existing law allowing minors to receive pregnancy care without parental permission. It passed, and this time Governor Reagan signed it. Beilenson and I also eliminated both the word and the concept of children being illegitimate with another bill that grafted the Uniform Parentage Act onto existing California law.

Although I loved working for Beilenson, in January 1975, after watching Governor Jerry Brown's inaugural address on the TV monitor in Beilenson's office, I submitted my resume to the Governor's office with a cover letter describing my years as a legal aid attorney and legislative assistant. I never received a reply. However, I soon forgot about it because Beilenson became Chairman of the powerful Senate Finance Committee in April and made me the committee's chief of staff. I supervised six analysts who, with the help of the Legislative Analyst's Office, reviewed each year's state budget. In addition, we reviewed every bill of fiscal consequence before it could reach the Governor's desk.

California's first major medfly infestation occurred in September 1975 in Los Angeles County. Farmers grew thousands of acres of citrus and other medfly host fruits in the 4,000 square mile County. No county in the state had more medfly traps in place than Los Angeles County, and none had a staff as large and well-trained. The medflies were discovered near the coast and only blocks from a major yacht harbor with international visitors. The Los Angeles International Airport (LAX) was nearby. Passengers from around the world arrived daily at LAX and on cruise ships from Hawaii, Mexico, and South America at the largest port on the West Coast in Long Beach. The flies could have come from anywhere. I heard nothing about it in Sacramento. Years later, I learned I didn't because there was no controversy. When the first flies were trapped, Paul Engler, the county's agricultural commissioner, immediately took charge. He ordered inspectors to put out more traps and to start cutting open fruit to look for signs of maggots. USDA and CDFA were alerted, and a joint federal-state-county eradication program was quickly assembled under Engler's command. USDA scientists had recently finalized the new SIT approach that relied on releasing sterilized medflies to breed with the fertile invaders out of existence. Therefore, this approach was implemented instead of the aerial malathion bait spraying. If the 1975 Los Angeles medfly program made the news in Sacramento, I didn't see it.

The Sterile Insect Technique (SIT) grew out of decades of research at the USDA and the International Atomic Energy Administration in Vienna (IAEA). The USDA research initially focused on another troublesome fly, the screwworm fly. Screwworm flies reproduced using the same four-stage process as fruit flies (egg-larvae-pupae-adult). However, instead of fruit, female screwworm flies placed their eggs in the open flesh wounds and eyes of wild animals and cattle. Their maggots fattened on the live host animals' flesh before tunneling through the animal's hide to drop to the ground and pupate. The exit wounds created more exposed flesh, allowing more flies to lay eggs in the animal. The result was weight loss, permanent scarring, and, in some cases, a painful death. Pesticide spraying provided only limited control of the flies. Releasing sterilized screwworm flies worked better in significantly lowering the total presence of new flies.

IAEA's research established the process of sterilizing flies in the pupal stage with the right amount of cobalt radiation to ensure sterility upon emergence while leaving the male flies vigorous enough to seek out and compete with wild males for mating opportunities with wild females. USDA and IEAE also perfected other critical elements of the SIT strategy, including protocols for attractants to detect the presence of medflies and the techniques required to raise millions of insects in a laboratory setting. They also established procedures for shipping the irradiated pupae from overseas labs to the infestation project and incubating the pupae until emergence. After sterile flies were released by air or ground, success depended on monitoring trap catches in the infested area to ensure that enough sterile flies were being released over a period of months to maintain a 100-1 ratio of sterile to wild flies. This required inspecting each fly caught in a trap for evidence of a florescent dye applied to sterile pupae. Undyed flies caught in traps were presumed wild until dissected and identified as wild males or females and, if the latter, whether unmated or mated. Experiments on a Caribbean Island proved the technique could eradicate screwworm flies from a limited area. Later tests in Hawaii on the island of Lanai and on Rota, an island in the northern Marianas infested with medflies, proved SIT could be effective in eradicating a medfly infestation in a specific geographic area.

The 1975 Los Angeles medfly invasion became the first real-world test of whether SIT could eradicate a medfly invasion on the U.S. mainland. Dr. Roy Cunningham from the USDA Agricultural Research Service (ARS) in Hawaii served as the principal scientific advisor on the 1975 project. By the end of week one, overseas USDA labs in Hawaii and Costa Rica began shipping irradiated pupae sprinkled with powdered fluorescent dye to Los Angeles. The project incubated each shipment of pupae on site to complete their emergence as adults, then released them by air and roving trucks over the next four months. A half-billion sterile flies were released over the course of the successful 1975 eradication. Technicians sorted the trap catches during the same period, looking for any flies without dye, to determine whether a trapped fly was wild or irradiated. The CDFA insect identification lab in Sacramento made the final determination. Over the next seven weeks, the eradication team trapped a total of 77 wild medflies and discovered 12 sites with maggots. On November 14th, less than 60 days after the first discovery, a trap yielded the infestation's final wild fly. After continued extensive trapping for six more months, California was again officially medfly-free.

Even though Senator Beilenson represented a coastal district in Los Angeles and served on the Senate Agriculture Committee, I never heard a word about the medfly or its successful eradication. The 1975 infestation went so smoothly under the management of the joint federal/state/county civil service operation that it garnered little notoriety or interest beyond Los Angeles and in the farm press. Medfly just was not on the political radar in 1975 like it would be in 1980.

Chapter 2. (Chief Counsel to Deputy Director of Agriculture)

As 1975 became 1976, my life seemed ideal. We owned a home on two acres with horses. My wife had become a school principal in 1974 at age 29. Our two school-age children were thriving, and I had a dream job. All that began to unravel at the end of April 1976 at a routine weekly hearing of fiscal bills. As I sat at the center of the horseshoe-shaped dais to the right of Beilenson, a staff member quietly mounted the dais behind us and slipped Beilenson a note. He read it and silently passed it to me. It read, "Jerry's father-in-law has died." I knew instantly that my life would never be the same. My parents were overseas. My wife was an only child. Her father, a professor at U.C. Berkeley's School of Forestry, headed the family. My wife and our two children spent summers in the woods with her parents. Now he was gone, dead of a heart attack at age 60. Two weeks later, in May, my wife's small rural school district advised that they could not continue her as principal for the next school year due to declining enrollment. Then, in early June, Beilenson won the Democratic primary for a seat in Congress. He would be moving to Washington, D.C., in November, and I would be out of work.

Sudden and unexpected changes controlled my life growing up. We moved frequently as my father served as a sergeant in the military. My three younger sisters and I lived for short periods with grandparents in Florida and Maine and on or near military bases in Texas, Hawaii, Alabama, North Africa, Delaware, Illinois, and Japan. I attended six elementary schools, sometimes two in the same year, and five different high schools. Beilenson urged me to move to Washington, D.C., as his chief of staff. I had promised myself that if I ever had children, they would have a stable home with a father who stayed in the same place. That place was now Sacramento. I said I couldn't do that and set my sights on becoming the chief counsel of the Senate Judiciary Committee. The position had opened, and I was the only candidate. However, on a Friday afternoon, the week before my interview, Beilenson called me into his office. He had just returned from lunch with Rose Bird, who had been his former intern when he was an Assembly member. Bird, the Secretary of California's Agriculture and Services Agency, was one of

21

Governor Brown's earliest and most important cabinet appointments. The Agency oversaw the work of ten major departments of state government, including the Departments of Labor, Consumer Affairs, General Services, and Food and Agriculture. Beilenson told me that at lunch, Bird had revealed her chief counsel was leaving to join President Carter's administration. Then he told me he had strongly recommended me to her as her new chief counsel. When I said I preferred the judiciary job, he lowered his voice and told me he had personally assured Secretary Bird that I would be interested and would meet with her. The following Tuesday, I did. She offered me the position, and two days later, I accepted. The next three months would be some of the toughest in my life. The new job proved to be far more difficult than expected.

Former Governor Reagan had created the Ag and Services Agency and other so-called super agencies by forcing formerly stand-alone cabinet departments into larger units. Grouping departments with similar missions such as the health and human services departments into a more governable structure made sense. The same was true for transportation-related departments and environmental departments like water resources, forestry, and fish and game. However, the new agency structure worked less well for major departments like Labor, Food and Agriculture, and Consumer Affairs, which had nothing in common and often took opposite positions on issues. Furthermore, these departments bitterly resented no longer reporting directly to the Governor, and they chaffed at being placed under a cabinet-level agency secretary whose approval controlled every major decision each department director could make. Governor Brown's first major achievement was the creation of the Agricultural Labor Relations Board, which supervised contentious labor disputes under a new law allowing farm workers to unionize. The ALRB was now also part of the Ag and Services Agency. Farmers especially despised the Board and Secretary Bird. A former law professor and public defender, Bird acted decisively and unapologetically in implementing Governor Brown's pro-environment, pro-consumer, and pro-labor initiatives, none of which California farmers welcomed.

For the next three months, I spent my days and nights trying to coax warring department directors to work together and move forward in the direction Secretary Bird and Governor Brown wanted. That often meant forcing changes on the conservative Food and Agriculture Department proposed by the more liberal Consumer Affairs and Labor departments. My assigned tasks included implementing administration goals such as reducing pesticide use, increasing safety for farm workers, and providing more opportunities for small organic farmers and consumers to sell and buy at local farmers' markets.

The day-to-day pressures and long hours were difficult. Governor Brown was single in those days and a night owl. My first face-to-face meeting with him took place in his office after midnight. It was one of innumerable late nights through the fall of 1976. I often did not return home until the rest of the family was asleep. They would have seen more of me had I accepted Beilenson's offer to be his chief of staff in Washington, D.C. However, I genuinely liked the department directors with whom I worked and Secretary Bird as well. I found her invariably warm, funny, and gracious in person, albeit inflexible on policies she felt were right. On my birthday in December, she arrived bearing a birthday cake she had baked herself. There were other kindnesses as well, such as agreeing to my request for a two-week family vacation at Christmas in Hawaii to reconnect with the family still grieving the loss of my wife's father.

While I was in Hawaii, my life took another shocking turn. When I returned to my office on the first workday in January 1977, I learned that I no longer worked there. Bird's deputy secretary met me at the door with the news that while I was in Hawaii, the Director of Food and Agriculture had resigned along with his deputy director. Bird had appointed the chief deputy to be acting director and me as his new deputy director. Bird's staff apologized for the lack of notice, explaining I was unreachable, then instructed me to immediately report to the department's morning staff meeting already underway.

In the fog of the moment, it never occurred to me to quit. I had never quit anything in my life. In a daze, I walked out of my former office and over to the Food and Agriculture conference room. When I entered, the conversation stopped. All eyes turned on me. Jim Youde, the acting director, now director, motioned me to join him at the head table. I sat down next to him behind a hastily prepared hand-written cardboard sign that read JERRY SCRIBNER, DEPUTY DIRECTOR. If it had been pinned to my chest with a noose around my neck, I could not have felt less welcome. Twenty senior managers, still in shock at the unceremonious departure of their former well-liked director, sat grouped around the large square conference table, grimly sizing me up. I was younger than their children. The managers knew I was not a farmer or even the son of a farmer. Nor was I a native Californian, having come to California to attend college and then law school in Berkeley. They also knew what little I knew about California's huge and diverse agriculture I had learned in the less than three months I had worked for Secretary Bird and that I was a liberal former poverty lawyer rumored to have been a confidant of Cesar Chavez, the head of the United Farm Workers Union. Most farmers were Republicans who had strongly opposed the election of Governor Brown and even more strongly opposed the unionization of farm workers. The Department's managers, not surprisingly, all had backgrounds in farming and most shared the same outlook toward Democrats as the farmers we regulated. That changed over time, as they recognized that I worked for a Governor who was at least as liberal as I was. They came to see me as a competent and fair manager committed to the needs of farmers, consumers, and employees of the department. However, the wider California farm community continued to see me as the political appointee I was, and worse, one poorly equipped to understand and appreciate the problems of production agriculture.

In February, Governor Brown appointed Dan Dooley, also an attorney, but more importantly, an agricultural economist from a prominent farming family in the Central Valley, as the department's new chief deputy director. Governor Brown also announced he was appointing Secretary Bird as the next Chief Justice of the California Supreme Court. In March he appointed Richard Rominger to be the new director of CDFA. Rominger, a fourth-generation California farmer in nearby Yolo County, was widely respected by the agricultural community even though, unlike most farmers, he was a liberal Democrat. Soft-spoken and willing to listen, he tirelessly supported the preservation of farmland and the conservation of renewable resources. More of an Aldo Leopold than a John Muir, Rominger dedicated himself to family, community, equality, and environmentally sustainable farming. His gentle patience, commitment to the land, and generosity of spirit awed thoughtful people in the corridors of power in Sacramento.

Before accepting the appointment, Rominger demanded the department be returned to its former eminence as a stand-alone department reporting directly to the governor. Governor Brown agreed to the change. Farmers applauded the decision. They also believed Rominger had demanded and received the authority to pick his own deputy directors. Most expected, one of his first acts would be to replace me and Dooley. Both of us were young lawyers further tainted by having worked for Secretary Bird. As political appointees, it would have been perfectly reasonable for Rominger to ask for my resignation so he could appoint his own deputies. To my surprise, he kept both of us and appointed a third deputy, Marc Faye, a fellow Yolo County farmer with deep roots in California agriculture.

Over the next four years, I supervised the department's Divisions of Administration, Marketing, Inspections Services, and Weights and Measures. Dooley managed the Divisions of Animal Industry and Plant Industry and took on the difficult task of creating a new and innovative pesticide regulatory program. The new system modified California's agricultural commissioner system of issuing pesticide use permits to farmers in a way that incorporated the environmental considerations required by the California Environmental Quality Act (CEQA). The result eliminated the need for separate, lengthy environmental impact reports for each permit issuance in a way that achieved the result both environmentalists and farmers wanted.

We all worked well together. Rominger approached decisions in his own way. He listened patiently, often taking notes on a yellow pad. I never saw him lose his temper or speak ill of anyone. His thinking came from deep inside, and decisions flowed from what he thought was right. My efforts to promote farmers' markets, better relations with consumers, and Dooley's to reduce unnecessary pesticide use were consistent with the direction Rominger wanted to go. Nevertheless, some in the agricultural community still objected to me and Dooley. In 1978, the widely read *California Farmer* published an article in which a prominent grower praised Rominger "as a high-class individual fighting hard for production agriculture." The grower then described me as a socialist who had been a problem in Rose Bird's office. The grower then went on to claim Dooley and I were close confidants of Governor Brown secretly carrying out his orders behind Rominger's back. None of it was true.

Chapter 3. (Medflies Discovered in Los Angeles and San Jose)

On June 5th, 1980, a Los Angeles County agriculture inspector recognized the orange banded wings of a Mediterranean fruit fly stuck to the bottom of a tent-shaped insect trap hung in a backyard orange tree. The inspector alerted her superiors, who flashed word of the discovery to the control and eradication branch in Sacramento and to USDA in Washington. Both agencies immediately ordered their most experienced medfly personnel to Los Angeles and initiated an eradication program based on the Sterile Insect Technique. Dr. Roy Cunningham again served as the principal scientific advisor. As additional personnel arrived from Sacramento and USDA, Los Angeles County inspectors were already out deploying more traps in a nine-square-mile grid around the first fly's location. Preliminary quarantine boundaries were established, and sterile fly-producing laboratories in Hawaii, Costa Rica, and Mexico were asked to begin shipping sterilized medfly pupae as soon as possible. Crews sprayed the orange tree where the first fly was trapped with malathion bait and the ground under it with a stronger pesticide, fenthion, designed to kill any larvae and pupae there. The L.A. staff also began randomly cutting open fruit in the area, looking for maggots.

On June 13th, fruit inspectors found medfly maggots in loquats not far from where the first fly, a male, had been trapped. A second male was trapped on June 20th in a grapefruit tree four and a half miles away from the first. Inspectors deployed more traps in a 9-square-mile grid around the second fly. Six days later, they caught a third one, this time an unmated female. It was one and a half miles from fly number two. After deploying more traps around fly number three, they caught the fourth and final fly on July 14th, also in a grapefruit tree. It, too, turned out to be another unmated female. No more maggots or flies were ever found. Catching only the four flies, two males and two unmated females, and finding the maggots in what turned out to be the locus of the new infestation confirmed the wild medflies had been caught early. That did not mean there were not thousands more in the vicinity since the best traps normally were lucky to catch one out of two thousand in the area. Millions of sterile flies were continuously released in the area over the summer and into the fall. The releases were then stopped while trapping continued in the target area and beyond it to ensure no more wild flies were present. None were. In December, the L.A. infestation was declared eradicated.

While all eyes were on Los Angeles beginning on June 5th, 1980, the wild medflies in the north exploded across San Jose and nearby cities. The lush Santa Clara Valley provided every advantage a foreign pest with no natural enemies could want. Nestled between hills to the west and east and San Francisco Bay to the north, the valley's Mediterranean climate proved perfect for growing fruit of all kinds. In the 1930s, the valley was carpeted with orchards of prunes, apricots, peaches, plums, and other fruit-bearing trees. Three dozen canneries, including Del Monte, and a dozen packing houses, including Sunsweet, were shipping fruit all over the country. In the late '40s and '50s, the orchards were replaced with a new crop—row after row of homes. By 1960, the Valley's 20,000 acres of apricots had shrunk to 12,000 acres. Still the area produced more apricots than any place in the United States. In 1930, only 57,000 people lived in San Jose. By 1980, the city had grown tenfold to a half million. California's fifth largest city was now surrounded by a dozen smaller communities with bucolic names like Sunnyvale, Mountain View, and Monte Sereno. They had grown, too. The area flowed together, a continuous metropolitan area of 1.2 million people. As computer companies like Hewlett Packard, Apple, Oracle, and other giants grew around Stanford University, the towns in the northwest corner of the county filled up. Los Altos, Los Altos Hills, Redwood City, and Palo Alto became home to more PhDs per acre than almost any place in the United States, and the area acquired a new name—Silicon Valley.

In 1958, a well-respected scientific paper, known as the Messenger and Flitters study, concluded it was too cold in the winter in California north of Santa Barbara for medflies to breed successfully. Nevertheless, the staff of the Santa Clara County agriculture commissioner hung 80 insect traps in scattered locations in the 1200 square mile county. In a bizarre and still unexplained coincidence, on June 5th, the same day as the Los Angeles discovery, an inspector checking the traps for the first time saw what he believed might well be two medflies stuck to the sticky floor of a Jackson trap hung in an orange tree in the city of San Jose. The trapper carefully preserved the two flies in alcohol, packaged them up, and mailed them to the entomology lab in Sacramento for dissection and confirmation. The lab identified them both as wild male medflies on the day they arrived. However, the package had taken twelve days to travel the 80 miles from San Jose to Sacramento. Worse, there was no way to estimate how long medflies had been breeding in the county. Finding two flies in a single trap suggested the medflies had been breeding far longer than the twelve days already lost. All the available federal and state medfly experts had been sent to Los Angeles. Therefore, the department control and eradication managers in Sacramento reassigned a small crew of personnel already in San Jose working on a gypsy moth infestation to assist the Santa Clara County agricultural commissioner in setting up a medfly eradication program there. USDA also began scrounging for employees in other parts of the country they could send to San Jose on rotating thirty-day assignments. More time passed before this cobbled-together and under-resourced team in the north could hang more traps. Not surprisingly, more wild medflies were trapped as soon as the additional traps were hung. At one location, a single trap contained ten wild flies. Days later, six more were trapped on the same property. Although it was clear almost immediately that this infestation was far larger and more established than the one in Los Angeles, the Flitter study lulled managers into believing the Los Angeles situation should remain the primary concern.

By the end of July, wild flies had been trapped at 24 locations in the north. Maggots had been discovered in 37. These numbers would each more than double by the end of August. In Sacramento, the increasingly worrisome statistics were delivered to the director's office by the professionals in the State's headquarters' control and eradication staff. The bad news was invariably accompanied by assurances improvements were underway. In September, the Department replaced the assistant director of the Plant Industry Division. In October, the state's medfly project manager was replaced. Still, the eradication effort continued to falter. Farmers and USDA officials in Washington called for dropping SIT and switching to the aerial bait technique that had worked in Florida and Texas. California resisted. Both the professionals and top management, me included, believed the aerial spraying of more than a dozen cities in the Santa Clara Valley with malathion was not a politically viable option.

I was born in Florida and lived there twice during elementary school. The earliest home movie pictures of me show me in my underpants swatting at insects in front of my grandparent's orange tree. Florida was hot, sticky, and buggy. It still was when I attended college there in 1960 before transferring to UC Berkeley as a sophomore. As a child in Texas, I and other kids played hide and seek as we ran behind trucks spraying clouds of DDT down the street of the poor neighborhood where we lived at the time. I doubted that what had been acceptable in Florida and south Texas decades earlier would be tolerated in liberal Santa Clara County in 1980. I was not alone. Those of us at CDFA believed the aerial spraying proposed by USDA would be viewed in northern California as nothing less than Orwellian. We doubted the USDA bombers would get off the ground. Based on the success in Los Angeles in 1975 and 1980, we also believed the SIT strategy was fundamentally sound and would succeed in the north with more time.

Dan Dooley left in mid-October to start a law practice. Pending Dooley's replacement, Rominger temporarily shifted the Plant Industry Division to me. On October 30th, USDA formally requested that the EPA issue a specific exemption allowing malathion to be used in an aerial release program for medfly eradication. EPA approved the request subject to a general requirement that USDA comply with all other applicable federal laws. At the time, no one recognized that an existing FAA (Federal Aviation Administration) regulation of general applicability required local governments to approve all low-level flights over their jurisdictions.

We knew that to succeed with SIT, we had to release more sterile flies. The only possible source of more flies was the large rearing laboratory in Mexico that produced sterile flies for their medfly eradication project. On November 12th, Rominger flew to a meeting in Mexico seeking more sterile flies. USDA, a partner with Mexico in their eradication effort, quietly urged Mexico to turn down the California request unless the state agreed to at least one aerial spray to reduce the number of wild flies to a manageable level. Mexico had previously faced a similar crisis in its medfly eradication program—too many wild flies and insufficient sterile flies. At USDA's insistence, Mexico had agreed to one or more aerial sprays to reduce the wild population. Biologically, it made sense. However, the local Mexican public violently resisted, including kidnapping the project director and holding him hostage for a week. The aerial spraying went forward, the director survived, the number of wild flies reduced, and SIT resumed. Mexican officials told Rominger they would not ship additional sterilized flies to California unless the state first aerially sprayed, and then not until February.

On November 20th, officials from USDA presented the medfly project's advisory committee, known then as the Technical Review Committee (TRC), with a series of options weighted toward ordering immediate aerial spraying. The committee members questioned the effectiveness of aerial spraying in winter, pointing out that few flies would be flying or feeding on the bait in cold weather. Chet Howe, the Santa Clara County Ag commissioner, a member of the committee, urged them to instead support a winter ground program of fruit stripping combined with more robust ground-spraying of the bait. The meeting ended with the committee neither approving nor rejecting either recommendation. A week later, at the end of November, the current project manager quit. No one knew what would happen next.

Soon after I arrived for work, early Tuesday morning, December 2nd, Betty Taylor, Rominger's executive assistant, appeared at my door. She said, "Governor Brown's office is calling asking for Rominger. They say reporters in San Francisco and San Jose are calling to ask if the Governor has approved aerial spraying of Malathion." She paused, then said, "Rich is out today. The Governor's office said they are referring the calls to us. What should I do?"

I was alone. Rich had said nothing to me about any such decision, nor whether he had even discussed the medfly situation with Governor

Brown. I looked back at Betty, then out my window at the Governor's corner office in the State Capitol, a few hundred feet away. Betty stood silently, waiting for my answer, her face unreadable. I knew even if she knew more, telling me was not her responsibility. I told her to refer the calls to me when they came in and to let me know if she heard from Rich.

My father had believed part of his job was to toughen his kids, especially his son. He insisted on obedience, telling the truth, and respect for authority. These values were reinforced as I moved up the ranks as a Boy Scout until I became an Eagle Scout at age 16. As a legal aid lawyer, I had ruthlessly cross-examined witnesses with loaded questions. Now, reporters would be asking me if killing flies justified crop dusting women and children with a nerve poison. I knew aerial spraying was under discussion. It might even be the only option left. I steeled myself to answer as truthfully as I could with the limited knowledge I had.

The first call came from a reporter with the *San Francisco Chronicle*. He first established that Rominger was out and that I was the highest-ranking person available, then bluntly asked if Governor Brown had approved aerial malathion spraying. I said I didn't know. As he asked further questions, I responded truthfully, admitting that it was under consideration and might be necessary. By the following morning, the *Chronicle* and other morning papers were reporting a 9:30 a.m. press conference scheduled to occur at the Santa Clara County Administration Building. Aerial spraying of malathion over cities might be announced, they reported. Further confirmation came later that morning when I received a telephone call from Dr. Ephraim Kahn, the chief epidemiologist for California's Department of Health. He knew more than I did because he had attended the press conference in San Jose after learning of it the night before from the County health officer in Santa Clara. He told me the press conference had been a public relations disaster and described in detail how a mob of environmental activists, ordinary citizens, and interested county workers had tried to squeeze into a tiny room that had been set aside. A county employee tried to clear the room by announcing that the meeting was for the press only. That announcement only increased the urgency of those trying to shoulder their way in, including Dr. Kahn himself. No one who could get in was going to miss this. Kahn reported to me that Director Rominger, Harvey Ford, the USDA administrator, and the County Agricultural Commissioner, Chet Howe, sat behind a conference table at the front of the room facing a wall of television cameras, reporters, and microphones. They told the press that aerial spraying would begin as soon as the planes could get in the air, and at least 100 square miles would be sprayed one or more times. Dr. Kahn then said he was calling me because he knew that the Santa Clara Board of Supervisors had demanded a health assessment of the possible impact of spraying malathion on humans be prepared before any spraying. Kahn said he expected to be told to prepare one. Kahn also told me that he had managed to hand a reporter a set of health questions related to Malathion, hoping the reporter would ask the panel how much Malathion would be used. That didn't happen. Dr. Kahn needed me to tell him how much malathion would be in the spray. I told him I didn't know but would get back to him with an answer as soon as I could.

After the press conference ended, telephone calls, telegrams, and letters began pouring into the offices of local officials, state legislators, and especially Governor Brown's office in Sacramento, demanding the spraying be stopped. The intensity of the public anger shocked farmers. It should not have. The decision to announce such a plan without prior notice or so much as a nod to human health concerns all but guaranteed the reaction that followed. The USDA leadership in Washington and farmers in California had badly underestimated the fear of pesticides in the proposed spray area and the public's low opinion of the right-wing agribusiness lobby. The urban residents and farmers lived in two different worlds. To farmers, the urban fear of Malathion was unreasonable, almost ludicrous. Most of the pesticides used by farmers required special permits and use restrictions, as well as protective clothing for applicators. Some were so toxic that fields, after being sprayed, had to have warning signs posted in English and Spanish prohibiting entry for hours or days after they had been treated. Malathion, on the other hand, required no permits or special instructions to buy or use. Anyone could buy it over the counter and use it around the home and in backyards to kill ants and other insects. It was also a common ingredient in dog and cat flea collars.

The antipathy the urban public felt toward big agriculture ran even deeper than their feelings about pesticides. Urban residents did not see California's farmers as thousands of small family farms, even though many of the fruit orchards in the Central Valley around Fresno were small family operations, planted and replanted by immigrant parents and grandparents who had settled the Central Valley generations ago. Nor did they believe farmers were stewards of the land as most farmers saw themselves. The farms that urban people saw driving down Interstate 5 on the west side of the San Joaquin Valley were huge. City dwellers viewed these farms as commercial operations focused on profit with little regard for the environment or the laborers who harvested the crops. They saw corporate agriculture, family-owned or not, as unwilling to provide their workers, primarily of Mexican descent, with safe housing, fair pay, and decent working conditions. Residents of the San Francisco Bay area had been at the forefront of the unionization of dock workers in San Francisco in the '30s and later of cannery workers in the Santa Clara Valley. Unions were popular and powerful. Residents had marched in support of civil rights and against the Vietnam War in the '60s. They also strongly supported the table grape boycott as part of the fight to unionize farm workers. Jerry Brown had marched with Cesar Chavez. As a result, the public had little interest in helping agriculture eradicate the medfly.

They saw Malathion differently too. More than a few supported organic farming both in their yards and in their shopping. Even those who used Malathion themselves viewed it entirely differently if the government sprayed it on them from the air. Their trust in government assurances of the safety of Malathion and chemicals, in general, was low. They had more confidence in the opinion of the Sierra Club and environmental organizations, all of whom opposed aerial spraying. In response to the claims that Malathion was safe, the universal reaction came down to one word—thalidomide. The government had said it was safe. Doctors did, too, as they gave it to pregnant women, only to learn later that it caused terrible birth defects. For many people, this experience confirmed that relying on past research on the safety of malathion or any other chemical was itself dangerous. Birth defects and cancer might well be shown to be problems in the future, especially with a program of mass spraying in the air over population centers.

The day after the press conference, the San Jose *Mercury* News published an editorial captioned "Let sleeping fruit flies lie." The editorial claimed nothing needed to be done because it was winter now, and the scientific research said the flies would not survive this far north. Furthermore, in winter, most medflies would be in the ground as pupae or in fruit in the larval stage. Thus, didn't it make more sense to wait for warmer weather and then consider spraying if the flies were still present? The editorial concluded, "All things considered, there doesn't seem to be a persuasive scientific case for spraying now." On top of the fear of malathion and lack of health assessment, this argument provided a one-two punch against any spraying in December.

Regrettably, in my view, the editorial trivialized the danger posed by the medfly, cavalierly suggesting that biological controls were available. This was false. The tiny wasp predators in Africa were unavailable and would not eliminate the medflies nor prevent their spread. Like other biological control strategies, the best they could do was reduce the amount of damage. Various biological control strategies had been tried in Hawaii for decades, beginning as early as 1915. None had ever provided a level of control that made it possible to grow fruit in the presence of the medfly without extensive pesticide use, and not even then. Biological control is not eradication. Control means living with the new pest by bringing in another pest to try to reduce the damage the first one causes. Sometimes, the control pest turns out to be ineffective, or it creates new, unforeseen problems. As with human disease, the best medicine is to not get sick in the first place. Consider the benefits to humanity of eradicating smallpox, measles, and polio compared to living with them and treating the effects of these horrific diseases. The editorial never mentioned the word eradication. Nor did it discuss the commercial reality that having any medflies present in California would itself lead to massive economic losses as other medfly-free countries and neighboring states would ban fruit from California that had not first been fumigated.

Both other states and countries were already warning that if the medfly were not soon eliminated, such a ban would follow.

Rominger, back in Sacramento, calmly repeated the need for aerial bait spraying, noting that all other efforts, including SIT, had not stopped the spread of the fruit fly. He said he believed that when people fully understood the grave danger the medfly posed and the minimal risk of spraying, they would recognize that the spraying was needed and safe. I doubted that was true, but I was glad it was not my responsibility.

In the first week of December, state and federal project officials appeared before city councils requesting local permission to fly under 1500 feet, as required by the EPA permit. Every city council unanimously voted it down. They also passed new city ordinances specifically prohibiting any aerial spraying of malathion in their jurisdictions. The Santa Clara County Board of Supervisors took the same action. So long as the permit required local approval, no aerial spraying program could get off the ground. Even if a new permit removed this impediment, local opposition would remain.

California agricultural leaders and farmer groups recognized they had seriously underestimated the public fear of pesticides and general distrust of corporate agriculture. Over the following weekend, Merlin Fagan, a lobbyist for the California Farm Bureau, aghast that years of efforts to improve relations with the urban public had been squandered by the rushed and poorly planned aerial spraying announcement, took his concerns to Democratic Assembly member John Thurman, a dairy farmer from Modesto in the Central Valley who chaired the Agriculture Committee. Thurman, a rural Democrat, was one of the farm community's few friends in a Legislature dominated by urban Democrats. His gruff exterior and colorful criticism of bureaucrats masked a big heart and brilliant political mind. A liberal in overalls, he cared deeply for the less fortunate as well as for his rural constituents and was loved by legislators on both sides of the aisle. Thurman agreed to do what he could.

On Monday, December 8th, he quietly laid the groundwork for a reset by scheduling a hearing of his committee for Wednesday,

December 10th. He said he was stepping in because both his urban Democratic colleagues and his farm constituents were calling him, upset about the medfly situation. The farmers wanted the spraying to go forward, while legislators in the infested area insisted the spraying be shelved in favor of continuing to release sterile flies. Thurman promised both sides his hearing would be a listening session focused on gathering the facts. Privately his staff reached out to the environmental community to assure them the hearing would be open and fair. It would focus on why Rominger and federal officials had not eradicated the medfly earlier and why they were calling for aerial spraying now without first doing a health evaluation. Thurman made sure the press would also be invited. The high-profile legislative setting and presence of the press would be advantageous to both sides. It would offer an opportunity to convince the public that it was essential to eradicate this nightmare foreign pest no one wanted. It would also emphasize that the aerial spraying had already been done safely in Florida and Texas. For the farm lobbyists, the hearing would bring needed urgency and attention to the issue while, at the same time, giving their membership a greater appreciation of the depth of public resistance state and federal officials were up against. For opponents, it offered an opportunity to flood the State Capitol with citizens adamantly opposed to a government program they believed posed unknown health risks, especially to children and pregnant women. Environmentalists also believed they could make a compelling case that aerial spraying in winter would be ineffective.

On the morning of December 10th, Bay Area residents and their representatives filled most of the seats in the already packed hearing room. They had come in buses and cars to testify against any plan to spray them with Malathion. Farmers, including many who, like Rominger, were third-and-fourth generation farmers, had come too. They had seen the frightening pictures of medfly maggots squirming out of oranges, apricots, pears, and other fruits from backyard trees in San Jose, and they had read the increasingly gloomy reports in the farm press describing the ever-worsening situation in the Santa Clara Valley. They knew that the State project manager had been fired in October, and his replacement had resigned at the end of November. At the monthly Farm

Bureau meetings, coffee shops, farm supply stores, and everywhere growers and shippers came together, fear that the medfly situation was spiraling out of control took center stage. Everyone knew medflies had been eradicated quickly and safely in Florida and Texas with aerially applied Malathion bait. What was the hold-up in California? For months, they had been calling their local representatives in the Legislature and Congress, urging them to pressure USDA and CDFA to do what was needed before it was too late. Now, they had come to Sacramento to show their strong support for aerial spraying as soon as possible.

Lobbyists and leaders of major grower and fruit-shipping organizations lined the wall on one side of the room. They included Lee Ruth of the Agricultural Council, representing many of the large farm cooperatives, and Bill Quarles, head of governmental affairs for Sunkist, the giant citrus cooperative with more than five thousand grower members. Sunkist marketed California's annual naval orange and lemon crop in over 37 countries. Merlin Fagan had come too, along with members of various chapters of the Farm Bureau from around the State. He was joined by representatives of the California Grape and Tree Fruit League and the Western Growers Association.

Across the room, waiting along the opposite wall, stood leaders of environmental organizations like the Sierra Club, Citizens for a Better Environment, and Friends of the Earth. They had brought along scientists to buttress the case against spraying at this time. In the audience as observers were lobbyists for the League of California Cities, the County Supervisors Association, and individual cities. All of whom had clients who needed to be kept informed of developments.

As Rominger seated himself at the conference table, those who had been talking sifted into seats saved for them or squeezed in next to those standing along the walls. As I took a seat one row back behind Rominger, I reflected on times like this during the years I had worked for Beilenson when I sat nervously behind him as he presented legislation I had drafted. I had no idea how the hearing would go. We had few friends in the audience. Rominger was more a target than a witness. We knew the script called for Rich, as the Director, to present the facts and then expect to be pummeled for the next couple of hours with criticism from all sides, including Thurman. As a legal aid lawyer, I faced angry judges and hostile agencies. Here, I felt helpless. There was nothing I could do to help my boss. I could only watch someone I wanted to protect be the scapegoat for an impossible situation. For a brief second, the tension and pent-up anger of both the residents and farmers at each other hung in the air. Then Thurman tapped his microphone, thanked everyone for attending, and asked Director Rominger to begin.

In his low-key manner, Rominger quietly covered the same points he had on December 3rd, starting with the grave threat facing the state. He acknowledged everyone's preference for using sterile flies, including his own, but said the infestation was now too big for SIT to succeed. He said the aerial spraying had been proven both safe and effective in Florida and Texas and caused no human health problems. As for winter killing the flies, he wryly noted that it was winter now, and we were still trapping adult medflies and finding live maggots. With spring approaching, there was no time to wait. His words changed few, if any, minds, but his thoughtful and detailed presentation significantly changed the atmosphere in the room. The resolute opposition to aerial spraying remained, but now it had been joined by a sobering awareness that the medfly was a problem and, if not eradicated, would require an enormous increase in annual pesticide use throughout the state. The farmers and their representatives felt well represented. Rominger had acquitted himself in the face of a hostile audience. He had made their case for a safe, common-sense approach to a frightening problem.

Thurman next invited the others to testify. One by one, they came forward to speak at the microphones set up at the foot of each side aisle. Some spoke as individuals, others as representatives of various environmental organizations. All were united in strong opposition to the aerial spraying of pesticides on an urban population. It was simply unthinkable, they said. The scientists generally acknowledged the medfly was a potential problem while offering a biologically based position favoring minimal pesticide use. The environmental representatives consistently spoke of the aerial bait program as a broad-spectrum spray that would kill all insects below indiscriminately. I do not recall any acknowledgment of the fact that the medflies would not be killed on the wing but instead die only if they ingested the bait. They proposed a host removal program as a winter alternative to aerial spraying. Something they said urban residents would wholeheartedly support. They were careful not to express opposition to all pesticides, instead emphasizing the benefits of integrated pest management. The possibility of unknown health consequences and significant impacts on non-target insects and aquatic species was raised over and over. The failure of the government to prepare any environmental impact report lent weight to their arguments for delay and more study. So did the fact that no health report had been prepared. Their claim, supported by the Messinger and Flitters study, that the medflies would not survive the winter, making aerial spraying unnecessary, made sense. Aerial spraying might not be needed at all, they said. Why not wait? Rominger's earlier statement that it would be too late to stop them by the time you realized winter hadn't killed them carried little weight.

The individual witnesses who followed the scientists and environmental spokespersons quoted Rachel Carson and emphasized how little we knew about the long-term health risks of Malathion. They said all the studies had been done only on laboratory animals, and all years ago. None had been done on asthmatics, pregnant women, or those with compromised immune systems, thousands of whom would be involuntarily subjected to the aerial assault. They noted that the potential health impacts of spraying Malathion on urban cities had not been studied at all. Thus, the absence of adverse reports during prior urban spray programs did not prove there were none. There could have been unreported or unrecognized longer-term impacts. Considering these unknown risks and the lack of recent studies, they argued no spraying should take place until safety could be assured.

After two hours of debate, Thurman spoke. He first thanked all who attended for their helpful testimony. Next, he roundly criticized all the government agencies involved. He praised the community advocates for their willingness to mount a massive, voluntary, community-based host removal program in December. Then, to the amazement of everyone present, he announced that an agreement had been reached to postpone aerial spraying until January 31st to allow the community to come forward with the fruit-stripping alternative. Stunned silence followed. There had been no agreement. USDA and CDFA had not expected Thurman to announce a delay; neither had agriculture. The proposal for a community-based host removal program had been more of a suggested alternative than a promise to do it. The environmental community had no authority to offer a voluntary program of this magnitude. Thurman again thanked everyone for coming and pronounced the hearing adjourned. His Solomon-like move left all present feeling like winners and losers at the same time. Thurman had declared an armistice without the agreement of anyone but himself. The room slowly emptied without a clear sense of when or if aerial spraying would go forward. Thurman had sidetracked immediate aerial spraying, but not necessarily forever.

Two days later, Rominger and Shannon Wilson, USDA's Emergency Programs coordinator, jointly announced that no aerial spraying would occur before the completion of a health risk assessment by the California Department of Health. Meanwhile, on December 15th, USDA formally petitioned the EPA requesting the removal of the local approval requirement. EPA promptly made the change. On December 16th, the Department of Health released its report titled: *Health Hazard Assessment of Aerial Application of Malathion in Santa Clara County*. The report concluded that even in high doses, Malathion posed little or no health risk to humans or other mammals. The report, prepared in haste, primarily addressed the chemical itself, declaring that Malathion's toxicity was so low that at 2.4 or 2.6 ounces per acre, no one would be harmed. The report also noted that "no public health hazards have emerged" from the extensive use of Malathion in mosquito abatement programs and from 30 years of widespread home and garden use. It said that "[a]n exhaustive review of the scientific and clinical literature reveals no information which would lead to any reasonable suspicion of a potential adverse public health impact under the proposed Malathion use conditions." Based on their review, the Health Department said the risk to human health of the aerial spraying program would be "insignificant."

This conclusion, which was all most people read or heard about, did not end the controversy. There was widespread skepticism that any pesticide could ever be truly harmless or insignificant if sprayed from the air. It killed not only medflies but also mosquitoes and other garden insects. Further, the report itself acknowledged that people had been killed by Malathion in suicide attempts and had died after mishandling the chemical and its breakdown products. The report's observation that in failed suicide attempts, the survivors recovered with "no evidence of prolonged or irreversible effects" did not satisfy those concerned about possible long-term health effects such as developing cancer later in life. Even less reassuring was the statement that "pregnant women who have become intoxicated with Malathion have had normal offspring." Again, what about some long-term effects on these normal offspring and the women?

The report failed to discuss whether there would be any meaningful exposure to the Malathion beyond noting that people would be inside and the amount to be used per acre was tiny. This allowed the public to draw on their own experience. Residents who had watched a farm field being sprayed by a crop duster pictured the aerial spraying as a ubiquitous milky cloud floating down. They could not imagine why this would not inevitably be drawn into the lungs of every human below. Those who had sprayed Malathion themselves or had sprayed insects with a can of aerosol pesticide could see what seemed to be an easily breathable spray. Malathion also has a distinctive odor. You can smell it. For all these reasons, it was hard to believe that the Malathion bait would not be inhaled. To the extent the public believed it would fall to the ground as sticky droplets too large to be absorbed in the lungs, they still refused to believe it would not somehow get inside them.

For the rest of the project, the health debate would continue to focus on Malathion as a pesticide and, thus, a chemical potentially no different than other chemicals claimed to be safe in perpetuity. Further research had shown that other chemicals earlier deemed safe were later found not to be. Based on past studies and use to date, Malathion might appear to be a reasonably safe chemical now. But would it be found unsafe by future studies? As with COVID-19, pseudoscience, confusion, and misinformation flourished as the public demanded a level of certainty greater than reason or science could deliver.

Chapter 4 (A Christmas Surprise)

Christmas music played in the background on Wednesday night, December 17th, 1980, as department employees and their spouses mingled over drinks and hors d'oeuvres at the annual Christmas party. Instead of work, conversations centered on plans for the holidays and hopes for the New Year. Children would be out of school. My plans included taking the next two weeks off to drive a bus-sized motor home the length of California with my wife, two kids, and our German exchange student. We would stop at Disneyland on the way to San Diego, then stay with friends and go whale watching on their sailboat before returning home after New Year's. The trip would be an opportunity to show our exchange student more of California and to give all of us a much-deserved rest after a busy year.

It had been a good year for me. After four years, I knew a little more about agriculture though far less than the career civil servants who worked for me. They had seen deputy directors come and go. Fortunately for me, personal qualities mattered more than political party. The staff respected my honesty, work ethic, and sense of humor. They sensed that I cared about them, their families, and their careers, which I did. I always tried to listen with an open mind yet take responsibility for decisions that were mine to make. As the son of a sergeant, I especially valued opportunities like the Christmas party to let every employee know how much I appreciated them.

Near the end of the party, I stood alone near the punch bowl, picturing our planned Christmas trip and wondering if I could manage driving my neighbor's borrowed motor home in LA traffic without an accident. I felt a light tap on my shoulder and turned to see Rich standing next to me, a worried look on his face. "Jerry," he said, "I hate to do this to you, but I need you to move to San Jose and take charge of the Medfly program."

I never saw it coming, even though I knew John Thurman had demanded that someone at the deputy director level or higher up at USDA or CDFA be put in charge of the program. I assumed it would have to be someone from USDA. They had a nationwide cadre of top-flight federal managers who had spent their careers fighting pests all over the country and the world. None of the three of us at the deputy director level in California had any pest management experience, least of all me. I learned later that USDA told Rominger it was California's problem. They would not take the lead.

Although caught by surprise, I felt oddly elated, as if my life had prepared me for this moment. Growing up in a military family the possibility that I would be called to fight in a war had been a constant companion all my life. As a male, I believed, from my earliest memories, that someday a call like this would come. My elementary school playground in 1951 overlooked Pearl Harbor and the sunken Arizona across the water. Both Hickam Air Force Base, where we lived, and Pearl Harbor were busy shuttling troops to and from Korea as they had been in WWII. Later, in junior high school, on an air base in Libya during the Suez crisis, I rode a school bus with an armed soldier standing in the well between the door and the driver. A sand-bagged machine gun nest sat on our playground near the eight-foot wall topped by broken glass that surrounded the base. As a child, I played with toy soldiers, and when I was older, I played combat games with other boys. We jumped into foxholes in Hawaii, pretended to fly a wrecked B-17 on the airfield in Libya, and fired imaginary machine guns from the slits of concrete pillboxes remaining from battles between the Germans and the British. As a teenage Boy Scout, I earned merit badges in first aid, lifesaving, hiking, signaling, and map reading. I led other boys as a patrol leader and then the whole troop as senior patrol leader. I knew Baden Powell created the Boy Scouts as boyhood training for being a soldier in war, and I was prepared to be one if called.

From elementary school on, I read dozens of books about past wars, including those by Bruce Catton on the Civil War, books on the Revolutionary War, and endless books on World War II. My wife's heroes were cowboys; mine were soldiers like Alexander the Great, Robert E. Lee, and Erwin Rommel, men who led men in battle. I admired the toughness of the Spartans. My mother once quoted a Spartan mother sending her son off to war with the admonition to come home carrying his shield or on it. That comment, more than any other, left me knowing that, for me, quitting anything was not an option.

Another book I read somewhere in elementary school or junior high gave me something else: boundless confidence. Howard Pease wrote a series of books for teenage boys starting with *The Tattooed Man* about a young cabin boy named Tod Moran who shipped out on a tramp steamer named the Araby. In the series, as I recall it, the cook was tattooed and a fount of wisdom. In a sequel, *Heart of Danger*, the cook tells Tod the safest course in a crisis is to go unafraid to the heart of danger. There, he says, you will find safety. Whether going to college with no money or being ordered to report as the deputy director of a department I was ill-equipped to lead or receiving this latest assignment from Rich, I believed plunging ahead and working my heart out was the safest course.

When I graduated from high school in Japan, the Vietnam War was beginning, and Americans were secretly filtering into Indochina as advisors to the counterinsurgency underway. They came through the base in Japan where my father, still a sergeant, worked in the air terminal. That summer, he paid me to type manifests for outgoing flights.

The Vietnam War changed me even before I left home. Being a war hero, if it involved killing people, lost whatever appeal it had ever had. I resisted my family's pressure to attend the Air Force Academy. At the end of the summer, I sold my car, and that, plus working part-time, got me through college in four years. At 18, I registered for the draft and took the two years of mandatory ROTC training required of all males enrolled in a land grant college. On the first day of class, the officer teaching the class said he was pleased to see we had all "volunteered" for Air Force ROTC. The word volunteered outraged every man present. None of us had volunteered for this mandatory no-credit class where the curriculum consisted of spit-shining shoes and marching in step. After a pause, the commander added, "You could have chosen Army ROTC." The incident remained a lifelong reminder for me that, though limited, there are always choices one can make.

When Rich asked me to take on the biggest challenge I had ever faced, it seemed logical that he would ask me rather than one of the other deputies more identified with agriculture. Although I was a deputy director at CDFA, I was seen as more liberal and urban than the rest of the department. All my life, I had been the new kid in school, an outsider, as I was in the department. Also, I empathized with the opponents. They were non-combatants in this war against the medfly. I did not want to aerial spray either. Standing next to Rich that night in December, I knew I was the right person to lead this fight. And I believed I could find a way to defeat the medfly without aerial spraying.

Rich had one more surprise for me. Thurman had scheduled a second hearing. This one would be in San Jose on Monday the 22nd, five days away. Thurman told Rich that on the 22nd he expected to see a new plan of action by the new manager. Rich's final words were, "Jerry, you can choose anyone you need in the department to help you."

Driving home from the Christmas party, I thought about how victory in war often resulted from speed and surprise. Between now and the hearing on Monday, three days before Christmas, no one would be expecting any change other than the announcement of a new project director. Thurman's new hearing on short notice opened the door for a reset, but only if we could seize the initiative. Accordingly, I decided on the way home our strategy would be to charge into the Monday hearing with a bold proposal for a comprehensive new plan, bigger than anyone expected. This would break open the deadlock and refocus attention on eradicating the medfly.

Secretly designing a massive surprise attack would be challenging, given that we had no army, no plan, and no time, and by morning, there would be only four days to choose a new team and write a new plan in time for Monday's hearing. It looked daunting, if not impossible, especially a week before Christmas. Working backward, I knew my wife, Penny, could manage our Christmas preparations without me. Putting the lights on the tree was my main Christmas responsibility, and I had already done that. I could come home next week for Christmas Eve and Christmas Day. Then, we would all take off in the motorhome for San Diego as planned. Later, I would have to figure out how to manage the medfly project during the last week of December and how to get the family and motorhome back to Sacramento.

Rominger had said I could choose whoever I needed from the Department to help me. Two key people immediately came to mind: Dr. Isi Siddiqui and Arnie Morrison. Dr. Siddiqui, a brilliant scientist, originally from India, had been sidelined as a supervisor of a small unit in the division of Plant Industry despite his obvious talent and managerial skills. He would head up the fruit stripping because that required a manager who was personable, flexible, and capable of organizing a dozen different cities and innumerable volunteer groups into an effective fruit stripping program. Thurman had halted the aerial spraying plan only until January 31, meaning we had only one month at most to strip fruit. I knew I could count on Isi in the same way Eisenhower depended on Omar Bradley. There would be no need for direction from me. The stripping program would be organized and ready to start on the first week in January.

I needed a much different kind of leader for the ground spraying program. Someone more like George Patton, hard-driving and willing to push his troops to the breaking point. Arnie Morrison had been tapped to take over the medfly program on December 1st after the previous manager quit. Aggressive, profane, and manic, Arnie approached each day so revved up that we all worried he might have a heart attack. The men he commanded in the Curly Top Virus program loved him. So did the farmers whose assessments paid for the program. I came to love him, too, even though he thought all Democrats were wimps—especially liberal ones like me. A natural leader, Arnie would deliver a 100% effort and let nothing slow him down no matter the obstacles. It also helped that despite our political differences, he admired my straight talk and hard work as much as I admired his. That Arnie was as conservative as I was liberal was another asset. Farmers distrusted Jerry Brown and me. I knew they trusted Arnie to tell them the inside truth about the program. Agriculture would have their man on the project reporting that we were fully committed to eradicating the medfly, and if we had to do it the hard way by spraying Malathion bait by hand, then by God, that was what we were going to do. What little I knew so far about the medfly had convinced me that winter would not solve the problem. Neither would fruit stripping alone. I also expected opposition to aerial spraying to be as strong on January 31st as it was now. With aerial spraying blocked, I believed our best hope was to go all out with the tools available. Those included door-to-door stripping plus ground spraying and releasing greater numbers of sterile flies. I also believed that although winter would not eliminate all the medflies, it would probably reduce the number of wild flies in the same way a one-time aerial spray had done in Mexico.

I needed two more key people to manage the remaining two essential elements of any SIT eradication plan. One person would oversee the quarantine program. The second would manage the detection and sterile fly release elements. Fortunately, the Division of Plant Industry had two experienced managers, both of whom had been actively involved in the eradication effort from the beginning. I decided to assign Dick Fehlman to head up the detection and sterile release program and Tom Collister to take charge of quarantine. Neither they nor the other two senior commanders had ever worked directly under me before.

Early Thursday morning, December 18th, I separately called each team leader and explained the situation. I told them to drop everything they were doing and plan to meet me Sunday afternoon at 5 p.m. in the conference room of the Santa Clara Motor Lodge. They each received the same authority Rich had given me—they could immediately choose four key lieutenants for their team from anywhere in the department. I said together we were going to write a new eradication plan Sunday night that would not include aerial spraying and that the plan had to be ready by Monday morning in time for a legislative hearing in San Jose called by Assembly Agriculture Committee Chairman John Thurman.

It was a lot to ask, especially one week before Christmas. I learned years later that Jim Rudig, one of Isi Siddiqui's four lieutenants, had signed a written landscaping contract to be completed during the two weeks he planned to be home in Visalia, California, over Christmas. To be in San Jose by Sunday afternoon, he had to find someone in Visalia on Saturday willing to take over the job and earn the extra money he had been counting on. He did. I spent the rest of Thursday reassigning, until further notice, all my other department responsibilities. On Friday, I arranged for the Department's Steno pool staff to come in to work at 5 a.m. on Monday morning to receive my call from San Jose. I warned them I would be dictating a new medfly eradication plan over the telephone. Their job would be to turn it into 50 error-free typed copies and to deliver those copies to Director Rominger by 8 a.m. He would bring them with him Monday to hand out at the Thurman hearing.

The meeting on Sunday at the motor lodge began promptly at five. The four teams, their leaders, and I were seated randomly around a square conference table. Except for me, nearly all were college-educated entomologists and biologists who had spent their careers in the field working on control or eradication projects. At least half had been on the medfly project since June. They were tired and discouraged. I had crushed their hopes for a brief rest over Christmas. And I was the third project manager they had worked under since July. They knew I had no agricultural or science background and no eradication experience. As a politically appointed lawyer, I'm sure they expected me to offer the empty equivalent of a football coach's pep talk before sending them onto the field now in the fourth quarter of a losing game. I had to convince them this would be different.

Back in 1977, CDFA had brought in Michael Doyle, the co-author of *How to Make Meetings Work*, to teach how to conduct effective meetings. The classes were mandatory for management employees. It was the most valuable four-hour class I ever took. On Sunday night, we started with introductions and my agenda for the evening. The first step would be a brainstorming session on the problems to date, coupled with suggestions for change. We agreed each team would take notes during the brainstorming session. The four project teams would retire for further separate team meetings over dinner. Their task at dinner would be to turn their notes into a rough draft of their portion of the new eradication plan. Next, we would reconvene at 10 p.m., and as a group, we would review and critique each team's rough draft. I would then collect the drafts and go to my room, and it would be

50

up to me to write the final plan. I asked them to trust me to produce a polished, typed plan by morning.

We then went around the room clockwise, with each person contributing a specific comment. The first few brainstorming comments and suggested improvements were helpful. Then, the third speaker began with a pessimistic disclaimer disparaging his suggestion before even making it. "Stop!" I said, slamming my hand down on the table. "If we doubt our new plan will work, how can we expect the public to get behind it?" Then I quietly added, "Assume whatever resources are needed to implement your suggestion will be provided. Now, please begin again." A shock went through the room. In that moment, the possibility that we might be able to eliminate the medfly if we formulated a bigger and better plan than anything they had seen before, took flight. New bold suggestions poured forth.

Over the next few hours, the tentative outline of an all-out winter ground offensive took shape. It would be much larger than anything attempted before. In addition to the release of twice as many sterile flies, it would center on two new elements. The first would be a mobilized city volunteer stripping program, like that proposed at the Thurman hearing, within which the project would itself mount a military-like door-to-door campaign of stripping all host fruit in the most heavily infested core. Second. trucks would follow the stripping crews in the core area, spraying malathion bait in every yard. We hoped by engaging the public in the battle, it would be seen as eradicating a community menace, and not solely as a problem for farmers or government to solve. The new plan called for repeating the door-to-door ground spraying every 7 to 10 days—in other words, the same rotation as aerial spraying. The plan would require a huge increase in resources for the stripping and ground spraying. The trucks needed at least a three-man crew and would have to tow a spray rig behind. The crew would drag long hoses into each yard and spray the foliage. If larvae had been found, they would apply a second pesticide, fenthion, known as Baytex, on the ground under the foliage.

Finally, the plan called for doubling the number of sterile flies released and increasing the number of insect traps deployed to a minimum of five per square mile. The quarantine would be tightened by adding inspectors at airports and increased public education efforts and roadside signage. At no point did I tell anyone present that we could not achieve each element of the planned changes. Our planning focused on what it would take to win on the ground. I emphasized our job was to ask for what we needed and assume we would get it. I said it would be my responsibility to get the resources needed. Each of the four teams then left for separate locations for dinner and to write up their part of the four-part plan.

At 10 p.m., we reconvened. The group reviewed each of the plans and suggested further changes and improvements. The changes were scribbled in the margins or on separate sheets of paper. By 11:30 p.m., I was pleased with what we had and confident I could pull it together with the help of the Steno pool staff. I thanked everyone for their work, then went to my room and pieced together a handwritten final draft of the new plan. By 2 a.m. it was in good enough shape for me to go to bed for a couple of hours.

At 5 a.m. I got up and telephoned the steno staff in Sacramento. Using the marked-up draft, I dictated the final plan over the telephone. They delivered 50 printed copies to Director Rominger when he arrived for work. He then drove to San Jose with the copies, arriving in time for a meeting with me and the team leaders. At a second meeting prior to Thurman's 1 p.m. hearing, Rich briefed key farm leaders on the new plan.

At noon, Isi and his fruit stripping team began their first meeting with representatives from the 16 cities who would be organizing the voluntary stripping programs. It soon became clear that the minute aerial spraying had been postponed, the commitment to stripping fruit had all but evaporated. Only one city, Palo Alto, had taken steps to implement such a program. The others said they were waiting for directions. Our team also learned that none of the cities had allocated any funding for staffing or any other resources. Isi asked me if we could offer to pay the salaries of the city volunteer coordinators. Without checking with anyone, I agreed we would. We needed their help, and like Teddy Roosevelt, sending the fleet halfway around the world, I intended to approve the resources needed until someone stopped me. The shock value of the new plan would fade quickly unless the public saw dramatic evidence we were serious. My goal was to exploit the initial surprise by pouring reinforcements into the Santa Clara Valley. Whether we could sustain the forward progress would depend on performance, not promises. Without additional resources, the new plan would fare no better than earlier ones. I was confident no one above me wanted that outcome.

At 1 p.m. as scheduled, Thurman gaveled his one-man hearing to order. Rominger had given Thurman an advanced copy of the new eradication plan and now distributed the remaining copies to the press. He then read it as his opening statement. The four-page plan described a broad military-like counter-offensive, complete with objectives and a timetable for achieving them. D-Day was set for January 5th, the first workday after the New Year's weekend.

The plan described how the most heavily infested areas, dubbed the "core," would be subjected to an unprecedented rolling ground attack on the flies. Residents would be contacted door to door and given written notices that stripping crews would arrive the following day to strip all host fruit from their yards, and a second crew would come a day or two later to spray malathion bait on trees and other foliage. The stripping in the core area would be completed by the end of January, with repeated ground spraying continuing every week to ten days for at least six applications. Residents in the rest of the infested area would be asked to voluntarily strip their yards of fruit. Rominger also presented the additional elements of the plan, such as tightening the quarantine, deploying more traps, and increasing the number of sterile fly releases.

Thurman was visibly pleased with the detailed written report and revitalized eradication strategy. He asked Rominger if Governor Brown should declare a State of Emergency. Thurman knew Rominger had blocked a request for an emergency declaration suggested by the county during the summer of 1980. At the time, Rominger resisted because neither the federal nor state officials believed that the medfly in the north was out of control. Declaring the situation an emergency would have sent the wrong message to Japan and other countries already nervously monitoring the program. If California had declared an emergency, these countries might well have decided to quarantine all California host produce at the peak of the harvest season, precipitating an economic disaster for farmers. Taking Thurman's cue, Rominger responded, "At this point, we do believe a declaration of emergency would assist us in getting the message across to everybody that this is a serious matter in Santa Clara County." He added that the intensified program in the next five weeks would also need public cooperation and more funding from the Legislature. As I had hoped, the public unveiling of a new aggressive eradication plan that did not involve aerial spraying dramatically changed the atmosphere. Momentum replaced resistance. Thurman's hearing scheduled to prod a stumbling bureaucracy into action had showcased an energized new alternative for eradicating the medfly with community support instead of opposition.

After the hearing, Rominger and I met privately with our USDA partners. They had been caught flat-footed with no plan except to continue to press for aerial spraying despite the overwhelming community opposition. They had expected the city stripping effort offered as an alternative on December 10th to fail to materialize, or if it did, to be too little, too late. Then when it was discovered that the medflies had not died in winter, the cities would have no basis for resisting the commencement of aerial spraying around February 1st or soon after. The new plan implementing a fruit removal program and ground spraying left USDA with little choice other than to go along with the proposal as written, at least until Thurman's announced postponement expired on January 31st.

At the end of a long day, Rominger invited me to fly back to Sacramento with him on the state's airplane. During the short flight, Rich and I drafted the Emergency Declaration. I believe he and Governor Brown huddled later that night to discuss the request and the additional resources we would need in Santa Clara to win the ground war.

The next day the news media gave broad coverage to Assemblymember Thurman's hearing and the new plan. The *San Jose Mercury* quoted Thurman describing the infestation as "a grave situation that could ruin state agriculture." This press coverage was a welcome change from the paper's earlier do-nothing stance. After the story ran, the San Jose City Council voted 7-0 to request that the Governor use "every means at your disposal—including the National Guard to help clear trees of fruit that serve as hosts for the fly." The city's popular mayor, Janet Gray Hayes, joined the chorus of officials, expressing concern that the medfly posed a potential disaster. She stated: "We're talking about a 12-billion-dollar industry."

The farm community appreciated the recognition that eradication had to be the goal. However, they viewed anything less than immediate aerial spraying as an unworkable prescription for disaster. On January 17th, the *California Farmer* published a scorching and largely misleading editorial attacking those opposed to aerial spraying as "a few hysterical politicians" and USDA and CDFA as "spineless."

Governor Brown issued the formal Declaration of Emergency on Christmas Eve. By then, I was home with the family packing up the motor home. In the accompanying press release, he announced that he had ordered the Office of Emergency Services to:

> Coordinate the mobilization of the California Conservation Corps, the State Departments of Parks and Recreation, Forestry, and Fish and Game, the use of Caltrans ground sprayers and crews, as well as any additional state personnel and equipment that might be needed. [and] directed Frank Schober, the Commanding General of the National Guard to prepare a plan of action to assist in the overall state effort if it should become necessary to use the Guard.

In addition to the National Guard, I knew the Governor could order the California Conservation Corps to help with the fruit stripping. B.T. Collins, the Conservation Corps Director, had privately offered to send us 200 CCC volunteers to help with the stripping. I told the press the new effort to strip the heavily infested core area of all host fruit and follow that with the malathion ground spraying of thousands of yards could cost as much as 10 million dollars.

Before the Governor's Declaration of Emergency, the *San Francisco Chronicle* published a major story on the front page under the headline: "The Secret Report on Fruit Flies." The author, Rick Carroll, accurately characterized the first six months of the medfly fight in northern California as a history of bumbling incompetence. Regrettably, he wrapped the facts in a theme of government conspiracy and secrecy that had only now been revealed through the intrepid sleuthing of an environmental organization. The article described the project's advisory committee minutes as confidential secret documents. There was nothing intentionally confidential or secret about the minutes. They were public records under California's Public Records Act. However, they had not been publicly released until a formal request was made under the law. Advisory committees were a standard part of cooperative federal/state/county pest eradication projects. They enhanced the coordination of a multi-agency endeavor and provided scientific advice and oversight to field managers on how best to manage the difficult task of eradicating a foreign pest in a new environment.

Carroll accurately reported that local, state, and federal officials all "moved too slowly…and, because of mismanagement failed to gain the upper hand against the fast-breeding insect." The emphasis on who to blame for the present impasse did little to illuminate the stark choices facing the public and the state. Assemblymember Thurman had colorfully described the eradication project as a disaster and government officials as incapable of organizing a three-car funeral. Reading of the screw-ups described in the committee minutes infuriated him further. Thurman told the press: "It never should have gotten this bad as it is. There should have been more liaison with citizens and the local governments. I think they are on the right track now." His comment was pure Thurman-speak. He simultaneously gave a nod to both the concerned public and worried farm community by slamming the government for putting everyone in the current situation, then he deftly pivoted to endorsing the current effort as on the right track.

The remaining coverage over the Christmas holidays lavished praise on Governor Brown for his prompt and decisive action with headlines such as "Brown mobilizes fruit fly SWAT team" (*Sacramento Union*), "State to tackle fruit flies" (*San Francisco Examiner*), and "Brown orders 1,000 workers to fight fruit fly," (*Oakland Tribune*). Even the *San Francisco Chronicle,* in a follow-up article by Rick Carroll, lauded the Governor. Carroll combined parts of his story from the day before and, in this second article, added that Governor Brown was committed to employing every appropriate means at his disposal to rid the counties of the medfly. These positive stories helped shift public support both locally and in the farm community in favor of the January effort. However, they did not change USDA's position in favor of starting aerial bait spraying as soon as possible. Nor did the favorable press weaken the resolve of the local governments to resist aerial spraying at all costs. The community's support for the new program included a better understanding of the need to eliminate the medfly and a grudging acceptance of ground spraying malathion as the lesser of two evils.

The Governor's emergency declaration and the press coverage over Christmas were a godsend. It allowed me and the rest of the staff a brief opportunity to rush home and spend Christmas with family. It also made possible the increase in resources the new plan required. Without Governor Brown's personal commitment to giving the project whatever it needed, the new plan would have quickly failed.

On Christmas Day, the family opened presents in the morning, and I began packing the motorhome in the afternoon. I continued to mull over how to manage the build-up in San Jose while needing to return the motorhome and family to Sacramento. We left the next day for San Diego. On Monday morning, the 29th, I called the project office and quickly recognized I needed to be there in person. My wife agreed to drive the motor home back through L.A. traffic after New Year's, and I flew back to the project on the next flight.

Chapter 5 (The Medfly Technical Advisory Committee Meeting)

When I arrived at the former Berry Elementary School in Los Gatos, I learned that the Berry School, our new Medfly headquarters, had been our headquarters for only a week or so. Unknown to me, the move had been planned months earlier and scheduled for the normally slow two-week Christmas break. Our ambitious surprise attack would have been difficult to mount from the previous headquarters, a collection of trailers and temporary buildings in the City of Campbell several miles away. On the other hand, the school had everything we needed, including a large parking lot, multiple wings of classrooms all on one level, and a huge open playground area. The classrooms became offices and sterile-fly-rearing facilities. My office, the former principal's office, was centrally located at the school's main entrance.

I had just settled in when the staff told me the Federal-State Medfly Technical Advisory Committee would be arriving for a meeting with me scheduled for the next day. The committee had not met since November 20th. In the whirlwind of writing the new eradication plan, no one had mentioned this meeting. As the title suggested, the committee's advice was central to our operations. Without their blessing, our new plan could be dead before D-Day. I also learned on Monday that USDA had also named a new federal manager for the project. He, too, was expected Monday afternoon at the latest. I added meeting him and preparing for the advisory committee meeting, now less than 24 hours away, to my to-do list for the day.

Already on my list were three major changes in how the eradication project would be run, the first of which I had announced to the staff after the Thurman hearing in San Jose on December 22nd. That change had started immediately that day. The staff, henceforth, would operate as one team. Regardless of the agency that paid their salary, each employee would report to and be accountable to their project superior. No longer would state employees balk at taking orders from a federal employee or a federal employee from a state employee. The Allied command in Europe under Eisenhower had employed a similar integrated command structure to keep the allies fighting the Germans and not each other. In the Korean War, General MacArthur ordered an even more radical merger. He integrated shattered South Korean army units into arriving units of the U.S. Army to stop the North Koreans short of Pusan. We used parts of both models as appropriate. For example, groups of workers sent to the project from various state agencies were sometimes reassigned individually as needed. Alternatively, we left intact the internal chain of command structure of the National Guard and California Conservation Corps. At the top of the unified command structure, Wayne Granberry, the new USDA manager, became my new deputy project director. We hit it off instantly. Arnie Morrison, Isi Siddiqui, and the other section chiefs, who were all current state employees, would now report to me through Granberry. USDA further agreed to change its policy of rotating its personnel in and out every 30 days, something that had been disruptive from July to December. From now on they would stay six months at a time. Granberry told me another federal manager would join us in a week. We agreed he or she would head the detection section covering both trapping and fruit collection. The current state detection manager, Dick Fehlman, would return to his other duties in Sacramento but continue as a member of the advisory committee.

On Monday, the 30th, I implemented the second change. This one involved eliminating delays in obtaining equipment and personnel. Delays in acquiring needed equipment and supplies had plagued the project from June until now. I asked Dick Knoll, the manager in Sacramento for the unit that approved equipment and supply requests for the department, to assign special staff to Los Gatos with the authority to approve our needs on the spot. If necessary, they could be purchased the same day locally. The personnel office in Sacramento similarly assigned a senior personnel analyst to my office at the project. From now on personnel decisions involving state personnel on the project would be initiated and approved in Los Gatos. If a problem developed, it would be elevated to me. Both the personnel office and supply sections reported to the division chief of administrative services in Sacramento. He reported to me. Thus, this second change eliminated several layers of bureaucracy that had contributed to the project's poor performance during the summer and fall.

The most controversial change was the one I announced on the 30th. I believed public trust and confidence in the commitment and integrity of our renewed effort would come only if we were completely transparent with the media. Accordingly, I announced to the staff that reporters, television crews, and public officials were welcome everywhere on the premises at all hours. Reporters could interview and ask questions of employees and of me as they wished. Furthermore, the advisory committee meeting scheduled for the next day would also be open to the press. The idea that our operations and mistakes would be fully exposed struck long-time civil service employees as extremely risky, if not insane. They foresaw an avalanche of articles like the December 24th article in the *Chronicle* becoming a daily disaster as our every screw-up led the local evening news. Most had little experience talking to the press and worried they might say the wrong thing. I told them the public had every right to know what we were doing. The press were the eyes and ears of the public whose support we needed and whose awareness of the gravity of the medfly problem was critical to eradicating it. I told the staff not to worry about making a mistake. We had nothing to hide. The policy proved to be a good one. The trust that came from openness far outweighed the few "gotcha" stories.

Meanwhile, I had no idea how to obtain the support of the advisory panel other than to put on a brave front and ask them to approve the new plan. I knew USDA fully expected our plan to fail and had reluctantly signed on only for January. They wanted aerial spraying to start on February 1st or soon after. My ignorance of this important advisory committee meeting and not knowing about the move to new quarters reminded me how unprepared I was to manage the project. It mirrored how unprepared I was four years earlier to be a deputy director of the largest state Ag department in the country. Then as now, I had no alternative but to plunge ahead and do my best. I hoped to get the new plan approved at least until the end of January. The committee had previously balked at approving aerial spraying in winter. It was still winter. Furthermore, they knew that if they voted to start aerial spraying on February 1st, it would be blocked again as it had been in December.

The day after the meeting would be Wednesday, the beginning of the New Year's holiday weekend. With many state offices and departments operating with skeleton staff for the rest of this week and none on the weekend, I could not see how we could be ready our new official D-Day on Tuesday, January 6th. We were counting on hundreds of new people and vehicles arriving between now and next Monday, the 5th. The city stripping coordinators would need direction and support. The CCC stripping crews would also need training and direction. The spray crews would require medical testing, and we would need to coordinate their work with that of the stripping crews. In addition, the complicated process of receiving shipments of sterilized pupae from overseas labs, rearing them to adulthood, and releasing them by the millions did not stop for holidays or weekends. Nor did the quarantine inspections. I could not be everywhere at once. Given the complexity and time pressure we were under, even if everyone worked 24 hours a day, being ready in one week might be impossible.

What made it possible turned out to be the outstanding work of the four managers I had chosen, plus the outstanding assistant leaders they each had chosen to help them. Isi Siddiqui's first call had been to Don Henry. An entomologist familiar with the medfly program, Henry had been a Green Beret intelligence specialist on a twelve-man team deep in the jungle in Vietnam before returning to finish college. John Pozzi, also a Vietnam combat veteran and an entomologist, was, like Henry, smart, soft-spoken, hardworking, and dependable. Pozzi would later convince me to approve his purchase of an Apple II computer. For the rest of the project, Pozzi and the computer would prove invaluable in calculating the life cycle of the medfly under varying temperature conditions.

While I was in San Diego Sunday night, the 28th, Pozzi and Henry had prepared a huge map of the infested area for use at the meeting. Using trapping records from the prior six months, they pasted red dots for flies and yellow for larvae—on the map at locations where wild medflies had been trapped or found in fruit.

Monday afternoon, I met with Henry and Pozzi and reviewed the map that would be the centerpiece of our presentation on Tuesday afternoon. Our plan, as outlined a week earlier, proposed an intensive ground program in a core area that we had only estimated at a maximum of sixteen square miles. However, our map showed not one but two clumps of dots. The sixteen square miles area covered the cities of San Jose and Santa Clara. Another clump of dots covered an area several miles away in the northwest corner of Santa Clara County around the City of Palo. Scattered red dots were sprinkled in between and elsewhere in what was the originally estimated 100-square-mile infested area. Our strategy assumed winter dieback would reduce the number of wild flies and increased sterile fly releases would be enough to eradicate the widely scattered and presumably less heavily infested gap area and periphery. I was cautiously optimistic the map, combined with our ambitious stripping and ground spraying plan would be sufficient to secure the advisory committee's approval the next day.

An hour before the start of the advisory committee meeting, a red-faced Arnie Morrison barreled through the open door of my office. "I just got off the phone with Caltrans," he said. "They only have ten spray rigs and twenty people who have volunteered. What do you want me to do?" "That wasn't the agreement," I snapped. "Let me see what I can do." Arnie turned on his heel and huffed off. I knew it would be impossible to spray tens of thousands of residential yards every seven to ten days unless the California Department of Transportation, known as "Caltrans," delivered the 100 trucks and spray rigs and their crews as planned. The Governor had promised we would have the support we needed. I picked up the telephone and called Rich Rominger in Sacramento. "Rich," I said, "Caltrans must understand that this is not a volunteer operation. We've got to have those spray rigs, or this isn't going to work." He calmly thanked me for the information without saying more. I hung up assuming he would talk to the Caltrans Director, and the situation would improve. I had no idea my call would prove far more critical to our success than I had imagined.

After Arnie left, the advisory committee convened for their eighth monthly meeting, and the first since aerial spraying had been soundly rejected by the public and then postponed by Thurman. I had scheduled the meeting in the school's combination gym and multi-purpose room and invited the press and public to attend. The committee members were aghast at my putting them in this situation. However, I viewed a public meeting as the only way to give the community an opportunity to see them for the low-key advisory committee they were, not the ominous secret committee behind the aerial spraying decision portrayed in the *Chronicle*. I believed that regardless of their discussion and recommendations, secrecy would only deepen the divide and create paranoia about our ultimate intentions. This way the press would be able to see the committee's reaction to the new plan and the public's essential role in it. Whatever they decided, hearing the debate about what to do would further the goal of educating the public about the catastrophic damage the medfly would do if not eradicated. It would also help them recognize that aerial spraying had to remain an option until the medfly was eliminated.

Like every move so far in the thirteen days since Rich asked me to take over, Obtaining the committee's support, or at a minimum, their acquiescence to our plan would be a high-wire act with little room for failure. USDA would be pushing the committee to recommend aerial spraying beginning on January 31st. I had never met the two USDA members or attended any previous meetings. My inexperience together with scheduling the meeting in public, risked everything up to this point. However, to maintain the momentum, we had to have their tentative approval of the plan at least until the January 31 end of Thurman's postponement. I hoped the Governor's Declaration of Emergency and the resources he had pledged would be enough for them to let us try. If they refused, I did not have a backup plan.

The committee's chair, state entomologist Don Dilley, opened the meeting by offering a brief opening statement clarifying their role as strictly advisory. It was up to management to decide how to run the program. While technically true, his purpose was to insulate himself and the committee members from criticism for an unpopular aerial spraying decision or the uncertain ground program I was proposing. Dilley then introduced the other members and the agencies they represented. Dick Fehlman from the Department, along with Dilley, were California's two representatives. Next were the two county agricultural commissioners, or their deputies, representing the two infested counties, Santa Clara County and Alameda County. The committee's most knowledgeable and powerful members were the two experts from USDA, Dr. Roy Cunningham, and Dr. Earl Osaki, a scientist with USDA's Animal and Plant Health Inspection Service APHIS) from Honolulu. Both possessed a lifetime of experience researching medfly behavior. My expertise as the new manager of the project was equivalent to that of a pilot flying a four-engine plane while leafing through a how-to-fly manual. They were the experts. I was not. On the other hand, our plan's virtue was that it was not aerial spraying in winter. Plus, it offered a temporary way out of the current impasse. It might only be an interim step but it made sense for now.

After the introductions, I outlined our new plan with the help of Don Henry and Isi Siddiqui. When I finished, the committee immediately pushed back, saying the 16-square-mile core area was too small. The map showed dozens of dots scattered outside our core area, far too many, in their opinion to believe the sterile fly releases throughout the unsprayed area would be able to achieve eradication. Dr. Cunningham led the committee's attack. He said a core area of 20 square miles wouldn't be enough. He suggested the minimum core area needed to be at least 50 square miles. The others agreed. They also suggested the stripping program should continue beyond the end of January to cover the additional area they were recommending. I knew USDA would oppose any further delay of aerial spraying. I had gone into the meeting banking on the committee approving the plan. Now it was being rejected in front of the press I had insisted be present. The only way forward was for me to accept their recommended changes. I thanked the committee for their suggestions and agreed to implement them. They then approved the effort to try. The plan was still alive at least until the end of January or maybe their next meeting.

The committee next took up the question of what to do if our plan faltered. Sensing their deadline of January 31st slipping away, USDA asked the committee to recommend a specific trigger that would require the project to switch to aerial spraying if the fruit stripping ground program had not been fully completed by the end of January. They also suggested an automatic trigger for aerial spraying be the discovery of any new flies after January 31st. None of the members of the committee either proposal was reasonable. We all knew some fly emergence in January was all but inevitable. Insects, from houseflies to mosquitoes, commonly overwinter in conditions far colder than anything in northern California. Logically, at least some medfly pupae already present in the ground or as maggots suspended in development inside fruit, and maybe even some adult flies, would survive. Thus, the USDA proposal was tantamount to an automatic requirement to begin aerial spraying after the end of January no matter how successful the ground program turned out to be.

The debate then turned to finding another benchmark for success or failure, preferably one the opponents would concede was fair. The public had asked to postpone the aerial spraying in favor of fruit stripping. USDA and some of the committee members doubted the community effort would meet expectations. If it didn't, the opponents would have no real defense to aerial spraying other more delay or accepting the medfly as a permanent state resident. I told the committee that fairness required success or failure to be determined by something based on science and rationally related to the problem. Whether the stripping succeeded or not did not answer the question of whether aerial spraying was necessary. The debate reminded me of the anecdote about a man kneeling under a streetlight looking for his lost car keys. When asked by a passerby, "Where did you last see your keys?" The man points to a dark corner down the street. The passerby asks, "Then why are you looking for them here?" To which the man replies. "Because the light is better here". Furthermore, no one knew what effect, if any, winter would have on medfly reproduction or even when winter would end. January 31st was too soon to know whether we were succeeding or not.

no later date was acceptable to USDA, and there was no agreement on the appropriate date to judge success or failure.

The science suggested that it would only require a few survivors after January for the medfly to quickly rebuild the infestation. From a biological perspective, any sign of new breeding after January 31st, such as viable larvae in fruit or trapping mated females carrying eggs, would be troubling. Therefore, the key issue became knowing when winter would end and when the emergence of new flies would begin. There was a general sense it could be as soon as February or March or perhaps as late as April. The emergence might well depend on the Santa Clara Valley's many micro-climates. With no agreement on timing, the entire issue was left unresolved until the next meeting except for a series of possible trigger recommendations that management could choose from if they wished.

After the meeting, I returned to my office. By chance, my call to Rominger had reached him as he was about to leave the office for a rare formal cabinet meeting scheduled for noon with the Governor himself in attendance. When I returned to my office after the advisory committee meeting, I received a call from the Deputy Secretary of the Transportation Agency to which the Department of Transportation reported. When I talked to Rich Rominger I had forgotten that Caltrans was part of the Transportation Agency. The Deputy Secretary first confirmed he was talking to me. Then he said, "Mr. Scribner, the next time you have a problem with one of our departments, please call me directly." Before I could respond, he continued, "My boss just got 'reamed out' by the Governor in the cabinet over this." Then he spat out, "You will have your trucks and crews by next Monday." I politely thanked him, took down his telephone number, and promised to call if further problems arose. From that day on, we had outstanding support from Caltrans and from all the other state agencies, too.

Not long after this call, Arnie arrived back at my office. "I don't know what you did," he said, "but Caltrans now says the rigs will be here Monday. They asked me if there was anything more they could help with." Arnie gave me a quizzical look and asked, "What did you do?" I said, "I made a call." Overnight, word spread through the ranks. The effect was electric. Morale and confidence shot up, and preparations for the kick-off of the ground program went into overdrive.

After the advisory meeting, Don Henry and John Pozzi revisited the map of yellow and red dots and tripled the size of the core area to a total of between 43.5 and 50.1 square miles. Was it enough? There was no way to know. In any case, we knew we simply did not have the resources to cover the gap between the core in San Jose and the concentration of larvae around the City of Palo Alto beyond releasing sterile flies in that area. The area targeted for the intensive ground program now covered half of the original 100 square miles, divided into two core areas with a gap in between.

Removing all the host fruit and ground spraying fifty square miles was triple what we had originally estimated we could do. Expanding to the 100-square-mile area originally targeted for aerial spraying was impossible. Our success depended on hoping that winter would reduce the population and our suppression efforts would reduce it further. Beyond that, it would be up to whether the available sterile flies could be released in large enough numbers to outcompete the wild males so that surviving females produced only sterile offspring. Finding new larvae would signal failure, and we knew it.

Having the meeting in front of the press paid huge dividends. The lack of any firm decision on aerial spraying left all the attention on the presentation of the new plan. The *San Jose Mercury News* ran a full-page article on the meeting, the first two paragraphs of which were colorful in ways a canned press release generated by a government project would never have been.

> SWAT teams" armed with ladders, plastic bags, and pruning shears will pour out of their tent encampment at the Santa Clara County Fairgrounds on January 6th to do battle with the Mediterranean fruit fly. The fight will rage for up to two months 'door-to-door, block-to-block.

Isi Siddiqui had used the "SWAT" moniker to help me present the plan. It stuck and was picked up by other news outlets around the state. The article went on to describe the plan in detail as laid out in the public presentation. The press coverage of the meeting gave the community a first-person inside look at the advisory committee debate and detailed information on what to expect. It was exactly what we needed.

BOOK

TWO

JANUARY – JUNE

1981

Chapter 6 (The First Month)

On Monday, January 5th, 1981, I left the family home in Carmichael, a suburb northeast of Sacramento, and drove south toward the project office in Los Gatos. Alone in the pre-dawn darkness, I knew I faced an uncertain future, if not an impossible situation. As I crested the Altamont pass from the Central Valley and coasted downhill into the Livermore Valley, the sun rose behind me and began to burn off the morning fog. My fear of failure yielded to the security of familiar surroundings. The Bay Area was the longest I had ever lived in one place. It was where I attended UC Berkeley and became the first in my family to finish college. It was the place where I met my wife, where we married, where our son was born, and where I graduated from law school. Maybe the project's new eradication plan would succeed.

The day marked the beginning of a new year, a new decade, and soon, the inauguration of a new president, Ronald Reagan. In Sacramento, re-elected and newly elected legislators would take their seats for the first day of another two-year legislative session. Traffic, now bumper to bumper, began to slow as I reached San Jose, then transitioned to Highway 17 toward the project headquarters in Los Gatos. I imagined the drivers around me were also headed to work, with some to a new job and others to a new semester in college. I doubted many were worrying much about the Mediterranean fruit fly.

When I arrived, medfly headquarters still looked like the elementary school it had always been, except now, instead of children and teachers, the parking lot overflowed with uniformed adults exiting 6X6 olive green National Guard trucks, government agency pickups, and a variety of other government and private cars. I parked my state-issued Pinto and joined the others hurrying into our new offices.

The staff had done an impressive makeover during the weekend I had been absent. On the outside wall next to the entrance, a 4X8 plywood sign pictured a giant blue-eyed medfly with lettering identifying the facility as the "Home of old Blue Eyes." Don Henry met me at my office and took me on a brief tour. Telephones were ringing continuously in a former classroom repurposed as the project's phone bank. I had no idea how the phone bank had come into existence, nor who arranged for it to be staffed mostly by unpaid volunteers from Creative Initiative, a Palo Alto community organization. Maps covered the walls, displaying lists of what to strip and where stripping and spraying crews were scheduled to arrive in the next few days. Callers were told to strip nearly all tree fruits and to also strip vegetables, like tomatoes and peppers, from their gardens. Only leafy vegetables and root crops were exempt. Everywhere I turned, the project was humming with activity. In one wing, the classroom windows had been darkened to enable the rearing of fruit fly pupae until they emerged as sterile flies ready to mate with wild females. In another wing, supervisors were dispatching trappers to service the hundreds of traps used to detect wild flies. In that wing, next door to the trappers, another room contained fruit collection teams reviewing maps of their assigned quadrants for the day. On the sidewalk behind the classrooms, government pickup trucks, each specially equipped with a screened hut in the back, were lined up being loaded with stacks of lidded paper buckets. Each bucket held hundreds of buzzing sterile flies ready for release. The buckets would be emptied one at a time as each truck slowly roved through its assigned neighborhood. Later, boxes of newly emerged adult sterile flies would be loaded and driven to a local airport for aerial release over the infested area.

In the covered walkway outside my office, TV crews were setting up cameras as reporters waited to ask questions. No formal press conference had been scheduled for this morning, but in response to media requests, they had been told I would shortly hold the first of what would become daily morning press briefings at which I shared new information and answered questions. The media had been at the project all weekend, ducking in and out of rooms and buttonholing staff for information about the plans for the coming week. They already knew more than I did about all that had been done to get ready for D-Day.

The morning headline in the *San Jose Mercury* read, "Fruit-fly campaign underway." A list of useful facts related to combatting the medfly appeared next to a story covering the build-up over the weekend. The details of how the stripping program would work filled four long columns on the back page, including Don Henry's promise that homeowners would be contacted personally before the stripping crews showed up. "We're not going to be the Gestapo," he said. "We're not going to march into someone's yard, saying we're doing this in the name of the State." This detailed coverage of what we were doing and why reinforced the message that we were all part of one big community effort. Further support came from Governor Brown's office in Sacramento in the form of a lengthy press release detailing again the multiple agencies pouring into the community to help defeat the medfly and reiterating his commitment "to employ every appropriate means at our disposal to rid the counties of medfly infestation." The *Mercury* reported the CCC members would be coming from as far away as San Diego in the south and Yreka near the Oregon border, and they would be uniformed and under the direction of experienced state employees as they went door-to-door helping with the stripping.

The media loved the CCC. They were the cavalry come to the rescue, fresh-faced reinforcements, the unsung heroes of the war. The National Guard had set up showers, portable kitchens, a medical aid station, and other support services on the Santa Clara County Fairgrounds. By nightfall on Sunday, the 4th, 450 CCC members had arrived and settled into their temporary home for the next month. That evening, they received a briefing on the project and then watched a training film our staff had prepared that described the work they would be doing.

Uniformed Department of Forestry personnel had arrived over the weekend and were put to work delivering notices to the residents scheduled for stripping in the first 100-block area. They continued going door to door on Monday, taking notes on what needed to be stripped and speaking personally with each resident if possible. At the Berry School, the ground-spraying staff administered blood tests to a long line of local applicants being hired to work with the Caltrans employees on the spray crews. The pre-work blood tests were part of the worker safety protocol needed to ensure that the spray workers did not experience any change in their level of cholinesterase. More spray rigs arrived. Although less than the 100 promised, we had all we needed to get started.

To accommodate parking and fueling the large number of trucks involved in the ground spray program, Caltrans commandeered a stretch of cleared state-owned land in the nearby city of Campbell, scheduled to become part of a new cross-town freeway. They turned the right-of-way into a huge, fenced dirt parking lot and maintenance facility. During operations, more than 100 truck-trailer rigs would start the day lined up nose to tail at this new satellite facility. Each night, the rigs would be serviced and refueled. By the next morning, they would all be lined up and ready to move out beginning at 8 a.m. Arnie Morrison's program staff at the school prepared maps and addresses for each day's operations of the spray crews and recorded what they completed. This process would be repeated daily, six days a week. Isi Siddiqui's staff similarly managed the paperwork for the CCC fruit-stripping crews. Another part of Isi's team coordinated the voluntary stripping programs being operated in 16 cities. Security staff guarded the headquarters in Los Gatos and the fenced equipment yard in Campbell twenty-four hours a day.

Monday afternoon, Dick Knoll arrived from Sacramento with the draft contract for constructing a new State sterile medfly rearing laboratory in Hawaii to complement the federal one. He had also arranged who would manage it. All I had to do was approve it and thank him, which I did. With luck, the new facility would be in operation by April shipping us 100 million sterile pupae a week. This would allow us to double the number of sterile flies released around the time we believed new emergence would peak. Rominger and the Governor quickly facilitated the layers of approval needed. Dick and I flew to Hawaii a couple of weeks later to meet with our new lab director, Nori Tanaka. By then, work on the new lab was well underway.

At Monday afternoon's press briefing, I told the press we were going to need more help to complete the stripping on time. I already knew Governor Brown intended to order another 400 CCC members into the fight. His announcement came later in the week. At five o'clock, I held the first of our end-of-the-day staff meetings. At each of these daily wrap-up meetings, I called on each manager around a long conference table to briefly report on their unit's progress and problems. In this way, everyone could see the whole picture, and any conflicts or needed coordination between programs could be ironed out on the spot. I kept the meetings positive, productive, and short. My presence allowed decisions to be made and shared quickly. The confidence and initiative displayed by team leaders strengthened every element of the plan.

After Monday afternoon's staff meeting ended, I went to dinner with Arnie Morrison and his four lieutenants. We all knew that no infestation this large had ever been eliminated other than by widespread pesticide spraying. In 1929, Florida had done it on the ground. After that, it had always been with malathion bait by air or sterile flies. The dinner was my way of impressing Arnie and his team on how critical I considered their role to be in winning this battle. In 1981, cell phones mostly did not exist. Most of the cheap motels we stayed in did not have telephones in the rooms, and there was no internet or texting. To stay in close touch with Arnie's close-knit team, I made it a point to stay at their motel every night for the first two weeks and met them for breakfast and dinner each day. As much as I believed in and supported the stripping and sterile fly elements, I knew SIT had succeeded only twice, and each time, it had been against a much smaller and more localized infestation. This time, the only way the sterile fly releases would have a chance to complete the eradication would be if Arnie's team succeeded in killing a substantial portion of the emerging overwinter population before they matured enough to start mating.

Fortunately, the environmental advocates and the public accepted the malathion use, provided it was not applied by air. The Sierra Club readily conceded that it was a weak pesticide and generally safe. Nevertheless, they opposed the aerial bait program because their membership would not accept aerial spraying. In addition, they argued that the ground spraying of foliage made better sense environmentally. It sounded plausible, especially since most of the aerial bait landed on streets and rooftops. However, those who have experienced the annoyance of common house flies and mosquitoes know they do not spend all their time on foliage. They land everywhere. The aerial bait drops would be everywhere a fly could touch down. That much of the bait would land on roofs, sidewalks, and streets was helpful, not wasteful, as environmentalists claimed. I could never understand their opposition to a small amount of pesticide use applied for a limited time if that would prevent the need for a far greater continuous amount of pesticide use.

D-Day on January 6th dawned bright and sunny. At the fairgrounds, the CCC troops were roused early, fed, and loaded into trucks and vans that rolled out to begin the fruit-stripping campaign. National Guard trucks followed them down each street, picking up the bagged fruit in the neighborhoods targeted for day one. Excitement rippled through the community. The possibility that aerial spraying could be avoided had seized the imagination of the residents opening their doors and yards to the young men and women of the CCC.

"Tree-Stripping Starts Today" led on page one of the San Jose Mercury, along with a huge picture of uniformed CCC members unloading cots from a National Guard truck. The project's deputy director, Wayne Granberry, was featured in a glowing profile on page two, as were the personnel from other agencies sent to the battle by Governor Brown. Not surprisingly, the coverage skipped any mention of the door-to-door malathion bait spray program scheduled to follow the stripping. This omission reinforced the impression that fruit stripping alone was the alternative to the feared aerial spraying. It was illogical but helpful in facilitating acceptance of our ground spraying. However, the emphasis on stripping and ground spraying as an eradication strategy would later undermine the public's support of aerially spraying malathion when that became necessary.

The paper's afternoon edition, the *Mercury News,* included another half-page picture of the huge Exposition Hall at the county fairgrounds jammed, front to back and side to side, with cots and CCC members. It recalled the iconic pictures of U.S. troops and their equipment before the landing in Normandy. The lead story and more pictures highlighted the significance of the day for the Corps and its members, noting that the medfly battle was the largest and most challenging assignment of their young lives and of the CCC's history up to this point. The story continued on the back page, covering all the columns save one on the far-right edge, squeezing in President Reagan's announcement of his new cabinet.

In another front-page story, Tom Harris, the *Mercury*'s highly respected environmental writer, led with:

> They have battled raging floods in the Delta, fought blistering forest fires in the Sierra, and helped trap squirrels with bubonic plague.

> Now the California Conservation Corps is battling the Mediterranean fruit fly...Their motto is 'Hard work, low pay...and miserable conditions.

He chronicled all the work the CCC routinely performed on behalf of the environment and the work experience and training opportunity it offered urban youth willing to be part of the tough jobs and discipline required. A box in the middle of this and other articles featured a new logo depicting a medfly inside a circle with a diagonal line through it. It bore the words: "Battling the fruit fly." This logo would appear regularly in future editions. Below the logo, readers were directed to medfly articles on pages 1B, 3B and to an editorial on page 6B. Like Harris' article, the editorial supported the project and urged the public to "Join the Medfly War." It recommended community cooperation by all, followed by a specific list of bullet points on how residents could help.

The evening television coverage of D-Day began with Governor Brown's visit to the project headquarters that morning. The cameras had followed him during the day as he watched the CCC climb ladders and strip fruit from a large grapefruit tree. They also showed the Governor in a meeting that afternoon with the County Board of Supervisors, where he briefed them on the newly released proposed state budget.

Something else occurred early Tuesday morning before the Governor and legislative entourage arrived at the project. Technicians entered my office and installed a bright red telephone with a smooth face and no dial. I learned of it later because when Governor Brown arrived, he took me aside and told me he had ordered it installed and that it matched a second one on his desk in Sacramento. He added that if either of us lifted the phone, it would ring at the other end. He told me to use it if needed and that he would too. I took it off my desk as soon as he left and placed it high up on a shelf behind me. I never intended to use it, and even more, I hoped it would never ring. I said nothing about it to the staff, and neither had the technicians, so far as I knew. However, I learned later that its presence and purpose were whispered among the staff. Combined with the earlier call from Caltrans to Arnie Morrison after I intervened, the presence of the red telephone suggested that Governor Brown and I were secretly in frequent communication. Receiving all the support we needed reinforced this belief. The truth, however, was more mundane. Governor Brown had endless other matters on his desk. The red telephone didn't ring, and I didn't pick it up for the next six months. But only two people knew that—Governor Brown and me.

Tuesday morning, we published our first edition of The Daily Medfly. A one-page, single-spaced fact sheet summarizing what had been done the day before and what we had planned for the current day. These daily updates on the eradication effort covered everything from the number of wild flies caught in traps to the number of properties stripped the previous day, the number sprayed, and the number of quarantine inspections conducted. The Daily Medfly also provided information on the advisory committee meetings, legislation in Sacramento and Washington, pending lawsuits, and occasionally human-interest stories related to the battle. Reporters could and did follow up with further interviews of project personnel on any matters they wished.

On January 8th, we caught the first fertile medfly of the new year in a trap in the City of Santa Clara near the center of the core area. Like a pitcher in a baseball game who comes to the mound with the bases loaded, this first find and the next one, maggots in a strawberry guava collected in the same city on January 14th and identified on the 21st, represented problems we had inherited. They proved only that winter had not eliminated the medfly. The fact that the fly, when dissected, proved to be an unmated female further supported the theory that it had recently emerged and no mating had taken place.

To speed up the fruit stripping, Governor Brown announced he was ordering another 400 CCC troops to San Jose to join the stripping effort, saying he was doing so to ensure "we have done everything possible to eradicate the medfly." Where to house these much-needed reinforcements when they were expected to arrive on January 19th presented a new problem. The fairgrounds were full, and other events were scheduled to start in a few weeks.

The campaign picked up speed during the rest of week one. In week two, the CCC members exceeded their goal of stripping 50 blocks a day. Many homeowners stripped voluntarily before we reached them, thereby further increasing our progress. The ground spraying crews that followed close behind found that most homeowners were fully cooperating. During the first two weeks, we experienced only 30 outright refusals, a 1% rate of non-cooperation. We released 102 million sterile flies during week two, exceeding our official goal of 100 million two weeks in a row. With the cool weather, we believed this number was sufficient for the number of flies emerging. We knew we needed to double that number but would not be able to do that until the new rearing facility being constructed in Hawaii came online in April.

On Friday, January 9th, the project published a huge full-page notice in the San Jose Mercury Garden section in large black letters. The notice led with: "TO ALL SOUTHBAY RESIDENTS WITHIN THE MEDFLY QUARANTINE AREA." Below that was a large map of the quarantine area next to which, again in huge block letters, appeared, "YOUR HELP IS NEEDED." Under the map, another headline read, "FRUIT REMOVAL CAMPAIGN" followed by sections on "Here's How You Do It" and a Q&A captioned "Will This Do the Job?" Finally, at the bottom, the notice listed the city phone bank numbers as well as one for the main project phone bank. Those calling received answers to their questions as well as referrals to their local coordinators. In addition, the project funded the leaflets being distributed by the city programs we had helped organize. City coordinators mobilized a wide range of community groups to help participate in the city stripping programs. The Boy Scouts in San Jose distributed 200,000 leaflets. Nine hundred individuals volunteered to help strip fruit in Palo Alto. In the cities of

Saratoga, Los Gatos, and Monte Sereno trash bins were made available at strategic locations as a convenience to residents. The project footed the bill for the bins. Girl Scouts folded leaflets in Saratoga, and community groups volunteered in Los Gatos. Some cities appropriated funds to support their volunteer efforts. In San Jose, the garbage company agreed to pick up fruit bagged in plastic bags without charge and to bury them under at least a foot of soil at the dump. Outside the core area, voluntary stripping by homeowners far exceeded expectations. By the end of week one, 13 cities had voluntary fruit-stripping programs in operation. Two more cities joined the next week.

These first two weeks of unprecedented community support and our own extraordinary efforts set the tone for the next six months. There might be no way to know until April or May whether our efforts, no matter how heroic, would be sufficient to achieve eradication. Farmers and officials in other states were in no mood to wait that long. They were even more impatient than USDA to see the swift initiation of what had worked in Florida and Texas—aerial spraying.

On January 11th, Doyle Conner, Florida's Ag Commissioner, announced a formal hearing would take place on January 27th in Lakeland, Florida, to consider whether their state needed to quarantine California since aerial spraying had not yet started. Director Rominger and I were invited to present California's case about why such a quarantine should not be imposed. At the same time, Florida dispatched Charlie Poucher, their chief of pest control and eradication, to California to thoroughly appraise the status. He, too, would be a witness at the hearing. The next day, I was summoned to appear before the Santa Clara Board of Supervisors to report to them on the progress of the eradication effort. They insisted the project drop any further consideration of aerial spraying now that the stripping program had been implemented, claiming that they had fully performed their part of a bargain in agreeing to do stripping instead of aerial spraying. There had been no such agreement. Only Assemblymember Thurman's unilateral postponement of aerial spraying until January 31st. I told the Board I was confident that the fruit stripping and ground spraying of malathion bait was working, and if it did succeed in eradicating the flies, aerial spraying would not be needed.

However, we would not know that for some time. Therefore, aerial spraying would remain a possibility because total eradication had to be the goal. California could not live with the medfly. I would repeat this message throughout the spring each time they summoned me to appear before them.

Charlie Poucher, a 30-year veteran of Florida's medfly battles, turned out to be every bit the expert we needed. I found him genial, free of artifice and possessed with an encyclopedic knowledge of the medfly. Despite the public pronouncements in Florida about the dire situation in California, he arrived with an open mind. We responded with the same candor as we had with the press and the community. We were in the hands of a fair referee. Soon after I met him, I would recommend he be added to the advisory committee. That happened in March when we expanded the membership to include Poucher and two others.

Poucher proved both his expertise and attention to detail when he discovered evidence the medfly could infest native vegetation in California not previously known to be a host. This discovery occurred when Poucher, while watching CCC crews stripping fruit, got out his pocketknife and probed the inedible plum-like fruit of a California laurel tree. To the surprise of everyone, it harbored dead medfly larvae. He and Wayne Granberry surveyed the ridges around the area and found that, fortunately, the laurel trees were not fruiting this year. It proved yet again how adaptable the medfly could be.

During his week on the project, Poucher thoroughly reviewed every aspect of what we were doing and met with everyone from the lowest level employee to me. Before he returned to Florida, he pronounced the project—

> This is the best-organized major campaign I've observed
> in a long time. I believe this effort will turn off some of
> the heat (for a quarantine). There's no doubt in my mind
> that you are going to eradicate it. These people are
> working doggone hard.

Shortly before the 400 additional CCC members were due to arrive, the federal government rejected our request to house them at the Moffett Naval Air Station in the heart of the infested area. Instead, the National Guard built a tent encampment for them on the spacious grounds of a nearby state hospital that was in the process of being closed. Modeled on the Roosevelt-era CCC, creating the California version had been a pet project of Governor Brown. B.T. Collins, a colorful and charismatic former Green Beret captain who had lost an arm and a leg in Vietnam, reportedly asked Brown to appoint him as the CCC director. The Governor did, but Collins' version of how he got the job had changed by the time reporter Susan Yoakum interviewed him for a February 6th article in the morning edition of the *Mercury*. He told her that Brown had insisted he take the job. Collins, who had previously served as one of Brown's legislative aides, said he told Brown, "No, no, a thousand times no. We had a terrible fight. He let me scream at him for a while. He has a way of leaning on you where you can't let him down." After his appointment, Collins instilled in the CCC a work ethic and sense of pride like that of the elite force he had been a part of in Vietnam. He also created their motto— "Hard work, miserable conditions, and low pay." The Corps members had previously been called upon to fight flood and fire emergencies. Now they began referring to their role as fighting "floods, fires, and flies."

The media could not get enough of the CCC, publishing article after article and doing human interest interviews on TV. One such article described how, after getting up at 5:30 reveille and working a ten-hour day stripping fruit, many had lain down on tables at the fairgrounds to donate blood. Their boss was right there with them, giving blood, too. A crew of eight nurses and four aides collected the blood. Collins told the nurses he needed thirty-four pints of blood to save his life in Vietnam. He said, "We are repaying California for the privilege of living here."

When I heard this story, I recalled the day when, as a deputy director, I had attended the annual meeting of the California Tomato Growers Association. B.T. Collins was the featured speaker. In an unusual speech, he shared what he told the mostly disadvantaged youth and high school dropouts who joined the CCC, kids whose lives up to that point had not gone particularly well. He said he told them how lucky they were. He told them they could have been born anywhere in the world. But they were lucky enough to be born in America. You could have been born in some other state but were lucky enough to be born in California. And then, he told them, you have been allowed to join the CCC. He reminded them that someone had fed, clothed, and housed them for 18 years. Now, it was their turn to give back, to contribute to the common pot that had nourished them instead of asking for more. He told them (and the audience), that he did not believe in making exceptions for women, minorities, or even the physically disabled. Everyone could and should contribute, he said. And he made a point of emphasizing their motto of hard work, low pay, and miserable conditions.

His message was well received, as you would expect from this group of hardworking, often self-made farmers, who, like me, mostly believed in the Horatio Alger view that we had each succeeded mainly through our own hard work. I and many in the audience nodded in awareness that our lives might not have turned out so well. We had been lucky. We, too, had been nurtured and cared for by others growing up. Much of our success was due to where we were born and the support of our parents, plus the work of others who had the foresight to build the schools, the water projects, the roads, the university agricultural research stations, and the overseas markets. We might have worked hard and chosen wisely, but so had others before us. I left the convention humbled by the reminder of my own path, one with no money for college, admitted to the University of California at Berkeley when tuition was $200 a semester, and then admitted to its law school, where I received a first-rate legal education and a law degree. I realized how lucky I had been to have had adults nurture me along the way at home, in school, in Little League, high school sports, Sunday school, scouting, the YMCA, and so many other institutions. Collin's remarks reminded me how much life depends on others and on circumstances beyond our control.

As the CCC moved toward completion of their part of the stripping program, director Rominger and I were swept up in a whirlwind of public appearances as the focus switched to what would happen after January 31st. On January 22nd, I appeared before the medfly advisory committee at their first meeting since the December unveiling of the new plan. The stripping and ground spraying had far exceeded what they had expected and believed possible. Dr. Cunningham spoke for the committee, saying, "You have exceeded our expectations." Privately they remained wary of any suggestion aerial spraying might not be needed.

In my presentation, I acknowledged the outstanding effort to date while being clear-eyed about the limitations and uncertainty ahead. I reported that our sterile fly releases of 100 million per week in two of the last three weeks exceeded the total number released every week of 1980. The committee was satisfied the number of sterile flies we were releasing was sufficient for the limited number of wild flies emerging during January.

Next, they took up the question of when winter would end, and spring emergence of a new generation of flies would most likely occur. Two wild flies had been trapped, one on January 5th and another on the 16th. Two more wild flies were trapped the day before the committee arrived. All four were unmated females, In the opinion of the committee, they were not indicative of any new breeding in 1981—at least not yet. The maggots found in the strawberry guava were also attributed to the post-winter emergence of larvae whose development had been held in check by the freezing weather in December. The committee then discussed the trapping and fruit collection statistics for January and made various technical recommendations for improvements in both efforts.

After acknowledging the progress of the ground program in the core area, the committee declined to assess whether we had succeeded or not. They also declined to predict a specific date when we might see new breeding in February. They debated but reached no decision on when the main emergence would be most likely to begin. Dr. Cunningham ventured that the main spring emergence could be in March, April, or even May. It all depended on the temperature.

During the meeting, a member of the public stood and proposed abandoning the aerial spraying option in favor of more extensive ground treatments. To my surprise, the committee members respectfully accepted his request and added it to their agenda for their meeting in February. The courtesy shown by both the requester and the chair demonstrated a growing acceptance that these meetings could be conducted in a fully open and transparent manner.

On January 27th, Rich Rominger testified in Lakeland, Florida, before a panel deciding whether to impose a quarantine on shipments of fruits and vegetables coming from California. I had prepared remarks and was scheduled to accompany Rominger, but I have no recollection of speaking at the hearing. Our progress in January, plus Charlie Poucher's strong support, convinced the Florida Ag Commissioner and his panel to hold off on any quarantine for the time being. We had dodged another crisis and gained a little more time, though it would turn out not to be much.

The following day, I testified in Sacramento at a televised joint Assembly and Senate Agriculture Committees hearing. Additional legislators from districts in the Bay Area also attended. I gave the same cautiously upbeat report of the first month as the one I had recently presented to the advisory committee and the Santa Clara County Board of Supervisors. Other witnesses, including representatives from farm organizations, testified favorably. The Chairman, John Thurman, and rural legislators especially liked hearing me say that our goal remained complete eradication and that aerial spraying would be an option if needed. My remarks about aerial spraying were widely reported in the media in San Jose, resulting in another summons from the clerk of the Board of Supervisors demanding that I appear in person again on February 9th.

On February 5th, the California Conservation Corps began pulling out. Although the advisory committee had suggested that two months might be needed to complete the mandatory stripping of all medfly host fruits and vegetables in the core area, it was completed in 30 days. As they packed up to leave, the local media had one more opportunity to thank them. A photo of a proud and happy B.T. Collins dominated the front page of the *Mercury's* metro section. Under the picture, a lengthy article lauded Collins' humor, hard-drinking, irreverence, and tough love. It quoted what Collins called his Martin Bormann speech, a talk he said he delivered weekly to his troops. According to the interviewer, the talk went something like this:

> I don't care about you. Your personal happiness is of no concern to me whatsoever. My personal credo is I can work you to death. Forget about democracy. You left democracy at the bus station…Now go out there and finish the job.

The article concluded with another picture of him in uniform surrounded by Corps members. It was a warm send-off by an appreciative community. The CCC and the community had stripped the core and 80% of the city areas. There would be no homecoming parades here or in their home camps all over the state. The war was not over. But the first major battle had been won. The stripping had hopefully removed maggots in fruit that had not developed due to the cold weather while at the same time limiting the host fruit available for mated females. The CCC had been the beating heart of a community effort that turned panic and anger into hope.

Now that the stripping was complete, we put the ground spraying on a seven-day-a-week schedule. However, the assumption that Fenthion would kill pupae in the ground as it did in Hawaii and apparently in Los Angeles was not the case in Northern California. We discovered this near the end of January when Arnie Morrison, ever the worrier, began questioning Fenthion's effectiveness. He recommended testing the kill rate. Staff buried sterile pupae in screened plots and then sprayed the ground with Fenthion. All the pupae survived and emerged as flies. Learning that Fenthion did not work meant it had been useless in 1980 and so far in 1981 as well. We had no idea why it didn't work but now knew that no pupae had been killed on the 59,000 properties we had sprayed in January. We shared the discovery with the media and public with a predictable hit to our credibility. After telling everyone we knew what we were doing, a simple field test proved otherwise. The press was gentler than I expected. The headline on February 4th was "Pesticide failed because of lack of data." They quoted me as follows:

> I know the public reaction is, 'Is this any way to run a railroad?'
> We are like Columbus sailing off the end of the world here. You take the information you have and run with it. There is very little research on the Medfly in Santa Clara County. Scientists have to play a guessing game based on Medfly problems in Hawaii, Costa Rica, and elsewhere. We could have done a better job earlier.

The headline in a second article the same day was "Useless Spray deplored by Medfly project chief." I took responsibility for our continued use of it until the initial doubts had been confirmed by further testing. I also said the decision to stop its use was unrelated to health concerns. "If it were killing the medfly, we'd still be using it," I said. Dr. Kahn confirmed that although Fenthion was more toxic than Malathion, it would not present any serious health hazard if used properly. Arnie Morrison and USDA continued evaluating several stronger pesticides to replace the Fenthion. Diazinon proved to be 100% effective against medfly pupae. We switched to Diazinon a week after discovering the problem and used it for the rest of the project.

Republican State Senator Dan O'Keefe, a persistent critic of the project, jumped on our revelation that Fenthion did not kill medflies and claimed Malathion didn't either. His attempt to create more controversy went nowhere at the time. His information appeared to come from a state entomologist who no longer worked on the project. I had reluctantly ended this employee's temporary assignment to the eradication project after he refused to follow the instructions of his superior, a federal supervisor. He then tangled with a fellow state entomologist. I returned him to his regular unit in Sacramento. From there, he continued to criticize the project and later sued me. Ironically, given my open-door policy with the press, he claimed that the real reason for the transfer back to his regular job was my objection to his speaking to the press. Senator O'Keefe continued unsuccessfully for the rest of the project to try and discredit me and the eradication project. Years later, a jury concluded I had not violated his rights.

On Monday, February 9th, I appeared before the five-member Santa Clara County Board of Supervisors as requested. No one's position had changed. USDA still wanted aerial spraying as soon as possible. The county board and local city councils wanted aerial spraying permanently shelved. My position continued to be that the medfly had to be eradicated, and until it was, aerial spraying would remain an option if needed. Because the stripping goals set by the advisory committee had been met, and no new breeding had appeared, USDA could not claim the new ground program had failed. However, the pressure from farm interests on USDA to force aerial spraying increased by the day. January 31 had come and gone. Farmers and ag officials in other states, along with their Congressional allies, could not understand why USDA did not take over and do the spraying themselves. The eleven-member Southern Plant Board, representing states from Texas to South Carolina, suggested shipments of California fruits and vegetables into or even through their states be barred unless California agreed to immediate aerial spraying.

Despite this pressure, USDA did not want to act unilaterally against California, especially without the explicit approval of the advisory committee. The committee's wait-and-see attitude had, by inaction, extended the January 31st deadline indefinitely. Long-standing policy also constrained USDA. They favored working cooperatively with state departments of agriculture in the same way that California's department worked cooperatively with each of the locally appointed county agricultural commissioners. For USDA to override a sovereign state would set a precedent they desperately wanted to avoid. It also might not work. A federal court might not agree that they had unwritten emergency power of this nature.

However, to buy more time for the ground program to succeed, we needed a reasonable biological definition of success or failure, one that would reassure fruit growers in California, other states, and the world that we had the will and foresight to move to aerial spraying if it became necessary. At the same time, a clear marker for success or failure would give the urban community notice that the medfly was simply too destructive to be ignored and allowed to spread throughout California and, ultimately, to the rest of the United States. In addition, Aerial Malathion bait spraying had been reviewed and approved by the California State Health Department as posing no significant health hazard and had been safely used in the past in other states to eradicate this pest. Irrational opposition to aerial application of what we were using on the ground was not a sufficient reason to allow medflies to ruin agriculture in California.

I began my report to the County Board on a positive note, pointing out all that had gone well so far. I told them that we remained optimistic we could win on the ground. If not, I said we cannot simply ignore the damage living with the medfly would create. Therefore, we intend to begin contingency planning for aerially spraying to be prepared should that become necessary. Ignoring the frowns of some and glares of others, I said the project wanted the planning to include a public discussion of the details of what might take place. For example, what kind of planes should be used? How high would they fly? What time of day might the spraying occur? How often? How many total applications would there be? Would only the core area be sprayed or the whole quarantine area? I told the Board that I believed these questions should be discussed publicly and with as long a lead time as possible. I appealed to their responsibility to recognize what living with the medfly as a permanent pest would mean to their own residents, the larger community of California, and the rest of the country. I said that even if the local community wanted to live with the medfly, their local actions would condemn the rest of California and ultimately the rest of the United States to a huge increase in pesticide use or to the enormous devastation that would inevitably result.

My appeal for rational public debate and responsible leadership met with stony silence, followed by a swift vote to instruct the county counsel to take all necessary legal steps to prevent any aerial spraying. Their reaction reflected provincialism at its worst. They seemed oblivious to the consequences that would result if their residents had to live with the medfly. They were equally unconcerned about the devastation their refusal would force on other communities in the state and nation. It came down to three words: malathion, aerial, and spraying, none of which, separately or together, posed any realistic threat of harm to the community or to human health beyond the risk of an airplane crash. That had been the Health Department's only expressed possible health concern. I recognized there would be no cooperation in preparing the public for an eventuality I hoped would not be needed. I ended my presentation where I had started, by repeating my belief that while aerial spraying currently appeared unlikely, it would remain a possibility because under no circumstances would living with the medfly be acceptable.

As soon as I left the board chambers, I returned to the project and held the afternoon press conference to reinforce that message. There I repeated the contingency planning announcement and explained why it was necessary. Reporters scribbled away as I shared further details about the aerial spraying planning to date, such as our plan to talk with aircraft companies about whether to use helicopters or fixed-wing planes. I said that we would also discuss with the Department of Health the need to update the health risk assessment. I also emphasized that our contingency planning would include consultation with the California Attorney General's office and USDA's attorneys about our legal authority to spray. With respect to timing, I pointed out that the most likely decision point would come in April when spring emergence would peak. We would know better at that time where we stood. I said, "We cannot lock the door on aerial spraying and throw away the key."

By stating that no decision was likely until April, I intended to reassure the community that no secret plans were already in place, nor was aerial spraying inevitable. However, my referring to April as the target for a decision triggered pushback from USDA and those calling for aerial spraying as soon as possible. They saw my candor as once again moving the goalposts down the road. Aerial spraying had been sought by some from August through November, announced in December, then postponed to January 31st, and then left undecided. Opponents suspected we might not be winning the war, but only delaying the defeat. Within a week, Texas would announce its intention to block California fruit from entering their state. Unknown to me, USDA also was ready to force the issue.

An editorial in the *Mercury* a day later helped calm the local fears. It first lauded the CCC effort, referring to my statement that they had finished two weeks ahead of schedule. It went on to state, "Chances are excellent there never will be a need to aerial spray with the pesticide malathion." Governor Brown also weighed in with a press release announcing another Mediterranean fruit fly emergency proclamation order. This one waived all state laws and regulations that would impede bringing the new sterile-fly-rearing facility in Hawaii fully online by April. He did this under the authority of the original emergency declaration. His support for winning with SIT and the ground program was reassuring to the opponents of aerial spraying who believed he would never approve it. I believed the Governor, like me, hoped it would not come to that, if for no other reason than its unpopularity. The Governor and I never discussed what he would do if aerial spraying turned out to be needed. Yet I also could not imagine that Rominger would have announced it in December without at least warning the Governor he was about to do that. Now, if we failed, there would be no other choice. I was confident Brown knew it was a possibility, especially after I announced the contingency planning.

The next advisory committee meeting was set for February 19th. A decision on what would signal failure could be deferred no longer. USDA wanted an automatic trigger. I wanted something more nuanced and settled on the word "criteria." I began preparing for the meeting unaware that events at home, far more important to me than the medfly, would soon require me to immediately leave the project. When or if I would return would be left up in the air.

Chapter 7 (My Mother is Hospitalized)

A secretary entered my office late Tuesday afternoon, February 10th, and said, "Your wife is on the phone. She told me to interrupt you." When I picked up the phone, my wife said, "I'm sorry to bother you. Your mother is in a hospital in Eureka. She has been diagnosed with a brain tumor and is scheduled for surgery to remove it tomorrow morning. You need to come home." My head spun. What was she doing in a hospital three hundred miles from Sacramento, where my parents lived? She had always been in good health, and at age 60, she still worked full-time for the federal government.

I threw a few things in a briefcase, explained the situation, checked out of my motel, and drove to Sacramento. There I learned that my mother had complained of headaches and memory loss over the weekend. On Monday while I had been in front of the Board of Supervisors, she had been seen by a doctor in Sacramento. Based on her symptoms and a conversation with my father, who had accompanied her to the appointment, the doctor recommended a CT scan and said it was urgent. The earliest appointment in Sacramento was three weeks away. My youngest sister worked in the radiology department at a hospital in Eureka, California. My father called her and learned the hospital could do the scan that evening. Within an hour, my parents left Sacramento for Eureka, five hours away. The scan was performed soon after they arrived. It revealed a large mass in her skull and surgery to remove it had already been scheduled for the following morning.

Before I arrived home, my wife had arranged care for the kids and animals. We jumped in the car and drove all night to Eureka, arriving in time for me to see my mother at 6:30 a.m. for what I thought might be the last time. As she was prepared for surgery, she wanted to talk about what I was doing on the medfly project but couldn't make the words she wanted to say come out. Each time she asked about fruit flies, she said fruitcakes. Other words did not work either. I held her hand until she was wheeled into surgery. We waited anxiously for word of the results. When the neurosurgeon came out, he said the tumor was malignant glioblastoma, an incurable fatal condition. He gave her three months at most.

After the surgery, she lapsed into a deep coma that continued in the ICU with no change. The doctor said it was doubtful she would ever regain consciousness. The family met and, per her wishes, agreed to have her disconnected from all medical interventions except a feeding tube. My wife had to return to Sacramento. I stayed in Eureka, waiting for the end, briefly checking in with the project. She was in and out of consciousness over the next few days. On Monday, the 16th, I flew back to San Jose with plans to return to Eureka on the weekend.

When I arrived at the office, the staff handed me a letter from Scot Campbell, USDA's newly appointed national director of emergency pest management projects. In the letter, Campbell called for aerial bait spraying to be automatically "triggered" upon the appearance of any wild medflies after March 1, 1981. No wild medflies had been caught in February and only the four unmated females in January. If any emerged in March, they too might well be from pupae already in the ground from 1980. Thus, the proposal would force the initiation of aerial spraying regardless of any evidence the winter effort had failed or any evidence that new mating was occurring.

I quickly drafted a response, then picked up the telephone and called Campbell in Sacramento. I urged that instead of a trigger, we agree on criteria for a change in strategy based on evidence the ground program had failed. I offered to drive to Sacramento and meet him for dinner that night to discuss the matter. He accepted. Campbell and I both respected Bill Quarles, the senior vice president for governmental affairs at Sunkist, and asked him to join us at the dinner. While aware of the pressure USDA faced from Japan and other states, Quarles also recognized how little the resistance had changed since December 3rd. His grasp of the national and international fear of the medfly spreading and his informed and perceptive appreciation of the political climate in California and Washington, D.C., was helpful.

When we met, I argued that the revitalized SIT program could eradicate a small number of wild flies if there was little evidence suggestive of new breeding. In 1975, the medfly had been successfully eradicated with sterile flies even though there were twelve breeding sites and over 75 wild flies caught. Knowing we would not be given that degree of leeway, I proposed criteria set at a much lower level—15 wild flies or three larval finds in separate locations. Campbell accepted the proposed criteria based on new breeding. I drove back to San Jose Tuesday morning to finalize the proposal for the advisory committee's February meeting, now less than twenty-four hours away.

Before the meeting, a new crisis arose. The elected Texas Agricultural Commissioner claimed California's failure to implement aerial spraying required him to act to protect Texas citrus growers. To do so, he announced that beginning on March 1st, all trucks coming from California carrying fresh fruits and vegetables subject to medfly infestation would be stopped at the Texas border and turned back unless the contents had been fumigated. We knew the real reason was that his citrus growers continued to resent California's quarantine of Texas citrus infested with another pest, the Mexican fruit fly. The existing multi-county quarantine in Northern California already banned shipments of medfly host fruit from our area. The trucks Texas now proposed to stop came from the Central Valley, and other parts of California, not infested with the medfly. The urban infestation in Northern California offered the Texas commissioner a political opportunity to make a splash in Texas and tweak both California and USDA. His stunt directly challenged USDA's national authority to determine the quarantine boundaries for an international pest.

Although USDA also wanted California to begin aerial spraying, it told Texas to drop its illegal blockade. When Texas refused, USDA joined California in opposing the Texas quarantine. Tuesday morning, Rich Rominger agreed to take the lead with Governor Brown and USDA on our response. The Governor wrote California's independently elected Republican Attorney General, George Deukmejian, asking him to seek a restraining order against the Texas quarantine. At the same time, USDA sent a letter to the Texas Agriculture Department pointing out that any quarantine greater than the USDA's California quarantine area of 500 square miles violated federal supremacy. Rominger also personally called the Texas Commissioner. USDA and Rominger's efforts urging Texas to voluntarily backoff failed. California would eventually have to sue Texas in the U.S. Supreme Court.

However, in the meantime, Wednesday's advisory committee meeting drew a large crowd of media and residents wanting to hear if aerial spraying would be ordered. I began my report with the fact that the stripping had gone exceptionally well thanks to the outpouring of community support. In addition, the ground-spraying crews were well into their second round of bait spraying 78,000 properties. No wild flies or larvae had been detected at all so far in February. The committee already knew the ground spraying with Fenthion had failed, and we were now using Diazinon. With respect to sterile fly releases, there were concerns with both the volume of sterile flies being released and their quality. We were releasing an average of 100 million a week, but that number was well short of our weekly goal of 200 million. I explained that there simply were not that many sterile pupae available from the USDA lab in Hawaii, plus those from the labs in Mexico and Peru. The lab in Mexico was sending us an average of 30 to 40 million a week, but Mexico needed the rest of their production for their own medfly program. Meanwhile, the new California lab under construction in Hawaii would not be online until April at the earliest.

The quality concern arose from the fact that the flies from Mexico were significantly smaller in size than the sterile flies from Hawaii and the wild flies. In addition, the pupae arriving from the USDA lab in Peru sometimes arrived in poor condition, with debris and other insects mixed in. This was not publicly discussed. Nor was the fact that the number of flies released did not match the number of pupae received. We had no way to count adult sterile flies being released. But we knew there were fewer adults than the number of pupae received because, like popcorn kernels, a percentage of pupae in each shipment would fail to emerge as adults during the four-day rearing process. The non-emergence percentage in some cases was as high as 18%. Despite this disconnect, the standard policy was to use the number of arriving pupae as the sterile release number. Thus, I announced at the February meeting that we expected to release 105 million sterile flies that week. The committee responded to this part of the report by noting that the assumed ratio of sterile to wild flies in the field, though less than hoped, still remained high enough in their view to prevent new breeding.

The advisory committee next considered the question everyone came to hear discussed—whether aerial spraying was still being consided. The answer depended on knowing with some certainty whether we were winning or losing the war on the ground. I said if there were significant evidence of new breeding, then aerial spraying would be needed. At that point, I handed out copies of the criteria we and USDA agreed upon. Immediately, I was challenged about how "significant" would be defined. I explained that 15 or more wild flies being trapped, especially females carrying eggs, or finding multiple larval sites or a combination of both would constitute significant evidence of failure. The discussion then turned to the underlying issue of when spring emergence would be expected to occur.

Dr. Richard Tassan of the Biological Control Department at the University of California in Berkeley addressed the committee on this issue. He noted that the generational development time in the tropics, Florida, Texas, and Los Angeles is generally estimated to be 28 to 30 days based on a steady temperature of around 80^0 F, 24 hours a day, year-round. In the Santa Clara Valley temperatures varied widely both f during different hours of the day and from place to place. In full sun, the ground might be warmer longer, while a nearby shady area stayed cool all day. Therefore, he had installed automatic temperature recording devices at various locations in the Santa Clara Valley to determine average ground temperatures in February. These recorded an average of 47^0 F for the low and 63^0 F for the high. Then Dr. Tassan told the committee that if it took 30 days in Hawaii, where in winter the daily temperature stayed close to 78 and in summer 85, then it would require about the same number of hours of warmth at those temperatures for medfly development to occur elsewhere. Thirty days with warm temperatures, all 24 hours, amounts to 720 hours of warmth. Using that as a yardstick for medfly development and matching it with hourly and daily temperatures measured in the San Jose area, Dr. Tassan told the committee he had created a model based on day-degree calculations of warmth to approximate how soon medflies could mature and create a first new generation in Santa Clara's various micro-climates. In Dr. Tassan's opinion, little spring emergence had so far occurred. That explained the lack of trapped flies in February. He told the committee the main emergence would probably not come until mid-March at the earliest, though a few flies in warmer areas would emerge sooner than others. He estimated the bulk of a first-generation emergence would appear by mid-April. He added that there might be some further laggard emergence in May.

Based on Dr. Tassan's research, the advisory committee endorsed the proposed criteria. Dr. Tassan agreed to appear at the next meeting to report further. He said more temperature devices were scheduled to be installed in early March, and these would provide continuous 24-hour readings on the ground temperature at a depth of one inch, which was the approximate depth of the pupae. Dr. Tassan's recognition that the length of time needed for medfly development in wildly variable climatic conditions could be determined by calculating total day-degree warmth in each location was a brilliant achievement. The calculations themselves were made substantially easier by the number-crunching ability of newly available Apple computers. Dr. Tassan worked closely with John Pozzi in determining when we could expect the flies in the ground to emerge and when we could feel confident that medflies in each area had been eradicated.

Our attempts to rely on science would continue to be riddled with unknowns, but for the first time since early December, I felt more confident we knew what we were doing. Over the next couple of months, all eyes would be on the level of emergence; that would determine whether aerial spraying was needed or not. We believed we would know in April whether we had failed or not. After this discussion, Dr. Cunningham said he was encouraged. "The program is going well," he said, "I am cautiously optimistic." Beginning with this meeting, Dr. Tassan became a key advisor to the project and the advisory Committee. He would eventually be added to the committee and serve on it for the rest of the eradication effort.

The committee next took up the proposal submitted by an audience member at the previous meeting. This person had requested that any further consideration of using aerial spraying be dropped in favor of using only ground spraying. A vote was taken, and the proposal was unanimously rejected. The rest of the meeting was devoted to technical issues related to fine-tuning the fruit collection and trapping protocols. The next meeting was scheduled for March 5th only 15 days away.

My mother regained consciousness soon after I returned to the project. However, she remained hospitalized in Eureka. Near the end of February, she was transferred by ambulance to the military hospital at Travis Air Force Base, located between Sacramento and San Francisco. A few days later, in the middle of the night, two highway patrol officers pounded on the door of my room at the Los Gatos Motor Inn. The officers reported that the military hospital had told my father he needed to come to pick up my mother since there was nothing more they could do for her. My father had called 911, panicked about dealing with my mother. He could not reach me because the motel did not have telephones in the roomsThe officers told me they would call him back and relay a message that I would call him back when it was light, and I had access to a telephone. When I got to the office and called him back, he begged me to intervene with the hospital to keep her as he could not take care of her. I called Congressman Vic Fazio and Congressman Bob Matsui that morning in Washington, D.C. They each called me back within hours and agreed to call the hospital. At their request, the hospital said they would keep my mother another day or two while my wife helped my dad arrange for home care with hospice.

Each weekend in March and April, I drove home to Sacramento to help my wife and other family members care for my mother. Sadly, she was incoherent much of the time, hyperactive, belligerent, or alternately incommunicative and docile. She hated losing her mind and wanted to die. The most difficult moment came when I was helping her in the bathroom. As I bent over to sit her on the toilet, she whispered in my ear, "Please kill me." It was the one thing she wanted most and the one thing I could not do to help her.

Early on the morning of April 27th, my wife reached me at the office with word my mother's ordeal had ended. She had been admitted to the hospital the day before and, at eleven that night, had drifted away peacefully. My wife stayed with my father through the night. I drove home to help with arrangements.

Governor Brown sent me a hand-written personal note that read:

You gave your mother much reason to be proud—in your outstanding work in the agricultural community and also in your humanitarian accomplishments. I hope this will be a source of comfort in this difficult time.

Jerry Brown

Chapter 8 (Cautiously Optimistic—March to June 1981)

In late February, after Governor Brown asked California's Attorney General to respond to the Texas Ag Commissioner's quarantine threat, a team of attorneys in the Attorney General's San Francisco office began working night and day to draft a request to the U.S. Supreme Court for a restraining order against Texas' action. On Sunday night, March 1st, Rod Walston, a senior California Deputy Attorney General, and the team leader boarded an overnight flight to Washington, D.C., to file the case. After he sat down, the flight attendant asked him what was in the banker's box on the seat next to him. He told her, "A suit." She offered to hang it up for him. He thanked her and then explained it held 60 copies of a case being filed later that morning in the U.S. Supreme Court, adding he did not want to let it out of his sight.

The press and court clerks were waiting when he arrived at the Supreme Court Clerk's office that Monday morning. They knew all about the case and its unprecedented nature and importance. Under Article III of the U.S. Constitution, the Supreme Court has original jurisdiction when one state sues another. In *California vs. Texas*, California claimed that the Texas blockade violated the Constitution's interstate commerce clause and usurped USDA's national quarantine authority. The California Avocado Commission, with the help of the project and A.G.'s office, made the same arguments in a nearly identical lawsuit they filed in the U.S. District Court in Dallas. They likewise requested a restraining order and preliminary injunction be issued. The Attorney General and USDA appeared in support of their case as well.

In Washington, the Supreme Court requested the U.S. Solicitor General advise them by March 4th of the U.S. government's position in the case. Meanwhile, the federal judge in the District Court in Texas took the matter under submission without issuing a decision one way or the other. Because neither court acted on the request for an injunction in time, the embargo went into effect as scheduled, resulting in trucks being stopped and turned back or rerouting their trip around Texas.

On Thursday, March 4th, the Solicitor General advised the Supreme Court the Texas action was illegal under federal law. We learned later that the next day, Friday, March 5th, the justices had voted 6-3 at their weekly conference to grant the restraining order. However, before any order was issued by either court, a settlement was reached over the weekend in the District Court case. Under the settlement, USDA agreed to conduct two public meetings in Texas to inform the public of the efforts to eradicate the medfly, and a Texas representative would be added to the medfly advisory committee. The District Court then dismissed the case based on this mutual agreement. Given the settlement, on March 9th, the U.S. Supreme Court stayed action in its case. It later decided not to issue an order prohibiting Texas from reinstating the embargo, assuming such behavior would not reoccur. The Supreme Court guessed wrong. Texas would do it again.

While the litigation was underway in Texas and Washington, D.C., I testified again at the Legislature in Sacramento, and Governor Brown met with the Legislature's Assembly and Senate Rural Caucus leaders and issued a long press release praising the U.S. Solicitor General for his support against Texas. The Governor also announced that he and Rominger had been in consultation with USDA Secretary John Block in Washington. Brown reported that all were pleased with the progress of the eradication effort. On March 4th, I appeared before the Santa Clara Intergovernmental Council, composed of local mayors and other elected officials from 22 local political entities, to update them on the status of the eradication effort.

On March 5th, the advisory committee returned to Los Gatos for meeting number 11. Dr. Cunningham did not attend because he had flown to Texas to testify as one of USDA's Federal District Court case witnesses. We reported that in the entire month of February, no wild medflies were trapped, and no larvae were detected. This was the first month since June 1980 without wild flies being caught in Northern California. Quarantine inspectors continued daily monitoring and inspections at airports, nurseries, landfills, and roadside stands. 1.8 billion sterile flies had been released to date, and the number of traps deployed set new records, as did the number of fruit-cutting collections. We were feeling more confident by the day that this might work, even though we worried that any day could bring an explosion of wild flies seemingly out of nowhere as had occurred in other countries.

As the clock ticked steadily toward spring emergence, public anxiety that aerial spraying might yet be ordered increased. We, and especially farmers, continued to worry about the adequacy of the existing quarantine. No actual barrier existed to keep the wild medflies confined to the areas where they had been found, such as would exist around a forest fire or a dike preventing a flood. Major freeways flowed with traffic 24 hours a day, bisecting the infested area. Flies could easily hitchhike inside cars whose windows had been left open. Sterile medflies were being trapped in the Central Valley as far south as Fresno and Tulare County and in Ventura County on the coast north of Los Angeles. If sterile medflies could turn up in these locations hundreds of miles outside the quarantine area, so could a wild one. So could larvae. Despite constant warnings of the danger of moving fruit out of the quarantine area, travelers departing local airports were caught carrying fruit in their hand luggage multiple times a week. There was no way to know if the fruit was homegrown or store-bought. Residents could also take fruit that they had stripped from their trees by car to relatives or friends without our ever knowing it. We worried every day that a wild medfly or larvae would be found outside the quarantine area. If that happened, it could easily trigger a statewide quarantine and the economic disaster that would follow.

At the meeting, I asked for advice on a series of hypothetical questions related to our contingency planning. The questions included whether to use helicopters instead of fixed-wing planes, the amount of notice that should be provided to residents, and whether the spraying would continue until eradication or be limited to suppressing the infestation to a point where the sterile fly release approach could finish the job. My questions were widely reported in the press, but the request for answers was deferred to the next meeting, scheduled for March 29th. Before that meeting, Dr. Frank Gilstrap, an associate professor of entomology at Texas A&M University, would be added to the committee, along with Charlie Poucher of Florida and Dr. Richard Rice, a University of California entomologist familiar with California's Central Valley citrus industry.

On March 6th, the day after the meeting, I drove to Santa Cruz, California, to speak at a seminar organized by Assemblymember Sam Farr on behalf of local farmers. John Thurman and the Agricultural Commissioners of Monterey, Santa Cruz, and San Benito Counties also spoke. The subject was both a progress report and a discussion of the criteria adopted the month before. The discussion opened my eyes to a fundamental problem with the criteria. While it provided an agreed-upon scientific basis for determining when it was time to move to aerial spraying, in practice, it would operate like the automatic trigger I had opposed. If the criteria were met, it would be all but impossible not to spray. In drafting the criteria, I had imagined multiple flies and larvae appearing simultaneously not one at a time spread over weeks or months. Like a doomsday clock, each tick of a new wild fly or wild larval find brought us closer to the trigger. The criteria had become a lit fuse, burning toward a requirement to move to aerial spraying as soon as the requisite number of flies or larvae was reached.

On Sunday, March 8th, a new crisis erupted sparked by the *San Jose Mercury's* publication of an explosive article claiming hundreds could die if any aerial spraying took place. This dire prediction was based on a letter signed by a group of 59 doctors writing as "Physicians in Opposition to Aerial Spraying of Malathion." Under the leadership of Los Gatos internist Dr. Allen McGrath, the letter stated that based on what they said was their study of the medical and technical literature on pesticides, aerial spraying of malathion would pose a "life-threatening risk" to one out of every 2,800 persons in the spray area. Their shocking conclusion was based on assuming many people might lack the liver-produced enzyme cholinesterase, which detoxifies the nerve-inhibiting effect of organophosphate pesticides such as malathion. Although the letter did not mention *Silent Spring*, the only basis for this entirely theoretical risk likely came from Rachel Carson's observation in Silent Spring that a person lacking the liver-produced enzyme that detoxifies malathion and other nerve-inhibiting substances could be at greater risk from exposure to Malathion.

There was no evidence that anyone in the spray area had such a deficiency, let alone that one in every 2,800 did. Nor was there any evidence that this had ever been a documented health problem in the multiple earlier aerial spraying programs for medflies and mosquitoes or the millions of uses of malathion by gardeners and others. Surely, if such a condition existed in human individuals or in animals, it would have been observed at least once during the many years of extensive Malathion spraying in backyards, aerial programs, and laboratory studies. The McGrath letter went even further, claiming, according to the article, that infants under two years of age were extremely susceptible to Malathion. There was no evidence for this stated in the article.

In the event of aerial spraying, the doctors recommended evacuating all individuals with health problems and establishing emergency health facilities to treat those healthy individuals likely to be stricken ill during any aerial Malathion spraying. This nightmare scenario of what aerial spraying might produce would linger in the public's mind for the rest of the program.

The *Mercury* contacted Dr. Ephraim Kahn, Chief of the epidemiological studies section of the California Department of Health, for his opinion. He told the reporter that the group's conclusions were "nonsense" and "absolutely naïve." Dr. McGrath, in turn, said, "Kahn is all wet." What I found maddening was the fact that no evidence whatsoever was offered by the doctors that anyone in the area or in California or the United States, for that matter, had ever been shown to be lacking the cholinesterase enzyme. Further, if such a person could be found, at 2.4 ounces per acre, how would any significant amount of malathion enter a human body such that it would need to be detoxified? The amount of malathion touching someone outside during aerial spraying would itself be insignificant, and most people would be indoors between midnight and 6 a.m. when the spraying was to take place. Thus, they would not experience any exposure at all. These doctors, like the public generally, simply assumed exposure and thus theoretical consequences while simultaneously ignoring the fact that there was no evidence that human health had been affected at all in any of the previous programs involving the aerial spraying of Malathion over human populations.

With respect to cancer, most of the studies of malathion and other pesticides were performed in laboratories and involved feeding rats high levels of the pesticide over a lifetime. The rats were then dissected to look for signs of cancerous tumors. Successive generations were also monitored for evidence of birth defects. These studies of Malathion were repeatedly negative for both cancer and birth defects (although one scientist disputed the absence of the findings with respect to cancer). However, opponents could and did argue that no formal studies had been conducted in which pesticides were sprayed on human beings, many of whom had a variety of existing health problems and ranged in age from babies to the elderly. The opponents also argued that the lack of reported health problems during the aerial spraying in Florida and Texas, and with Malathion spraying for mosquitoes, did not prove none existed because there had been no follow-up health studies on the possible long-term effects of aerial spraying on population centers. The inchoate fear of unknown risks proved all but irrebuttable.

The debate and the impossibility of proving any substance could be guaranteed safe in every imaginable situation reminded me of a cartoon from an earlier controversy involving the Food and Drug Administration (FDA). The cartoon showed two FDA scientists in white lab coats standing on a podium in front of a glass case with an upside-down, obviously dead rat. The caption below read: "And then on a diet of 100% garlic." In the case of Malathion, the rat studies found neither cancer nor teratogenicity despite large doses fed over lengthy time periods. Nevertheless, people still argued that Malathion, because it was a poison, should not be sprayed over a populated area because not enough was known to prove that, in the long term, it would not cause cancer or birth defects. After all, science had said thalidomide was safe. (Actually, according to *Wikipedia*, thalidomide was never approved by FDA for use in the U.S. However, it had been approved in West Germany. The birth defects in the U.S. arose because sample doses of thalidomide were distributed free to doctors by pharmaceutical company representatives as part of an unapproved effort to secure FDA approval. But that is another story.)

To its credit, the *San Jose Mercury* followed the Sunday article with a thoughtful editorial on March 11th. The editorial, titled "Unfounded fear of spraying," chided the doctors for "raising alarms on the basis of tenuous or nonexistent evidence" and for letting "their concern get the better of their judgment." The editorial stated that:

> Malathion has been aerially applied to populated areas at least three times…without any apparent sign of the calamities McGrath and his colleagues fear. Even die-hard pesticide foes concede that Malathion appears relatively innocuous at least in terms of immediate human health effects.

The editorial changed few minds. The public wanted absolute assurance of safety, and that assurance went beyond what past research and experience elsewhere could provide. I believed in December and January that as we sprayed Malathion on tens of thousands of yards repeatedly, and people learned what an economic and environmental disaster living with the medfly would be, they would recognize that a couple of ounces per acre of Malathion mixed with corn syrup bait sprayed from the air was safe. I could now see how naïve my assumption had been. If the ground program failed and aerial spraying became our only option, the explosion of public anger and fright would be every bit as misinformed and ugly as it had been in December 1980. The only way that could be avoided would be succeeding on the ground.

To keep the public up to date on the project, we continued publishing *The Daily Medfly*. George Farnham, a CDFA public information officer, Barbara Kohn from USDA, and later, Jacki Montague-Wynne and others served as editors. In addition, on January 9th, we had kicked off the voluntary fruit-stripping program with full-page informational advertisements in the *Mercury* and other newspapers. We did this again on March 15th, in a report to the community on all that had been done up to this point.

George Farnham was especially good at mixing in human-interest stories and background pieces on fascinating details of medfly behavior. Here is one from the February 13th edition of *The Daily Medfly*:

TO KILL A MEDFLY

We have several weapons in this eradication program that sometimes appear to clash—as they did yesterday. Sterile fly roving crews passed a residence near the core area in the morning distributing flies. Several hours later a spray crew came by the same residence, and the homeowner was disturbed about the spray crews killing the steriles. It does seem like a waste, but the fact of the matter is that very few of those flies were lost. Sterile flies are fed as they are reared in our facility here. When they are released, they are looking for mating opportunities – not the food portion of the protein bait attractant being sprayed. On the other hand, the newly emerged wild fly goes directly to the nearest food – hopefully, the protein bait containing the malathion which will zap them. At the moment we are trying to reduce the population of wild flies so that our steriles will be able to finish the job and breed the wild pest out of existence. It would be a scheduling nightmare to try to avoid clashes like this, but we do expect them to happen occasionally again. The loss of steriles is minimal and right now the most important tool is placing that bait attractant in the core area.

The most important story was always whether any new wild flies had been trapped. If none had been, as was most often the case, Farnham would run a banner "NO FLIES," often followed by a statement about how long it had been since the last one was caught. On March 18th, the lead in *The Daily Medfly* was the discovery of the first wild fly trapped since January.

"WILD FLY FOUND," blared the headline. Trapper Anthony Domingo had found the fly in a trap in Mountain View on March 12th.

When it did not fluoresce under black light, it was sent to the lab in Sacramento and dissected. On March 18th, word was flashed to Los Gatos that the fly was a wild, unmated female.

Trapper Anthony Domingo made the news again on April 23rd under the headline WE HAVE A HERO. Here is that story:

> Anthony Domingo, a young trapper, was one trap away
> from completing his day's work yesterday on LaVerne
> Way in Los Altos when a lady dashed into the street with
> a very ill baby. Domingo, who is planning to go to
> medical school hoping to follow in the footsteps of his
> mother, a doctor at Kaiser Hospital, recognized the
> symptoms immediately---convulsions, a febrile seizure.
> He put the mother, Linda Sharp, and 20-month-old
> Amanda in his vehicle and sped them to the nearest
> hospital, Veterans at Foothill and Hillview. Today all is
> well. Mother and child are doing fine, and Anthony is out
> on his trapline starting with the one he missed last night.
> Nice going, Anthony.

On April 6, 1981, Citizens for a Better Environment, joined by Santa Clara County and the cities of Palo Alto, Mountain View, Saratoga, Los Gatos, and Sunnyvale, sued CDFA, EPA, and USDA in the U.S. District Court in San Francisco. Their lawsuit requested an immediate Temporary Restraining Order (TRO) and Preliminary Injunction, prohibiting aerial spraying until after an environmental impact report was completed and public hearings held. The *San Francisco Chronicle* article the next day reported that the lawsuit claimed the project intended to dump up to "80 tons" of the controversial pesticide on up to one million people in the County. To further hype the imagined danger claimed by the plaintiffs, the *Chronicle* bracketed a quote in large type in the middle of the article reading, "Malathion is 'recognized as a nerve poison,' say parties to the action."

The plaintiffs alleged the spraying was imminent, as required to support a request for a restraining order. Spraying was not imminent, and for that reason, the court would later deny their request. The other claims in the lawsuit were also weak. First, they said the exemption issued by EPA allowing USDA to aerially use Malathion exceeded EPA's statutory authority. It didn't. They also claimed any spraying required the preparation of an environmental impact report (EIR), and lastly, the U.S. Constitution required public hearings before any spraying could occur. I was familiar with each of these legal arguments from my previous four years as a CDFA deputy director and earlier as a legal aid attorney, where I had obtained restraining orders in both federal and state courts. The opponents were correct that government actions impacting the environment normally did require the preparation of an EIR or, under federal law, an Environment Impact Statement (EIS). However, in an emergency, such as a forest fire, flood, or, in our case, a devastating explosion of crop-destroying insects, the time-consuming preparation of either of these would be unworkable. So, too, would be the normal public hearings and litigation that typically follow the release of a formal report. Such litigation often leads to delays of years or even decades. In our case, even a relatively short delay to prepare the report would have ended any possibility of using aerial spraying to eradicate the medfly before it spread beyond the ability to ever stop it.

Two days after the suit was filed, the *San Jose Mercury* courageously published a lengthy editorial, systematically rebutting every element of the lawsuit. First, they pointed out that no decision to spray had yet been made and might never be needed. Secondly, the Governor had declared a state of emergency; thus, the lawsuit was "probably…an exercise in futility." In addition, they wrote, "At most, the lawsuit might delay spraying for a while and cost state and local taxpayers a lot of money." Lastly, they noted, "If spraying is delayed for weeks or months by court hassles, the Medfly population will explode, and the pest will spread into other areas." The editorial concluded with this observation:

> To be concerned about the effects of pesticides is reasonable, but to oppose all pesticide use under any circumstances, regardless of the potential damage to others, is parochial and myopic. It would have been best for everyone if the anti-spraying suit had never been

brought; it would be better for everyone if it could be quickly and quietly forgotten.

However, the court filing sounded the trumpet of fear, summoning the court and the public to believe people were about to be subjected to a dangerous, unthinkable risk. I doubted the judge read the editorial in the *Mercury* or, if he did, that it influenced his decision. Instead, I was confident he and his clerks read all the pleadings in the case before he called the attorneys into chambers for a brief discussion. Rod Walston from the California Attorney General's Office appeared on our behalf. He was armed with detailed knowledge of what was and was not being planned. He told the court there was no present plan to aerially spray. It was only a possibility, and then only if circumstances changed. I provided a declaration to that effect under penalty of perjury. In addition, Walston, on behalf of the state, agreed that should circumstances change, we would not do any aerial spraying without giving a minimum of five days' notice to the plaintiffs and their clients. A formal ruling denying the request for a restraining order was issued on April 10th. In his ruling, the judge stated that he was not satisfied there was a real imminence of irreparable injury without the possibility of a hearing. He then set April 28th for consideration of the request for a permanent injunction. The *Chronicle's* headline the next day on the ruling was less than straightforward. It read, "Judge Evades Medfly Spray Issue."

"NEW FLY FIND" was again the headline in *The Daily Medfly* on April 9th. Of 106 flies found in one trap, two looked suspicious and thus were sent to the lab in Sacramento. One turned out to be sterile, the other was an unmated wild female. That the sterile flies outnumbered the one wild fly by 100-1 was encouraging, as was the fact that the wild fly in the trap had not mated.

More wild flies were trapped as the April emergence continued. Three additional unmated and immature females were identified on April 13th, followed by another unmated immature female on the 16th, and four more unmated immature females the next day. On April 20th, *The Daily Medfly* reported ominously: *SIX FLIES TRAPPED*. Four were again unmated females. However, the other two had mated. Worse, five of the six were trapped in the core area, the heart of the infestation in 1980, where we had stripped and sprayed malathion this spring. Two more unmated females were trapped there the next day. Obviously, winter had not killed these medflies. Neither had our ground spraying program. The criteria of multiple fertile flies in multiple locations had been met. The two mated females further confirmed that at least some new breeding was going on. Based on the Criteria, it could have been argued that it was time to call for aerial spraying.

However, we had all believed all through February and March we would have a clear sense by April of whether significant numbers of wild medflies had survived the winter and the extent to which the ground spraying campaign had mostly worked. Now, it appeared that the limited number of flies caught in April could be both the last gasp of spring emergence and, at the same time, an indication that only minimal mating had occurred. Alternatively, the two mated flies could be seen as proof we were seeing the beginning of a major blow-up. We simply didn't know—and neither did anyone else. Privately, those of us on the project did not believe it was time to start spraying, even though some wild flies were present and some new breeding had obviously occurred.

One reason for our reluctance to believe we had failed was the arrival of reinforcements in the form of more sterile flies from the new lab in Hawaii. The sudden availability of many more sterile flies increased the likelihood we could manage a surge in emergence. Dick Knoll, Nori Tanaka, and others in Hawaii had worked around the clock, seven days a week, to bring the new lab into production in 90 days. The first shipment of 20 million sterile flies arrived on April 16th. The following week, we released 115 million sterile fruit flies. We believed that even though there were more wild flies present than we had hoped, the new and larger sterile flies arriving would tilt the odds in our favor going forward.

On April 23rd, the advisory committee arrived in Los Gatos for the next meeting. The day before, The Daily Medfly had trumpeted, "NO FLIES," and on the day of the meeting, led with "AGAIN NO FLIES." The committee was as mystified as we were that all the trapped flies to date had been female. Not catching any males was perplexing, especially since the traps were designed to be more attractive to males. Why weren't they showing up in the traps? Furthermore, if significant breeding was occurring, where were the larvae? We had not found any since January. The most likely explanation at the time appeared to be that the flies being trapped were primarily attributable to the continued emergence of pupae in the ground at the start of the project.

The timing was consistent with the prediction of peak emergence around mid-April. Because all but two had been unmated immature females, that too suggested recent emergence. Finally, although the lack of males was concerning, all the wild females, mated and unmated, had been found in traps containing a hundred or more sterile flies. Thus, the sterile fly numbers appeared adequate to address some occasional minimal new breeding. Further support for a wait-and-see approach came from medfly research in other countries. There, catching mostly unmated females had, in some cases, been indicative of an infestation in steep decline. Accordingly, the advisory committee chose to postpone any decision on aerial spraying pending more evidence of new breeding, such as finding larvae.

Later events proved that the lack of males in the traps and catching mated females despite the 100-to-one ratio in each trap should have triggered more head-scratching than had occurred. Starting from the day I was put in charge of the project, I knew that success depended on the sterile flies seeking out and finding the fertile ones and mating, and I knew that this was an exceptionally elusive pest. The traps were not a reliable indicator of anything more than the fact that some wild flies were out there. The only sure way to find them was with sterile flies meeting up with them or by aerially supplying such a ubiquitous supply of poison bait that newly emerging flies, hungry for a meal, would find one nearby and never make it to a trap. I did not want to question the basic assumption underlying the SIT approach. Either the sterile flies were doing their job, or if not, we would fail. If we did, I secretly hoped that the failure would be so obvious and overwhelming that there would be no dispute that aerial spraying was the only way to save California.

My hope for a clear sign and, therefore, an easy decision was naïve. In April, the local citizenry continued refusing even to entertain the possibility we might need to move to aerial spraying. Resistance was, if anything, stronger than it had been six months earlier at the beginning of December. Technically, the criteria had been met. But neither we, the committee, nor even agriculture was calling for implementing aerial spraying. For now, aerial spraying would remain in reserve until we knew for sure where we were.

Early in the project, someone gave me a 12x15-inch sign reading, "NOTHING IS LESS IMPORTANT IN LIFE THAN THE SCORE AT HALF-TIME." I posted it on the wall behind my desk as a reminder that although December had ended with the medfly well ahead, January marked the beginning of the second half of the contest. I believed we were going to come from behind and win this thing with a strong second-half ground campaign. We were holding our own in April, but the odd weather and microclimates in San Jose did not answer the most important question. Were the females caught in April first-generation flies that had recently emerged, or could they be second-generation flies resulting from mating by the first flies caught in January? All four of those were unmated females, but that didn't mean there were no others that could have mated at that same time, producing a second generation in April. No wild flies had been identified in February and only one (unmated) in March. No larvae had been found. Under the modeling Dr. Tassan and the advisory committee were doing, the April flies could be the result of mating after January or new emergence. Was there a possibility that mating was going on under our noses?

The rest of the meeting went well, including a visit by Dr. David Nadel, a renowned expert on the sterile-fly technique at the International Atomic Energy Agency in Vienna. The advisory committee's notes reflected his observation that below 60 degrees, medflies are poor flyers. He said this could explain our failure to trap more wild flies, assuming they were present. However, after the meeting, in a casual conversation with me, he went out of his way to warn me not to put too much reliance on the limited number of wild flies that had turned up so far. He said his experience in Tunisia with apricots had been one of trapping only a few flies before suddenly, overnight, they were everywhere. Most of the medflies trapped in July 1980 had been found in apricots. The Santa Clara Valley had large numbers of apricots, both commercial and in backyards. Dr. Nadel's Tunesia experience sounded much like what happened to General Douglas MacArthur in the Korean War. In 1950, after a few Chinese soldiers were captured in North Korea, he and his staff adamantly refused to believe they could be part of a larger presence. When American troops reached the hills overlooking the frozen Yalu River, five divisions of Chinese troops materialized behind them from positions where they had skillfully remained hidden from aerial surveillance. I hoped we would not be faced with a sudden explosion like the one Nadel described. If that happened, I knew we would need to move to aerial spraying as soon as possible. Even then, it might be too late.

As we reached and passed the peak of emergence with signs pointing to only a minimal amount of new breeding, I signed on to the committee's view that there was no cause for alarm, at least not yet. Our contingency planning slowed down. However, two key elements of any aerial spraying program had already been decided. First, it would be done by helicopters and not by fixed-wing planes, as had been the case in Florida and Texas. The thought of a USDA fixed-wing plane going down over a city had haunted me ever since aerial spraying had first been proposed. As a teenager on an airbase in Tripoli, Libya, I witnessed a jet fighter crash on take-off and explode in a skidding ball of flame, immolating the pilot. The crash of a low-flying multi-engine plane in a city neighborhood would be far worse. Helicopters were smaller, safer, and made less noise. They were also a familiar presence to urban commuters on crowded freeways with their radios tuned to the eye-in-the-sky traffic reports and to those who lived near hospitals used to hearing the coming and going of life-flight helicopters transporting patients for emergency care.

In addition, using a helicopter in an eradication program had been done before in San Jose. After gypsy moths defoliated millions of acres of trees in the Eastern U.S., they were discovered in 1977 in California. A CDFA mapping process determined the parameters of the infestation in San Jose. Next, eradication staff sprayed a two-block area around infested properties by hand with the pesticide Sevin (Carbaryl). Later, they followed up with two aerial treatments by a helicopter spraying an insect growth regulator, diflubenzuron (Dimilin), to eliminate any surviving gypsy moth caterpillars that might have hatched. This use of a helicopter in an urban eradication program occurred in a 19-square-mile area of San Jose's Willow Glen neighborhood. Ten thousand residences in a 4-square mile area (2,500 acres) were sprayed by a Bell Helicopter 212, flying at 150 feet. No more adults or egg masses were found, and there were no complaints or human health consequences.

We decided in the event medfly aerial spraying turned out to be needed, we would employ the same pre-spraying public notice and education elements pioneered in the gypsy moth program. There, hand-delivered, door-to-door notices to residents and extensive coverage in the media had preceded the spraying. Don Henry, Isi Siddiqui, Jim Rudig, and CDFA's public relations staff implemented the successful Willow Glen strategy. Now, they were all part of the medfly program. The helicopter belonged to San Joaquin Helicopters, based in Bakersfield. Arnie Morrison, as the manager of the Curly Top spraying program, also used San Joaquin for his rural spraying program. We were already meeting with San Joaquin as part of our medfly contingency planning. We would later learn that USDA had put out a nationwide solicitation for helicopter spraying as part of their separate contingency planning. However, they and the low bidder, Evergreen Helicopters of McMinnville, Oregon, were unable to agree on a contract. Evergreen wanted a hold-harmless clause that USDA said they had no authority to offer.

By the end of April, a total of 25 wild flies had been trapped, along with more than a million recaptured sterile flies. Measuring the success of the program relied on the delicate task of sorting through piles of dead flies brought in from traps that often held 100 or more. In theory, it was easy to see which had been dyed in the lab and which had no dye on them. In practice, it was difficult. In April, more flies were being examined than at any time since the previous October. On a typical day, tens of thousands of recaptured flies were processed through the I.D. lab,

114

and of these, up to as many as a hundred suspicious flies were sent each day to the Sacramento lab for further microscopic examination. On April 29th, for example, the project lab examined 39,056 flies. Ninety-four were sent to Sacramento. All 94 turned out to have been irradiated. Ten of those did have some dye on their bodies but not enough to be sure. The next day, 58,177 flies were examined, a new record. 95 were sent to Sacramento. One turned out to be an immature female who had mated. Female medflies normally mate only once. In the mating process, the male transfers a sperm-filled cartridge, called a spermatophore, into the female's spermatheca. As eggs pass down the follicular tube, sperm is released to fertilize as many eggs as she can produce.

In April and May, a total of 33 wild flies were identified at the lab in Sacramento. But all but seven turned out to be immature, unmated females, indicating they had only recently emerged, and this cartridge had not been transferred into their bodies. Four mated females were identified in April and three more in May. By the end of April, the total number of wild flies clearly exceeded the criteria. But, with only seven of them mated females and no larvae found the view was that we were winning. Furthermore, Dr. Tassan's model of when overwintering emergence would peak matched what we were seeing. If this was the peak of overwintering emergence, we were doing well. It was too early to recommend aerial spraying.

I was quoted in the *Oakland Tribune* on April 28th saying I was optimistic, even as I admitted that for every wild fly caught, there were probably a thousand in the vicinity we didn't catch. These, we hoped, were mating with the millions of sterile flies. Whether or not we would need to go to aerial spraying would depend on evidence of larvae turning up. So far, none had. Michael Greene, the Alameda County Agricultural Commissioner, was also quoted in the article in the *Tribune*. He, too, said he was "cautiously optimistic."

On May 21st, the advisory committee met again. They endorsed the project's decision to reduce the malathion ground spraying to only those properties within a half-mile of finds. The committee devoted much of the meeting to discussing what level of trapping would be necessary to formally declare the infestation eradicated. They also reviewed and approved Dr. Tassan's day-degree modeling. It had accurately predicted the April emergence. The modeling now predicted that if significant mating were taking place, the next generation would begin appearing near the end of June or early July. We remained optimistic there would be few in this or later generations, and therefore we could see an end to the program occurring by late fall after a period of intensive trapping at the rate of 25 traps per square mile to confirm eradication had been achieved. As if to confirm our optimism, no wild flies were caught during the rest of May.

On June 2nd, the *Sacramento Bee* led with "War Against Medfly Appears Successful." The article mentioned that the ground spraying was winding down and that we had initiated the layoff of half our current 650 non-civil service employees. I also announced that if all went well, eradication might be declared by December. Another light-hearted article captioned "Likeable Yet Detested Medfly Losing" observed that the flies didn't bite and described them as cute and lovable as they crawled all over one of the employees in the rearing lab.

Only a few new wild flies were trapped in early June. However, several were mated females that had been trapped inside the core area. Two more mated females were trapped on the outer edges of the project, one northwest in Redwood City in San Mateo County and the other northeast in the city of Fremont in Alameda County, south of Oakland. All but one of these flies were in areas where wild flies had been trapped in 1980. These discoveries should have been viewed as more troubling than they were. Instead, because we were releasing 125 million sterile flies a week and finding no larvae, we and the advisory committee were not unduly alarmed. Rominger nevertheless ordered the quarantine zone expanded as a precaution.

In the fall of 1980, long before I had any idea that I would be assigned to fight the medfly in San Jose, my wife and I had signed up and pre-paid for a sailing vacation in mid-June in the Bahamas with a group of friends. During spring emergence, I had one eye on winning and the other on whether I would miss the trip because of a flare-up of wild medflies. A flare-up of new finds or larvae seemed highly unlikely, but after Dr. Nadel's warning, one could never be sure. There were no wild flies caught during the week before I stepped on the plane to fly to Nassau with my wife and friends. The vacation of scuba-diving each day off the boat, usually anchored near a different isolated, uninhabited island, was exactly what I needed. From June 11th to the 21st, I was completely unreachable, and for the first time in the last six months, I was able to relax.

The day before I returned, the *Sacramento Bee* published an editorial titled "Medfly: The Good Fight." In it, the editors admitted their fingers were crossed that the fly would be declared eradicated by fall. However, they labeled it "The Good Fight" because the State had resisted the pressure from USDA and certain others "to dust the affected region from the air." When I read it after I returned, I liked the part heaping praise on me, Governor Brown, and especially John Thurman, to whom, in my opinion, much of the credit was due. Less positive was seeing their use of the word "dust" to disparage aerial spraying and convey the false notion that Malathion was unreasonably dangerous when sprayed from the air but wisely used and safe when sprayed by hand crews going door to door. This was nonsense. I had spent the last six months trying to bring people around to recognizing that letting the medfly become an endemic pest would be an enormous problem for them as homeowners, for agriculture, and for the rest of the country; and that, aerially spraying fly bait with a small amount of Malathion, if necessary, would not harm anyone.

The media's willingness to adopt the opponents' misleading characterization of the bait-spray program using words like "tons," not ounces, "bombers," not helicopters, and "dusting people with a nerve poison," had sensationalized a safe, commonly used backyard pesticide in a way that distorted any possibility of rational decision-making by the public. Now, on the eve of victory, instead of taking a bow, I found myself saddened by the realization that I had failed utterly to change the public's wildly inaccurate understanding of the importance of eradicating the medfly, as well as their hysterical overreaction to a pesticide they used themselves and one that had been extensively used for eradicating previous infestations without any evidence of harm.

On Monday, June 22nd, in addition to the editorial, I learned no more wild flies or larvae had been found during the time I was away. Since this had included a spell of hot weather with higher temperatures, the lack of any new flies or larvae was especially encouraging. The good news further raised the confidence level of everyone on and off the project. More positive news articles also appeared, suggesting the fight was all but over, even if it might be too early to break out the champagne.

On June 25th, the advisory committee met. The members again continued to view the absence of any sign of larvae and the lack of wild flies caught since June 10th as further cause for optimism. They believed we were now dealing with a low-level infestation that the increasing volume of sterile fly releases appeared to be eradicating. Particularly encouraging was the absence of wild males. "We feel it can mean one of two things," said Shannon Wilson, who had been the USDA coordinator of emergency projects back in 1980. "Perhaps the stress of overwintering and host stripping tended to lower the male portion of the population more than the females." He added, "We found in Mexico that every year, there's a decline in the male population at the beginning and the end of a season." His conclusion was "either we're at the very tail end of a cycle or at the beginning of a build-up, and males have yet to appear." Finally, he said, "[I]n general our feeling has been good about the program." We, on the project, all believed it was now a question of mopping up the stragglers, then continuing intensive trapping for three generations and declaring eradication. Even the state's farmers were beginning to tip their hats to a job well done. After the meeting ended, I drove to Oakland, where I was the featured speaker at a meeting of the Western Branch of the American Entomological Society. At the end of my talk, the attendees gave me a standing ovation.

BOOK

THREE

JULY 1981

Chapter 9 (Aerial Spraying Becomes Unavoidable)

After my talk in Oakland, I returned to the project. As I got out of my car, Don Henry met me with stunning news—medfly larvae had been found in the Mountain View gap. The first call came in minutes after I left for the meeting in Oakland. A homeowner in the city of Mountain View reported finding white worms in his apricots. He thought they might be medfly maggots. The fruit collection staff promptly drove out and picked up samples. Formal confirmation came the next day, along with more maggots in apricots called in by a second homeowner in the same area. The first three finds, localized in the Mountain View gap, met the aerial spraying criteria of three or more larval finds. No one, however, wanted to call for aerial spraying yet. This wait-and-see posture changed overnight as more larval properties popped up the next day. By June 29th, we had seven confirmed larval sites. We began urging homeowners to inspect their fruit for worms and to call us. Surprise and disbelief swept over the project and the public in the face of the unmistakable and heartbreaking realization that we had failed. The abrupt reversal from apparent success to obvious failure was captured by columnist Leigh Weimers in the Mercury, who wrote:

> No one knows the fleeting nature of glory better than Jerry Scribner…At a recent convention of entomologists in Oakland, he was given a standing ovation for successfully directing the fight against the Mediterranean fruit fly here. Within minutes, it was announced that fly larvae had been found in Mountain View and the battle was on again. Sit down, Jerry

The media coverage of optimism and congratulatory articles ended. The next day's headline suggested aerial spraying might be a step closer. We scrambled to spray Diazinon and Malathion bait on all properties in a three-block radius of each larval find. Crews were called back and began stripping fruit from the same properties. Wayne Granberry announced the project workforce would increase from 300 to 500 as those we had sent home were recalled to action. Five days after the first discovery, the number of larval properties had multiplied ten-fold to 38. Larval finds had now been found in five cities—Palo Alto, Los Altos, Sunnyvale,

Mountain View, and Cupertino. Peaches, nectarines, and figs joined apricots among the fruits infested. What we had hoped might be only a local hot spot now looked like the shocking explosion that Dr. Nadel warned might happen.

During the first week of July, the situation worsened by the hour. The media coverage could not keep pace with the number of new larval discoveries being reported twice daily at project headquarters. By Friday, July 3rd, 61 larval finds had been confirmed. By the following Monday, it would be 86. I did not hide my disappointment as I calmly reported what we were finding, what we were doing, and what next steps were expected. When asked about aerial spraying, I said, "It's a very significant possibility." On June 30th, The State Attorney General's office sent the required five-day warning letter to Santa Clara County and the five cities who had sued earlier, advising them that aerial spraying was now a substantial possibility and it might begin as soon as July 9th or 10th though no formal decision had been made yet.

On July 1st, Director Rominger and I, along with USDA's Harvey Ford, appeared together in Sacramento before an overflow Legislative panel. The hearing was televised and widely reported. We described the outbreak and said that aerial bait spraying appeared to be the best, if not the only, option at this point. The advisory committee had been summoned to meet on Tuesday, July 7th, to make a recommendation. Rominger revealed that preliminary plans were already in place to begin spraying as early as July 13th. Ford told the assembled legislators flatly, "We simply must succeed in our eradication, and we must succeed now." The use of the word now sent an unmistakable signal that USDA would wait no longer, regardless of the committee's recommendation. No one doubted that the committee would recommend aerial spraying as soon as we could get the helicopters in the air. Summer was here. The infestation was widespread and growing daily. Keeping it out of the U.S. was USDA's number one priority. Spraying had to happen, and soon.

On Friday, July 3rd, the Attorney General's office filed a new lawsuit requesting the court declare invalid the city and county ordinances prohibiting any aerial spraying. The *Mercury* covered the lawsuit, the hearing, the new finds, and details from the project on the aerial spraying plans. To anyone following the news, it appeared all but certain that aerial spraying would begin as soon as Monday night, July 13th. The paper also pictured Wayne Granberry pointing to a large map of the urban area with indications of where larvae had been found. Many of the dots appeared far outside the Mountain View Gap. In the article below, he said, "I'm afraid it is uncontrollable from the ground now. A reasonable person couldn't say it any other way."

From the beginning of the contingency planning, it had been public knowledge that Governor Brown would have to approve any recommendation involving aerial spraying. I had never spoken to Brown about aerial spraying, and not all since January. I had no idea whether Rich Rominger had or if he and Governor Brown were already discussing the next steps. The Governor's staff in Sacramento read the daily press clippings. From my years with the Legislature and as a chief counsel and deputy director, I knew government functioned much like an anthill. A decision on what to do would involve information rising through layers of officials and requesters to the palace guard. The Governor, like the queen, would be cossetted in the inner sanctum. His advisors would provide input on the pros and cons of various possible responses while preserving for as long as possible his decision-making discretion. So far, Brown had said nothing about what he might do if the ground program failed. He had said nothing publicly in December 1980, when USDA and Rominger had announced aerial spraying, nor did he comment when it was postponed by Assemblyman John Thurman. Beginning in January, Rich Rominger and I had pledged privately to the farm community that if the ground program failed, we would move to aerial spraying. Nevertheless, when we testified before the Legislature on July 3rd that aerial spraying was now the only way to eradicate the medfly, we, and everyone else, knew that our commitment did not commit the Governor. He would have the final word.

The prospect of aerial spraying rekindled the hysteria of December 1980. Opponents bombarded the Governor's office with telephone calls, letters, and even telegrams, demanding he shelve any thought of aerial spraying. They all described the dangers of Malathion in apocalyptic terms untethered to any scientific basis. Regrettably, environmentalists, including those at the California Resources Agency, advised Governor Brown that aerial spraying could have environmental consequences. As with human health, these broad-brush environmental arguments did not hold up in the face of careful analysis. They were premised on the same assumption the public had always had that the spraying would involve releasing a broad-spectrum pesticide in an atomized mist instead of the tiny dots of fly bait deposited in previous urban medfly eradication programs. None of the parade of horrors being offered up as theoretical risks had occurred in the earlier bait spray programs. I believed Governor Brown would see through these wildly exaggerated theoretical claims of environmental and health risks. However, if he did, he did not say so publicly.

Gray Davis, the Governor's Chief of Staff, told the press that Brown would make the final decision. Simultaneously, he set the stage for what I hoped would be a decision to protect the entire state from the economic disaster that would follow from failing to eradicate the medfly. Davis helped prepare the public for what had to be done. He said, "At stake may be the economic viability of our largest industry and the well-being of a great many of our citizens. A decision of that magnitude should be made by the governor." He added, "Aerial spraying has always been the option of very last resort. If the evidence leaves us no other option, obviously, we'll have to exercise it."

Davis was right. There was no other option. Lee Ruth, the executive director of the Agricultural Council of California, said he could not imagine the advisory committee reaching any other decision at their scheduled July 7th meeting. The Texas, the Ag commissioner renewed his threat to reimpose Texas's quarantine of California unless the spraying was ordered. In the Santa Clara Valley, the lawyers representing the county and cities sent a telegram to Governor Brown requesting he call out the National Guard and federal troops for another massive ground program. Advised of the telegram, I told the press, "I know what it took just to mobilize the 2,000 people we had at the peak of the winter program. There are human limitations. You can't turn over every leaf in the county, at least not in the time we have left."

While the decision process played out, Arnie Morrison and his team scrambled to make up for lost ground. July 13th was the earliest we could get the helicopters in the air with the guidance systems and ground support required and all the other myriad details worked out. As we called back workers and moved as fast as we could to ground spray the rapidly proliferating larval finds, environmentalists accused the project of deliberately dragging its feet. They demanded a new ground program of fruit stripping and ground spraying in lieu of aerial spraying. We ignored their fantasy that such a program made sense in the middle of summer and continued planning for aerial spraying while fighting the larval sites with every resource we could muster.

For six months, from January to the end of June, we worked night and day seven days a week. While I had had a vacation in June, almost no one else had been able to take any time off. The staff, both state and federal, had families. They had been on the project away from home for months at a time all year. I knew there would be few days off for the rest of the summer. I therefore scheduled a skeleton crew to work the weekend of Saturday, July 4th, a state and federal holiday, and Sunday, July 5th. A few critical staff responsible for rearing and releasing sterile flies and quarantine inspectors at the airports would still have to work the weekend. But the rest were sent home, knowing it would be the last break they would get for the foreseeable future. I volunteered to be in my office on Sunday, the 5th, as the officer of the day, answering as many calls as I could from residents weighing in against aerial spraying or asking questions.

On Sunday morning, July 5th, I parked my car in the empty parking lot and walked through the fog to the darkened principal's office. When I snapped on the light, staring back at me, was the halftime sign behind my desk. The belief that we could come back to win in the second half now seemed insane. Blind enthusiasm and hard work had failed to overcome millions of years of survival adaptation by the medfly. We had been defeated by nature. I sat down at my desk, feeling as alone as I could ever remember. All week, maggots had turned up on properties we had stripped and sprayed repeatedly, then flooded with sterile flies. Where did they come from? Some on the project thought we had released a batch of unsterilized flies from the lab in Peru by mistake. Others believed the flies had simply been breeding under our noses and errors had occurred in sorting the trap catches in the I.D. lab. They believed more wild flies had been caught but not identified as such.

Whatever the cause, I felt helpless and hapless, unable to even explain to the public or the Governor what had gone wrong. Nothing we had done appeared to have worked, and now, lulled by the euphoria of believing we had won, we were not prepared to get the helicopters in the air as quickly as events required. Even if, as expected, the advisory committee recommended aerial spraying at their meeting on Tuesday, as I sat there Sunday morning, I knew the earliest we could start spraying by air remained July 13th, more than a week away. That assumed no other problems arose in the meantime. We had recalled all the employees we had recently laid off. I told myself we had done everything humanly possible. Yet we had clearly failed. Why no longer mattered.

The ringing of the telephone brought me back to the present. It was the first call of the morning. As I reached for the phone on my desk, I expected either a caller with a question or an angry lecture about the dangers of Malathion. Either way, I thought, the caller would have the satisfaction of talking with the director of the project. I picked up the telephone. There was only a dial tone. The ringing continued. After a moment of confusion, I realized the ringing was coming from the dusty, never-used, red telephone on the shelf behind my desk. I swiveled around, stood up, and picked up the receiver.

"Good morning," I said.

"Is this Scribner?" said the voice on the other end. It was Governor Brown himself, not a secretary or staff member.

"Yes," I answered.

There were no pleasantries.

"I see you have been saying that aerial spraying is now the only option left to defeat the medfly."

"I believe it is, Governor," I said.

"I haven't made that decision yet," the Governor snapped, with enough emphasis on the word "I" to remind me who was in charge.

My mind, now fully engaged, remembered it was his decision, not mine. Before the Governor could say more, and without thinking, I blurted out, "If you don't order aerial spraying, Governor, you will be a hero in the Bay Area, but you won't be electable as dog catcher in the rest of the state." I should have been fired on the spot. But instead, after an awkward pause, the Governor said, "Scribner, you worry about the medfly. I'll worry about the politics. Is that clear?"

Having been raised on military bases around the world by a military father, it could not have been any clearer.

"Yes sir!" I answered. I repeated, "Yes sir!" twice more as he repeated the instruction. The Governor then calmly asked me to be in his office in Sacramento the next morning to discuss the matter further. He suggested that, in the meantime, I avoid any more pronouncements about aerial spraying. I quickly agreed.

After the call ended, I telephoned Rich Rominger at his home in Winters, California, and related the exchange with Governor Brown. I had no way of knowing what was going on above me in the chain of command. I hoped Gray Davis's suggestion would be where we would end up. However, so far, the Governor did not say what he would do. Rich listened quietly without offering any hint as to what had been discussed between him and the Governor or even if they had talked. At the end of my report, Rich asked me to be in his office in Sacramento early the next morning to discuss the next steps before we met with the Governor.

I honestly have no recollection of the rest of that Sunday. I know I kept working, taking calls all day and into the evening. I am sure I went over and over in my mind what to say the next day. Being fired appeared

126

likely. I could live with that. The strategy had been mine. We had failed. I had done my best. Success had never been guaranteed, though I believed we had come tantalizingly close. On the eve of the D-Day landings, Eisenhower wrote two short messages, one to be used if the landings were successful, the other if not. The other read in part, "The troops, the air, and navy did all that bravery and devotion to duty could do. If any blame or fault attaches to the attempt, it is mine alone." As the leader of the medfly war, I had bet everything on the ground program. We had gambled and lost.

A calendar my wife kept said that I arrived home from San Jose Sunday night at 11:30. Early Monday morning, Rich, the other deputies, and I huddled in his office. We reviewed the biological, environmental, and health arguments for aerial spraying. We discussed our assessment of USDA's position, plus that of the states and foreign countries that were threatening quarantines. We did not discuss any alternatives to aerial spraying because, in our view, none existed. We revisited the article that likely precipitated Brown's ire—a front-page story in the *Sacramento Bee* on Wednesday, July 1st. The headline read, "Medfly Area Expanded.   Aerial Spraying Is Only Way to Halt Medfly, Official Says." I was the official, and I had said there was no reasonable alternative except aerial spraying, adding, "I think it's a fairly easy choice." According to the article, a spokesperson for the Governor pointed out that he had not made up his mind on the issue and was asking for information about other alternatives, as well as about "what health effects could occur from spraying." We believed that the Governor, despite his reservations about pesticides, understood the gravity of the situation and the fact that USDA would not tolerate a refusal to spray. A decision could be avoided only until Tuesday when the advisory committee would meet and make their recommendation. We all knew what that decision would be.

After our deputies' meeting wrapped up, Rominger and I walked silently across the street to the Governor's office, alone in our thoughts, expecting a difficult meeting. In the beginning, the Governor listened patiently to our update of the many new larval finds and our belief that aerial spraying was now the only workable choice. We emphasized the fact that it was safe and that it had been proven so by actual prior use. The Governor, famously skeptical of conventional wisdom, asked questions that suggested he had internalized many of the opponent's theoretical health concerns. He, like the residents, harbored profound reservations about the safety of pesticides no matter how, when, or where they were used. It did not matter how much research had been done. This position left little room for him to recognize the fact that almost no one would experience any exposure to the Malathion bait. He clearly heard the economic arguments but doubted these too, believing they were exaggerated, worst-case estimates by an industry prone to pessimism. He also discounted the potential devastation that would result from the presence of medflies as a permanent endemic pest.

For the latter, it was clear that he relied in part on advice from Dr. Kenneth Hagen, a distinguished U.C. Berkeley entomology professor and an acknowledged expert on the medfly. Dr. Hagen's doctoral thesis on the medfly established the effectiveness of the protein bait in attracting medflies. He continued to insist, as he had in December, that the Northern California climate would not support an ongoing endemic medfly population. Brown had also talked to Professor Donald Dahlsten, another entomologist at U.C. Berkeley. Dahlsten headed the Division of Biological Control and happened to be a personal family acquaintance of mine whom I respected. Since Professor Dahlsten was a passionate advocate of biological control, I believed he, too, opposed the aerial spraying and likely the concept of eradication itself. The presence of only these two experts made it obvious the Governor had opted to surround himself with academics whose views aligned with his preference for biological control and avoidance of pesticides if possible. Both Rominger and I also favored biological control and integrated pest management (IPM) strategies. That was why we had fought so hard to make the sterile-fly approach work. The inconvenient truth was it hadn't worked, though why was still unknown. Furthermore, in a hundred years, no biological control solution, such as using predatory wasps, had been found to be more than minimally effective in controlling the medfly's destructiveness. No wasps were available, but even if they had been, the continued presence of medflies in California would guarantee that other countries and states without the medfly would proceed to quarantine California. And that farmers and homeowners would use substantial quantities of pesticides to control them.

What Professors Dahlsten and Hagen proposed to the Governor was the possibility that another ground program bigger and better than the previous one could eventually work. Neither they nor the Governor recognized the pent-up pressure and anger coming from all those scared to death of the medfly and worried it would soon show up on their farm, in their state, or, in the case of Japan, in their country. I knew continuing to try what had failed over the winter and spring could not be justified in summer weather, given the extent of the explosion of larvae we were experiencing.

Facing one of the most difficult, no-win decisions he had encountered in his six years in office, we recognized that Governor Brown was hearing the views of his Resources Agency, U.C. Berkeley's entomologists, and the medical concerns of medical opponents while failing to reach out to anyone besides Rich and me in agriculture. Dr. Beverly Myers, the director of the California Department of Health, was not present at the meeting, and no one else offered a credible and substantive basis for rejecting the Department's conclusion that the risk to human health was "insignificant." Nor was there any discussion of the fact that under the proposed spraying plan, no one would even be exposed to the Malathion. To experience harm, the medflies had first to ingest it. Humans would not be doing that. It wasn't a breathable mist and anyway, the spraying was proposed to take place overnight when residents would be indoors sleeping.

A critical question the Governor asked that I could not answer was why, after it appeared we had won, medfly larvae turned up everywhere. One possibility was that in early June we had released 50,000 medflies received from the lab in Peru that had not been sterilized. In other words, we had almost succeeded in eradicating the infestation and then accidentally reintroduced it. For some of us, including me, that seemed more plausible than believing that nothing we had done for six months had made any difference. The belief the ground program had worked only to be undone by a release of fertile flies lent weight to the idea we could do the ground program again and thereby continue to avoid aerial spraying. Unfortunately, even if fertile flies had been accidentally released, it was now the middle of summer. A ground program had no chance of success in the summer, as Rominger and I attempted to make clear.

After the Governor listened attentively to Rich and me for over an hour, he said he wanted to wait for the advisory committee's recommendation before making a final decision. We were not surprised. It was only one more day, and this delay would buy him a little more time and strengthen his position if the panel said he had no choice but to order the spraying. We left the meeting hopeful he would make the right decision.

As I drove back to the project to prepare for the committee meeting the next day, I felt some relief at not having been fired, at least not yet. However, like all lawyers, I could not avoid reviewing the arguments I could and should have made. I especially regretted that neither Director Rominger nor I told the Governor point-blank that he did not have the final decision. USDA did. We knew without a doubt that if he balked at following the advisory committee's recommendation, USDA would force the spraying. I cannot speak to why my boss did not push this point with the Governor when we met with him on Monday, except doing so would have been out of character for Rich. Another reason might have been that John Block, who knew Rich personally, had not alerted Rominger to their plan to quarantine California if Brown balked. It is also possible the Governor thought USDA might step in and do the spraying themselves. That might have taken him off the hook and been something he would have been OK with. I know I did not speak out more forcefully on Monday. I had already pushed my luck on Sunday. What did cross my mind afterward however, was my military father's warning to me years earlier when he said, "Jerry, I can't make you do it; I can only make you wish you had." It applied perfectly to USDA's superior authority here, and Brown's situation.

In Los Gatos, reports of finding more maggots continued to pour in. The latest round of bad news included finding larvae in the town of Portola Valley, several miles west of the Mountain View Gap. As with the earlier finds, we immediately stripped the fruit and sprayed Diazinon and Malathion bait, but we could not hope to keep this up. Arnie left the ground spraying up to his team and threw himself into planning for the aerial program. The cities and county filed a new lawsuit, this one in state court. Again, the argument was no spraying could occur until after completion of an environmental impact review. Their attorney, Walter Hays, conceded that "[I]t really doesn't look like we have much of a chance because now it really does seem like an emergency."

Monday afternoon, July 6th, the Sunnyvale City Council requested my appearance at an official emergency public community meeting of council members. The cities of Mountain View, Los Altos, and Los Gatos were also invited. The meeting was to be held in the Sunnyvale city council chamber. I had only enough time to prepare a brief four-page statement and make copies to hand out before a city police department squad car arrived to pick me up. A standing-room-only crowd of upset opponents and the usual TV cameras greeted my arrival. After speaking, I took questions from the council members. I acknowledged and praised both the huge community effort and that of the project before stating that the medfly had roared back for reasons I could not explain. I said the problem was now much bigger than the one we started with. I discussed the two options of another ground program versus aerial spraying, noting the advantages, disadvantages, and prospects for success of each. I emphasized that the infestation was now growing exponentially, and the warm weather and abundance of fruit made success with another ground program nearly impossible. I also stressed again that the aerial bait program had been successful and safely used over cities in Florida and Texas. Finally, I said that unless eradicated, the medfly's presence would devastate their community and the state and would lead to widespread permanent pesticide use.

The mayor and council members conducted the meeting with impressive courtesy and civility, given the exigency of the situation and the passionate feelings in the crowd. I felt those present appreciated my willingness, as the head of the program, to appear and discuss the situation. I had no answer for why we had failed, though the possibility that there had been an accidental release of non-sterile flies still seemed to me the most likely. I repeatedly challenged the audience to consider the problem and what we, the people, were going to do about the situation as it now existed. As with the Governor, time prevented a detailed discussion of the lack of any real health exposure. I made clear that the bait was not a breathable spray and that people indoors at night would have little or no actual exposure to Malathion. As the police drove me back to the project, I knew few minds had been changed by my remarks.

As I was appearing before the city councils in Sunnyvale, Gray Davis was meeting with reporters outside the Governor's office in Sacramento to share with them Governor Brown's decision-making process. According to Davis, the Governor had devoted much of his weekend and virtually all of Monday to being briefed by state officials and consulting with experts on both sides. I knew the first part was true. According to Davis, the Governor had not ruled out any alternative. What I did not know was that beginning on Sunday, members of the Governor's office and the California Resources Agency had been busy putting together another massive fruit stripping and ground spraying program.

On Tuesday morning, before the advisory committee members arrived for their critical meeting, we emptied the school parking lot of all project and personal vehicles, stashing them on nearby state property. As the 10 a.m. start time for the meeting approached, the school parking lot and nearby residential streets overflowed with cars. Hundreds of concerned residents, including local political leaders, assembled in the school's grassy interior courtyard. The day had dawned sunny and warm. Children played tag on the grass, and parents and friends from prior protest events reconnected. A local musical group circulated through the crowd, playing a banjo and hawking their recording of a blues song about the medfly crisis. It felt familiar, reminding me of my own participation in similar liberal protests in past years.

The seriousness of the issue and the unrequested presence of police failed to dampen the crowd's sense of history in the making. Many of the children and babies had signs pinned on them saying, "Don't Spray On Me." One asked, "Do I look like a fruit fly"? Adults carried signs too, including "Stop the Cancer Mist," "Better Med than Dead," and my favorite, "They Said Thalidomide Was Safe." While there would be no mist and no legitimate concern about cancer, there was no denying that scientists had gotten it horribly wrong on thalidomide and other chemicals as well. Who could say thirty years from now that science might also conclude Malathion was unsafe after all? Before the meeting got underway, reporters interviewed some of those waiting to speak, including a woman quoted in the paper the next day who claimed the spraying would unleash a "holocaust." As more families streamed in, reporters set up TV cameras and taped microphones to the lectern, facing a row of cafeteria tables and chairs.

At 10 o'clock I tapped the lectern's microphone and announced we were going to start the meeting and that everyone who wished to speak would have an opportunity to address the committee. Rich Rominger thanked people for coming and asked the members of the panel to introduce themselves. After that, the lectern was then turned around and prospective witnesses lined up to address the committee. Visibly pregnant women holding babies or small children led the long line waiting to speak. Each woman implored the committee not to approve aerial spraying because of the risk of birth defects and the possible harm Malathion could do to their children. Next in line were more mothers pushing strollers, most with additional children in tow or clinging to their skirts. They, too, urged aerial spraying be rejected. A few fathers with children spoke as well.

Approximately sixty or so people, out of the 600 to 800 in the crowd, spoke one after the other over the next six hours. Many addressed both the health risks and their fears of the possible environmental consequences of spraying a nerve poison over a diverse, populated area. The claim that Malathion had come about because of Nazi experiments with poison gas was mentioned often. The Chairperson of the Santa Clara Board of Supervisors, Rod Diridon, drew a round of applause when he said: "If it etches the paint on a car, what does it do to a baby's skin?" Zoe Lofgren, a member of the Board of Supervisors, also spoke. She said, "We must and will fight you in court and any possible forum to prevent aerial spraying of Malathion." Several speakers pushed for another ground-based program of stripping fruit and spraying from street level instead of from helicopters. A man from the California Farm Bureau in Kern County was the only speaker I recall who spoke in favor of aerial spraying.

The members of the committee listened carefully as the parade of witnesses continued without interruption through the noon hour and into the afternoon. All the members had spent long careers in insect research or eradication or control programs that used biological control, pesticides, or a combination of both. Dr. Cunningham had spent his entire career studying the medfly. Every member of the committee was thoroughly familiar with Malathion and knowledgeable about pesticide toxicity. They had no idea as to why we had failed so dramatically, but we had. There was little doubt they would recommend aerial spraying begin as soon as possible. No other alternative, including another round of fruit stripping and door-to-door ground spraying, had any chance of eradicating this infestation before it spread beyond its present area. The committee members had been reluctant but willing to try to win on the ground when it was winter and too cold to spray anyway. For a time, it seemed to have worked. Now it was summer, fruit, and larvae were everywhere. There was no time to waste. Yet, they recognized that this public meeting was an unavoidable, maybe even a necessary part of the process, at least in California. And that was why every member listened patiently in the bright sun and heat to the heartfelt worries of those who saw only something immoral, dangerous, and wrong.

At its core, we could not win the argument that under no circumstances could anyone among the hundreds of thousands in the area be harmed, no matter how young, old, or sick they might be. No amount of experience with spraying Malathion by air without reported health effects could meet the level of certainty demanded. Nor could the absence of any medical reports of harm occurring to the legions of home users of Malathion. The least reliable to the doubters were the decades of scientific studies of rats fed high doses of Malathion without developing cancer or birth defects. Pesticides killed living things. This fact alone, combined with the ubiquitous nature of aerial delivery, effectively trumped any willingness to consider whether there would or would not be exposure or some possible unknown long-term harm. As had been the case in December, it was impossible to eliminate the concern that some unknown health or environmental risk might be discovered at some point in the future.

I personally believed that pesticides were, in general, overused and hazardous to people and the environment. That was part of the reason I had been appointed a deputy director in the first place. Except for the risk of an aircraft crash, I believed the aerial spraying had been shown to be safe. Furthermore, from an environmental perspective, there was a compelling need to use a few ounces per acre of Malathion now to prevent the need for widespread use of even more toxic pesticides throughout the state in the future. Yet, as I listened, I could not help but acknowledge the sincerity of those fearful and angry at having to face any risk at all when they had no control over it being imposed on them.

By 4:30 in the afternoon, we had almost reached the end of the line of speakers. Everything that could be said had been said. The committee would soon be taking a vote. At that moment, every head turned as a young woman came out of the project office holding a sheet of paper in her hand, making straight for Director Rominger. She handed him the paper and after reading it, he stood up to announce that Governor Brown had telephoned the project to request the committee withhold any decision until they could meet with him personally the following morning in Sacramento. The committee agreed to temporarily adjourn, and for one more day, the opponents could hope the community's appeal might yet succeed.

The Governor's temporary delay pleased his constituents in the Bay Area but increased the concern of other interested parties. Caught between those fearful of Malathion and a major agricultural disaster, he had no way to avoid a decision sure to anger one side or the other. USDA proceeded to announce what Rominger, and I had known but not put forward in our meeting on Monday. No further delay in moving to aerial spraying would be tolerated. In Washington, D.C., a USDA spokesperson told the press bluntly, "The state is simply in a position where it has no choice. If the state doesn't opt for spraying, USDA will probably move to put the whole state in quarantine."

The warning by USDA appeared on the front page of the *Mercury* on Wednesday morning. Nevertheless, the *Mercury's* editors ignored it. They published an editorial titled "Aerial Spraying Not Yet," in which they urged the Governor to defer aerial spraying in favor of "an all-out ground war." They also wanted him to appoint a new, more objective panel to review the health ramifications of aerial spraying. They suggested that the new panel include local medical experts and "pharmacologists from major universities." There was nothing special or better about local medical advice other than the presence of a vocal minority of local medical doctors opposed to aerial spraying. This editorial made no sense and ignored the paper's earlier editorials sharply criticizing the exaggerated health claims being made by these same local doctors, as well as the lawsuits meant to block the spraying. Now they were insisting the Governor ignore their earlier advice, his state health department, and the USDA threat to quarantine the entire state.

California's Department of Health Director, Dr. Myers, continued to stand firmly behind her assessment that the risk to health was insignificant, noting that "Even pregnant women and the fetuses they are carrying would be in more danger from cigarette smoke than this dose of Malathion." Later, she would go further, pointing out that the residents would put themselves in greater danger using the freeways to flee than they would by staying put. The paper's reference to pharmacologists from major universities was particularly disingenuous since it all but specified by name, Dr. Sumner Kalman of the pharmacology department at Stanford University, a vocal opponent of aerial spraying. In a crisis, someone needs to keep their head. The local political leadership in the Santa Clara Valley and the editors of the *Mercury* miserably failed that test.

The USDA, warning that they would quarantine the entire state if the Governor did not order aerial spraying, failed to register not only with the Mercury but also with just about everyone else, including the Governor and his staff.

At 10 Wednesday morning, Rominger, I, and the advisory committee members were ushered into Governor Brown's office in Sacramento. Dr. Ken Hagen and Dr. Don Dahlsten had been invited to attend and were present when the rest of us arrived. The Governor initiated a discussion that focused on his concerns about the health and environmental drawbacks of aerial spraying. He asked good questions but received no support from the advisory committee members, who believed it was time to move to aerial spraying and had no reservations about either the safety or efficacy of the bait approach. Professors Hagen and Dahlsten acknowledged that aerial spraying had worked elsewhere but argued that the ground program had worked before being undone by a release of unsterilized flies. They favored continuing that strategy. I, too, believed the ground program had worked, and I shared the Governor's environmental leanings. But beyond conceding that we may have released unsterilized flies my recollection is I said very little at the meeting. I don't recall Rich Rominger saying much, either. I had made it clear in the telephone call from the Governor on the 5th that we had to spray and Rominger and I maintained that position on Monday. We had nothing to add to that.

Having personally ordered the release of the questionable flies from Peru, I know I felt sick about the possibility we failed because of that. However, at this point, it didn't matter why we had failed. We had. It was summer now with fruit and medflies everywhere and spreading fast. Governor Brown continued to press the committee members to explain why a ground program would not work again. All the committee members except for Dr. Cunningham resolutely refused to budge. Dr. Cunningham opened the door a crack, saying aerial spraying had a 98% chance of success, and at this point, he favored it strongly while conceding there was a possibility a ground program might have a 60% chance of success, but only if there were more sterile flies available.

When the Governor could not win over even one member of the committee, he abruptly ended the meeting by announcing that he had decided in favor of a new, more intensive ground program. Angered and dismayed, the committee members rose as one and were ushered out. The Governor, with me and Rominger in tow, moved to the Capitol press room across the hall from his office, where reporters awaited his decision. Brown took the stage, seated behind a table with Rominger to his right and me to his left. Speaking directly into a half dozen television cameras, he announced his decision to reject aerial spraying using the following words:

> There are human beings out there. The risk to people of aerial spraying is too great. There are too many unknowns about the long-term effects of Malathion. No definitive studies are available on the effects of widespread aerial spraying of Malathion on humans and the environment.

> As a governor, when I see a feasible alternative, I'm going to take it.

He then announced that he was re-mobilizing the National Guard and CCC, plus hundreds of state employees along with four hundred spray rigs, to undertake a renewed and far more extensive ground spraying program. He further announced that he was also ordering Highway Patrol roadblocks on major highways in and out of the infested area to prevent fruit from leaving. Finally, he ordered residents in the 700 square mile quarantine area to strip all host fruit by Monday, July 13th, or face fines and arrest by the Highway Patrol and National Guard. None of these plans had been shared with Rominger or me.

When the Governor finished, one of the reporters said, "Governor, Mr. Scribner has been saying that aerial spraying is the only viable option. Now you are saying you believe it can still be done on the ground. Does Mr. Scribner agree with you?" The Governor turned to his left and handed me the microphone. I ad-libbed something like, "When I said aerial spraying was the only option, it was before the Governor committed the enormous resources he has announced today. With twice as many people, I believe we can succeed on the ground." The

Sacramento Union described me as "grim-faced." I'm sure I was. They quoted me as saying: "I believe ground application could work if we have the kind of cooperation I think we're going to get." The Capitol press corps accepted my answer as one expected of a political appointee asked to repudiate his boss in public and moved on to another question or two before the press conference ended. As Rominger and I left the room, Jacques Barzaghi, one of Brown's aides, pleased with my defense of him, whispered to me under his breath, "Nice job!" I felt miserable and compromised. I disagreed with his decision but understood the Governor's reluctance to spray a million people with Malathion. I had felt the same way in 1980 when the aerial spraying was first proposed.

While the press conference was taking place, the advisory committee moved the rest of their meeting across the street to the Department of Food and Agriculture conference room, where they formally voted unanimously for aerial spraying and made other recommendations. Their one-page recommendation, later typed and formally addressed to me, did not mince words. It stated:

> The Medfly Technical Review Committee unanimously recommends the aerial application of Malathion bait sprays be applied in Santa Clara County until Medfly is eradicated. They further recommend the sprays continue, on a 7-10-day cycle, for 55 days after the finding of the last fly or maggot.

Brown's obvious insincerity in requesting to meet with the advisory committee in person left a lingering bitterness that would surface at their next meeting in August.

Years later, Brown would tell me his decision was motivated entirely by political considerations. He chose what his supporters wanted in place of what his opponents in agriculture urged. That may be true, though I believe it was more complicated than that. Certainly, his political choices in July 1981 were unenviable. He said so himself at the time. Approving the spraying would have enraged his most ardent supporters and undermined his reputation as an environmental champion. The spraying itself might not go as planned leading to unforeseen problems he would own. Refusing to spray could be even more problematic because it would anger powerful economic constituencies, and it risked making the Governor look indecisive and weak and unwilling to make an unpopular but necessary decision because a local constituency opposed it. It reminded me of the crisis of conscience and political dilemma his father had faced as Governor two decades earlier in May 1960, when he was forced to decide whether to allow the death sentence of convicted serial rapist and kidnapper Caryl Chessman to go forward or not. His father chose not to intervene. Chessman was executed, and Pat Brown was re-elected as Governor two years later. In the case of the medfly, the opposition was primarily local but with a wider constituency wary of the impact of pesticides on the environment. People outside the spray zone, especially those whose livelihood would be affected by not eradicating the fly or a statewide quarantine, wanted the medfly eradicated before it spread to them and damaged the state's economy. The same was true of other states. To Brown, mobilizing an even bigger ground program may have appeared to be the least risky political bet for the moment.

After the press conference, Governor Brown flew to San Jose to a "hero's welcome from local officials hailing his decision." The County's Rod Diridon called Brown's decision a "courageous action." The *Chronicle* reported Brown's remarks drew loud applause. He then traveled to San Francisco for a 6 p.m. press conference at which he again outlined to an approving audience his fruit stripping and ground spraying plan.

Elsewhere, though, over the next 24 hours, his refusal to spray prompted a firestorm of criticism in both California and across the country based on the belief that the Governor and a misinformed vocal minority were putting the entire country at risk. Thursday morning, nearly all of California's major papers ran headlines and articles sharply critical of Brown. In the Capitol, the influential *Sacramento Bee* headline read, "Decision is Roundly Criticized," followed by detailed coverage of the universal condemnation from around the state that erupted after Brown's decision. Simultaneously, the *Bee* revealed a potentially even more damaging criminal probe of the Governor's office was underway in an unrelated matter.

Wednesday afternoon, while the Governor was in San Jose and San Francisco receiving the grateful appreciation of voters there, the 40 member state Senate voted 28-0 to require aerial spraying. The roll call was kept open, and by the end of the day, the final tally stood at 34-2. In the state Assembly, the Speaker, Willie Brown, announced he was calling the Assembly back from their summer recess for an emergency meeting on Friday morning in Sacramento for a vote to force spraying. The Republican Assembly leader, Carol Hallett, reported she was working with USDA in Washington to have them overrule Brown. The Republican minority leader in the Senate, Ken Maddy, called for Rich Rominger's resignation. In response, however, industry representatives jumped to Rominger's defense, saying that he wasn't the problem, Brown was. They urged the anger be targeted directly at Brown. Typical was Fred Heringer, President of the 96,000-member California Farm Bureau Federation. He called Brown's decision "playing Russian roulette with California Agriculture…[W]e are facing a disaster." he said.

In Texas, the Ag Commissioner said: "We're talking about an insect that is a threat to the food supply of this nation." Twelve southern states, once again led by Texas, demanded a national quarantine of California produce unless aerial spraying began by July 15th. The Texas representative on the advisory committee, Dr. Frank Gilstrap, called Brown's decision "the most crass (sic) political move he [Brown] could have made." He added, "We were used." Overseas, the Japanese government joined the chorus, promising to quarantine California if aerial spraying was not in operation by the following week. In Washington, D.C., 28 of the 43 members of the California Congressional delegation called on federal officials to overrule Brown's decision. California's senior senator, Alan Cranston, reported that USDA officials were considering "…a federal go-ahead for aerial spraying…" even though it wasn't immediately clear they could override the state.

Editorial cartoonists had a field day depicting the Governor's awkward political situation. One cartoon pictured him dropping flyswatters from a helicopter. Others drew various versions of Brown complaining, "Waiter, there is a fly in my soup." The best one, in my view, captured Brown's predicament by picturing him crouching helplessly in a tent-shaped medfly insect trap hanging in an orange tree.

The Governor's decision temporarily sidetracked the opponents' legal cases aimed at preventing any aerial spraying. In the state court case, Judge Bruce Allen turned down the County's request to block aerial spraying on the ground that no decision to aerially spray had been made. In San Francisco, the State Attorney General's office temporarily stopped moving forward with their federal court case seeking to invalidate the local ordinances banning aerial flights over their cities since no flights were now planned.

Assembly Speaker Willie Brown, on Thursday morning, formally ordered Assembly members to return to Sacramento by Friday morning at 10 a.m. to meet as a so-called Committee of the Whole to consider a bill requiring the Governor to order spraying. Director Rominger was notified he would be summoned as the first witness. The Governor was invited to appear, though not expected to attend. He would be in Los Angeles. A meeting of the Assembly as a Committee of the Whole was unlike anything I had ever seen. From 1971 to 1976, when I served as a legislative staff member in the state Senate, nothing like this had ever happened.

Wednesday afternoon and Thursday, July 8th and 9th, thousands of employees from a dozen state agencies arrived in Los Gatos. I scrambled to stay on top of the rapid buildup as we worked feverishly to implement the new ground program. The CCC and Guard units were again put to work to help with the fruit stripping. The Guard had 100 trucks ready to pick up the tons of fruit expected to be stripped by local citizens before Brown's 5 p.m. Monday deadline. The Guard erected a tent city on the grounds of nearby Agnews State Hospital to house the CCC while other state employees scrambled to find local accommodations at inexpensive hotels and motels. The State reimbursement rate was impossibly low. In the two years I lived in Los Gatos, I lost money every night I spent away from home. I am sure other employees did, too.

Thursday morning, ground spray workers from Caltrans began arriving in trucks, each towing a spray rig. We expected a total of 400, ten times the 40 we had on hand. Hundreds of the new hires stood in lines at the school waiting to be blood tested and formally hired to augment the ground spray crews. Jim Rudig and Don Henry on Isi Siddiqui's team took charge of briefing the arriving uniformed park rangers and forestry employees. Their assignment would again be going door to door distributing the ground spraying notices.

Thursday night, the Highway Patrol began setting up the fruit inspection roadblocks on four major multi-lane freeways leading into and out of the quarantine area. State and federal quarantine inspectors would do the actual inspections of the cars and trucks that were pulled over. On Thursday morning, Governor Brown appeared at the CHP inspection operation on Highway 101 leading South toward the Salinas Valley. Traffic had backed up two miles as CHP personnel pulled 300 cars an hour out of traffic and directed them into the search lane. Many were found to be carrying fruit. Inspectors seized home-grown fruit from people claiming they had never heard of either the medfly or the quarantine. The volume of seized fruit highlighted the risk that a motorist carrying infested fruit might transport the medfly into California's rich farming areas less than 30 miles away or even farther. TV cameras filmed the enormous amount of fruit already confiscated. These video clips and still pictures in newspapers received wide coverage. The Governor called the results "terrible and very disquieting."

On Thursday, I received unexpected executive office reinforcements. Huey Johnson, the unabashed environmentalist Secretary of the California Resources Agency, had volunteered half a dozen members of his executive staff. They were led by Rich Hammond, a personable, Harvard-educated lawyer who served as Johnson's deputy Agency Secretary. I believed, without proof, that beyond supporting the Governor's ground program, Secretary Johnson's help included making sure we did not slow-walk the ground effort as we had already been accused of doing. My staff, especially Arnie Morrison, initially bristled at this unrequested help from those he believed had advised the Governor against aerial spraying. However, we all quickly came to appreciate the infusion of talented, can-do individuals committed to helping us. I personally hit it off right away with Rich Hammond, even though he did not hide the fact he was also reporting directly to the Governor's office. That didn't faze me because I felt Brown had every right to want to stay on top of the effort. His political future was on the line. Rejecting aerial spraying and ordering the ground program was an enormous gamble on his part. I knew, we were doing everything we could to succeed on the ground despite believing it impossible. Over the next weeks and months, I got to know Hammond and each of his team better as our executive team met each day over early morning breakfasts. All the members of the resources team were exceptionally bright, competent, and tireless. They worked out of my office or wherever assigned, making an impossible management situation workable.

Chapter 10 (Brown Orders Aerial Spraying)

"MEDFLY CRISIS—THE FULL STORY" in huge black letters topped the front page of the *San Francisco Chronicle.* on Friday morning, July 10th. Two ground sprayers, covered from head to toe in protective white overalls, gloves, boots, and full helmets with face shields, were pictured below the headline, pointing spray nozzles directly at the reader. They looked ghoulishly like workers at a nuclear disaster site. Below the masthead, additional headlines competed for space, followed by articles on the battle. One pictured a clogged freeway captioned "Forbidden Fruit." Another was captioned "The Medical Debate Over Malathion's Effects." Two more articles appeared on page 1A: "Huge Battle Begins—New Calls for Aerial Spraying" and "Threat of U.S Quarantine."

The front-page "Forbidden Fruit" article continued on page 4A under yet another headline, "Brown Leads Battle as the Big Medfly War Begins." Further coverage inside the paper featured a photo of Brown, labeled "The Commander." It showed the Governor inspecting a box of apricots seized at one of the CHP roadblocks. The article reported that despite the limited number of cars being checked in the random inspections on the first day of the new ground war, the CHP had confiscated more than 5,000 pounds of produce. The coverage closed with news that more larvae had been found and worse—This time, the maggots appeared in the middle of the heavily treated core area. Dr. Roy Cunningham said, "finds in that original core area makes me more doubtful of success." He also pointed out, "We've got two infestations—the old one in San Jose and the new one on the [San Francisco] Peninsula."

Meanwhile, in Sacramento, 70 of the 80 State Assembly members had returned from recess to attend the emergency session scheduled for 10 a.m. that morning. Senators had also stayed in town for a possible afternoon session of the Senate if needed. Protesters from Santa Clara picketed outside as Capitol Police patrolled the legislative hallways. A legislative staffer said, "My God, they've got guards everywhere." The Assembly's chief administrative officer claimed the extra security was unrelated to threats of violence. He said there had not been any threats against Legislators. "My main concern," he said, "was not knowing how many people would show up."

State security had also been set up at the entrance to the Department of Food and Agriculture building. On the top floor, Director Rominger was meeting with his deputy directors to prepare for his testimony. I was in Los Gatos, linked into the meeting by speakerphone. Rominger would be the first witness at the hearing. We discussed what he should say. Other witnesses from the farm community and the public were scheduled to follow Rominger. The bill, authored by Democratic Assemblyman Rick Lehman from Fresno, required the Governor to order immediate aerial spraying. Based on the Senate vote and the general mood in the Assembly, it appeared certain that there were sufficient votes to pass it and override any veto.

In Rich's office, the mood was grim. We had earlier pledged to the farm community's leaders that, in return for their support of the winter ground program, aerially spraying would be ordered if that failed. Now unable to keep our word, we had prepared a joint letter of resignation to be included in Rominger's opening statement. Moments later, Rich's executive secretary, Betty Taylor, entered to report that the Assembly hearing was canceled. Governor Brown had notified the Speaker he was ordering aerial spraying to begin Monday night as planned.

We later learned that President Reagan's Secretary of USDA, John Block, had reached Governor Brown by telephone in Los Angeles about 6 a.m. Pacific Time and told him he planned to order a quarantine of all of California "immediately." Brown asked for a delay. Block refused. Unless Brown backed down and agreed to order the aerial spraying as planned, the quarantine order would be issued forthwith. Even if Brown agreed to proceed to aerial spraying, Block said the statewide quarantine might still be imposed if, for any reason, the spraying was delayed. Walling off the state's fruit and vegetable exports to save the rest of the country from the medfly's spread would have been a disaster for California growers and shippers. Only host fruit that had been fumigated could be shipped overseas or to other states. In July 1981, California lacked the capacity to fumigate more than a tiny fraction of the harvest. Moreover, the chemicals used for fumigation, such as ethylene dibromide (EDB), were exceptionally toxic. Brown had no choice but to reverse course and order aerial spraying to begin as planned.

The Governor's sudden about-face Friday morning stunned his supporters, who had traveled to Sacramento in force to oppose the special Assembly session. According to press reports, the Mayor of San Jose, Janet Gray Hayes, "looked shocked," even as she acknowledged the Governor had no choice. "Some of my pregnant friends are leaving the spray area, but I'm staying," she said.

In Los Gatos, I ended my call with Rominger and the other deputies and stepped out of my office to report the new development. Then we went back to work. We still had thousands of people committed to a ground program that would have to continue at least until the aerial spraying started. The Governor said the aerial spraying would begin on Monday night, the 13th, as originally planned. I did not know if this was still possible. We had lost three days. Monday night was a little more than 72 hours away. I asked one of the nearby staff members to find Arnie Morrison. "Tell him it's urgent," I said.

When Arnie Morrison appeared, I assumed he had been fully engaged in the ground spraying scramble as we tried to keep up with the burgeoning larval discoveries. I learned instead that he had turned everything over to his exceptionally capable number two, Don Bowman and had continued to focus on aerial planning. As a result, Arnie could report that we had a handshake agreement with San Joaquin Helicopter Service in Delano to arrive on site by Monday, the 13th, with one and hopefully two helicopters, including ground crews. Arnie said we were going to need three to four more helicopters. Jim Josephson, San Joaquin's owner, had a lead on a third one to be flown in from Alabama and was negotiating to lease another one from a company in Washington State. Morrison said he had also been in touch with the base commander at Moffett Naval Air Station in the City of Mountain View in what was now the heart of the infestation. We had preliminary approval to base the helicopters there.

Moffett had been a major base during WWII. It was still in active use, now serving as the headquarters for the Lockheed P-3 Orion aircraft that flew long-range reconnaissance and anti-submarine patrols over the Pacific. The Air Force also used part of the base for satellite tracking. Navy carrier-based jets had flown in and out in the fifties and sixties. The base, with its iconic 175-foot-high hangers built for blimps, remained visible from Highway 101. It offered everything we needed for helicopter operations, including a secure perimeter. That would help solve another problem. After Brown's announcement, Congressman Norman Mineta's office had received threats to sabotage the helicopters on the ground or shoot them down. The calls had been duly reported to the police and the project. Flying from inside a restricted base would help us avoid both civil disobedience and the risk of sabotage. Because of the threats, Morrison refused repeated requests from the media to reveal where the helicopters would be based. He also had a backup plan in case we needed a second airfield. The San Jose County airport had the necessary facilities and security and lay within the spray zone.

I had picked the right man in choosing Arnie. He was exactly who we needed now to get the helicopters in the air on schedule. The air operations needed FAA coordination and approval. Arnie reported that Josephson already had a meeting scheduled with the FAA on Saturday afternoon to brief them on our planned air operations and secure any necessary approval from them for the low-level flights.

More good news arrived Friday afternoon from Assistant Attorney General Rod Walston. The federal court in San Francisco granted our motion for a restraining order against enforcement of the local ordinances blocking aerial spraying. The judge ruled the Federal Insecticide, Fungicide, and Rodenticide Act, known as FIFRA, preempted local government authority over pesticide use and that the state would suffer irreparable harm if aerial spraying were impeded.

That left one more big problem to solve before we could spray at midnight on Monday—how to guide the helicopters at night.

Agricultural spraying typically took place over crops in rectangular fields with the planes guided by flaggers on the ground, marking the beginning and end of each pass. The gypsy moth spraying in California and the aerial bait spraying in Florida and Texas had both occurred in daylight. We were committed to doing this at night, something that had never been done before. As we had for the logistics in the ground war, we turned to Caltrans for help with the guidance. Their engineers proposed creating straight lines of lights held aloft by kytoon ballons for each spray pass. We mapped the area to be sprayed by drawing a mile-and-a-half circle around each larval site to create a total spray area of 97 square miles. We then divided this into four numbered zones. We planned to start with Zone 1 at midnight on Monday the 13th. It covered parts of the cities of Palo Alto, Mountain View, Los Altos, and Los Altos Hills, the areas where the first new larval finds had shown up. Zones 2, 3, and 4 would follow on successive nights. To achieve eradication, at least six applications of the bait spaced a week to ten days apart would be the minimum required.

As with the ground program, written door-to-door notices would be delivered to each home at least 24 hours in advance of the first spray. There were 315,000 homes in the four zones. We scheduled delivery of the notices in Zone 1 for Saturday and Sunday. The detailed block-by-block system of medfly notifications for both fruit stripping and ground spraying from January to July 1, 1981, had been designed and managed by Jim Rudig. I first met Rudig in December at our initial hotel planning meeting. It did not take me long to discover that behind Rudig's broad-shouldered biker appearance of sunglasses, shoulder-length hair, beard, and boots lay a soft-spoken competence and natural leadership ability beyond that of anyone I had ever worked with on or off the project. He was largely self-taught after working part-time in agriculture beginning at age 15. He managed to finish high school but never made it to college. He had been working in Fresno on a control project there before being reassigned to the gypsy moth eradication project under Don Henry. The notification system for the aerial helicopter spraying for gypsy moths became the template for our program.

On paper, getting the aerial spraying underway on time looked doable. However, the failure to be better prepared to switch to aerial spraying if needed was entirely my fault. In early May, Arnie Morrison had urged me to sign a contract with San Joaquin Helicopters that would have enabled them to line up more helicopters; I had said no because I doubted they would be needed. By then, the likelihood we would have to spray had diminished, and contracting for more helicopters would send the wrong message. By the end of May and into June, even the skeptics believed we were close to eradicating the medfly on the ground, negating any need to spray by air.

After Morrison left my office Friday morning, promising to redouble his efforts to line up more helicopters, I moved on to worrying about other potential problems ahead, including a renewed legal effort to obtain an emergency restraining order blocking spraying until after the preparation of an EIR. On Friday, a new motion to block the spraying was filed in San Jose Superior court. The hearing was scheduled for Monday morning July 13th, and I was ordered to appear as a witness to what was planned.

On Friday afternoon in Sacramento, Governor Brown held an angry press conference, denouncing the Reagan administration for sabotaging the new ground program and thus forcing the spraying. He said doing so denied California any opportunity for that alternative to succeed. In a prepared statement released to the press, he also offered a new rationale for why he had reversed course and ordered the aerial spraying. Now, it wasn't the danger of Malathion but that of a different pesticide, ethylene dibromide (EDB), the use of which would be necessitated by USDA's threatened state-wide quarantine. He said he yielded once he realized that,

> The quarantine would require a massive fumigation program, imperiling the lives and health of thousands of produce workers. That is not acceptable. Fumigation requires the use of deadly poisons. They kill humans. They are a hundred times more deadly than Malathion, the Medfly spray.

The new justification failed to gain traction as the reason for rejecting aerial spraying because fumigation had not been mentioned at all when the Governor said his decision was based on the danger of Malathion. By highlighting a pesticide a hundred times more deadly than Malathion, he reminded everyone that Malathion was a weak, relatively safe pesticide.

Many of Brown's supporters believed the Reagan administration's quarantine threat was driven by politics. Accordingly, his supporters in San Jose applauded Brown's claim that,

> The action of the Reagan administration in threatening a quarantine is sabotage.... (it) has effectively taken away the ground spraying ...for a program which takes this country further and further down the road to increased use of deadly and toxic chemicals...in our environment and in the food we eat.,

Dr. Gilstrap and others saw politics only in Brown's equivocation. Having worked for Governor Brown during all or part of his four terms as Governor, I believed his resistance to aerial spraying arose from something more profound, a moral choice not unlike his opposition to the death penalty. Brown knew he would pay a high political price if he refused to spray. Ordering the spraying of pesticides on people ran counter to everything he stood for. He said, when he made his decision that he knew full well the serious political consequences involved. My view then and now is that Brown faced a defining moment, not only in his political career but in his life. What primarily drove his refusal to spray was his environmental opposition to pesticides, coupled with his distrust of big agriculture. Politically, it was a lose-lose choice. Jerry Brown chose who he was, both politically and morally. He viewed spraying people with a pesticide as simply wrong. In announcing his decision, Brown said:

> Subjecting that many people, including pregnant women, infants, and the sick and elderly to six or more aerial applications of a toxic pesticide, is just not an acceptable

alternative, not when there are experts questioning its long-term safety.

Tom Harris of the *Mercury* wrote: Brown's decision to hold off spraying was reached after what some of his top aides – and legislative allies – described as his most intense personal involvement in any issue since he was elected governor in 1974."

> One of his aides, who asked not to be named, (told Harris) 'I've never seen him spend that much time on any issue. He was at it for three days and three nights, an incredible amount of time. In the end, I think it was his deep philosophical leaning against our increasing dependence on chemicals, of society being ruled by Big Brother and a few experts who tell people what is best for them that convinced him to give it a try.

John Vasconcellos, the powerful chair of the Assembly Ways and Means Committee and a close ally of Brown, was quoted saying the same thing. "It was more of a deep, personal thing for him." He added: "Jerry has a curious, long-range sense of things. This is his strength, and I think that is the instinctive thing he went with."

Confirmation that Vasconcellos' view (and mine) that Brown's rejection of aerial spraying ran deeper than choosing what he saw as the politically safest course was confirmed when I started to write this book. In an old box of medfly files, I was surprised to come across a 1980 paperback, *The Pesticide Conspiracy*, written by famed University of California entomologist Dr. Robert Van Den Bosch. Clipped to the front cover was Governor Brown's business card. I swept the dust off, opened the cover, and saw for the first time the handwritten note he had addressed to me and its date. It read: "Jerry, --- Explore, Serve, Protect— the Earth. Jerry Brown. July 14, 1981". I do not recall him handing it to me that morning in July when we met after the first night of aerial spraying. Perhaps he had it delivered to my office later that day.

In April 1982, Brown was interviewed by Ronald Powell of the Sacramento Bee. He told Powell that he was "not impressed" with the presentation from his Department of Health Services and was instead persuaded by the arguments made by the Santa Clara and Stanford physicians. He also said he felt "duty-bound" to try another ground program before agreeing to the aerial spraying. He believed the ground program would provide more time for people to come around and more time to organize the aerial spraying if required. He did not get it, and whatever his motivation was, his refusal to make a locally unpopular but necessary decision on behalf of the whole state quickly turned into a political disaster.

Friday night and throughout the day on Saturday, the 11th, the telephones rang non-stop as thousands of people called the project seeking more information and help stripping their trees and gardens. We continued to release millions of sterile flies from the backs of trucks and in airdrops while ground spray crews dragged long hoses into yards in the Mountain View gap and elsewhere to spray recent larval finds. Our goal was to spray three blocks in all directions from each of the more than 80 separate larval finds. Traps were being checked, and a separate team of fruit collection workers continued responding to homeowner call-ins of worms in their fruit.

On all the major freeways, rivers of traffic slowed to a crawl, then inched forward, bumper to bumper past CHP checkpoints. Highway patrol officers randomly pulled out vehicles so inspectors could check for contraband fruit. And everywhere throughout the more than 660 square-mile quarantine area, residents frantically stripped trees of ripe fruit and ripped out gardens they had nurtured all spring. In January, it had taken residents and the CCC four weeks to strip 50 square miles. The Governor's order impossibly demanded an area ten times larger be denuded by Monday at 5 p.m. The fruit had to be bagged in plastic and then dragged to the curb for pick up by National Guard trucks. Many homeowners loaded their bags into the trunks of their cars and drove to the dump themselves, only to wait in lines of cars so backed up that many dumped their bags by the side of the road and left. Stores ran out of plastic bags.

The CCC stripped public properties and helped seniors and the disabled. We dutifully supported the fruit stripping, first because the Governor had ordered it and second because we believed it might be marginally helpful pending the start of aerial spraying. An unknowable percentage of ripening summer fruit was likely infested. More was being infested every day by female medflies, putting eggs into fruit still on the trees. Stripping and burying fruit would help dispose of these eggs and larvae before they became new flies. Also, the stripping would help if aerial spraying was blocked by the courts. Since the bait sprays eliminated the flies as they emerged and sought food before mating, host removal had never been used with bait spraying in Florida and Texas other than in the immediate area of a fly or larval find. Whatever its merits in July 1981, it was an impossible task in the time available.

The project's focus remained ground spraying and getting the helicopters airborne. For opponents, it was getting the courts to intervene on Monday and block any aerial spraying. The lawyers for Santa Clara County and multiple cities had already alerted the State Supreme Court they planned to appeal there on Monday night if the lower court on Monday refused to issue the restraining order they were seeking.

Beginning on Saturday morning, park rangers and forestry workers began going door to door distributing notices to the thousands of homes in Zone 1. In addition to informing residents the starting date and time would be Monday midnight to 6 a.m. Tuesday morning, the notices urged residents to stay indoors; close windows; cover fishponds, kiddie pools, and children's toys; and garage or wash off cars to prevent damage to their paint. We also included information on the safety of Malathion and telephone numbers to call for more information. On Saturday, the major papers helpfully offered similar advice.

The Governor's office created a new local Medfly Health Advisory Committee on Friday that held its first meeting on Saturday morning. Before we completed distributing the notices, the committee ordered them to be rewritten to tone down the health language we were using. They said our health warnings overstated the risks of Malathion. We printed 100,000 new notices overnight in Sacramento with their new language. By Sunday morning, more larvae had been found, requiring an increase in the aerial spraying area to 120 square miles. We therefore modified Zone 4 to become Zones 4A, 4B, and 4C. We also expanded the ground spraying using the 150 spray rigs that arrived on Saturday.

Soon after I arrived Sunday morning with the new notices, Arnie Morrison appeared in my office with a stunning new development. President Reagan's Secretary of Defense, Casper Weinberger, had canceled our permission to use Moffett Naval Air Station as our base of operations for the helicopters. While Reagan's Secretary of Agriculture was threatening to quarantine California if aerial spraying didn't start immediately, his Secretary of Defense was pulling the rug out from under our efforts to do so.

On its face, it appeared to be a transparent move to embarrass Brown. The Governor and I said so publicly. If the White House had not ordered the reversal, we believed they would restore our use. However, efforts to reach Reagan's Attorney General, Ed Meese, and President Reagan himself were unsuccessful. Both Secretary Block and Director Rominger personally talked with Secretary Weinberger. He said it was his decision after he heard about the protests and threats to shoot down the helicopters. He did not want the base involved. We learned later that Weinberger's decision had originated with news reports that we might base the helicopters on the stretch of unused land in the City of Cupertino, where the Malathion and hundreds of spray rigs were based. That had never been our plan. However, the possibility unnerved Cupertino's elected mayor, who promptly panicked at the specter of opponents descending on his city bent on blocking the spraying by any means possible. His concerns were reinforced by news reports of anonymous callers claiming to be Vietnam vets, threatening to shoot down the helicopters. The papers also reported that non-violent protesters wanted to learn the location for staging the aerial spraying so they could engage in civil disobedience. According to Robert Moore, a protest leader, they were organizing search teams with citizen-band radios to find the trucks that would deliver the pesticide. "Wherever the trucks are, we're going to be there with a vigil at 8 p.m. Monday," he said.

Cupertino's mayor had hurriedly scheduled an emergency city council meeting to prohibit the "Malathion-laden helicopters," as the San *Jose Mercury* had dubbed them, from using his city as their base. This, in turn, spurred Congressman Norman Mineta to call Casper Weinberger and recommend Moffett as an alternative. Weinberger, a Californian born and raised in the Bay Area, was unaware the base commander had already approved our use. He reacted the same way the mayor did. He told Mineta that "he didn't want people to be storming Moffett Field" either. He had then picked up the phone and called the Navy, telling them under no circumstances was Moffett to be used for the spraying program. This was California's problem. He did not want his Defense Department involved. The politics of the situation led to more political cartoons. One of the best was by Carl Mauldin in the *Chicago Sun-Times*. In his cartoon, a pilot in a WWI flight suit and cloth helmet carrying a giant can labeled Malathion is shown saluting President Reagan at his desk in the White House above the caption, "Never mind the Medfly, did you get Jerry Brown."

The next shoe dropped late Sunday afternoon when the City of San Jose notified us that they planned to ban our use of their airport. Monday morning, their City Council met and voted to deny use of the airport for medfly spraying. The mayor, Janet Gray Hays, told reporters, "We're getting caught in a political battle between the feds and the state, and I don't want to be left holding the bag." A member of the City Council, Tom McEnery, who opposed the spraying, said, "The police force in San Jose would bear the brunt." Arnie told me not to worry. He had a second fallback plan. I admitted to the press we did not currently have an airport. "We possibly won't go at 12:01 Tuesday morning," I said. "That is our goal, but we are not talking about a change of more than 24 hours." In the back of my mind was the Wednesday deadline Texas and the other southern states had set as the date they would quarantine all of California if spraying did not start by then.

While we were trying to start the aerial spraying on time, the media began reporting that residents planned to flee the area to avoid Malathion. County supervisors Rod Diridon and Zoe Lofgren announced they would be among those leaving. Lofgren revealed she was three months pregnant. Diridon and other officials predicted the local economy would experience a mass exodus of workers concerned about the potential danger of the Malathion. The Red Cross announced that they were opening four shelters outside the spray Zones to accommodate those fleeing their homes during spraying. The shelters would be in Fremont, San Mateo, and Milpitas, and there would be an overflow shelter at the University of California in Santa Cruz with 1,000 dormitory beds available.

The Governor's health committee said the shelters were unnecessary. I weighed in as well, noting that "People don't leave because of other health risks such as the smog that eats away the sides of buildings. Nor do they leave when their neighbors spray a whole bottle of Malathion." I tried to reassure the public the spraying would be safe. But our efforts to take extra precautions to prove we were sensitive to the health concerns had heightened, not lessened, the fear of unknown risks. For example, we had initially promised to ground-spray sensitive areas around hospitals and nursing homes. We dropped this after the health committee said this was unnecessary. The conflicting announcements on health issues only added to the general confusion.

In addition to creating the local Medfly Health Advisory Committee, Governor Brown ordered the establishment of a detailed monitoring program to address the lack of data from the earlier aerial spraying in Florida and Texas. State environmental agencies would conduct environmental monitoring independent of the project. The State's Air Resources Board was assigned to monitor the air inside selected schools, hospitals, and residences. Teams from the State Water Quality Control Board would take water samples from pools, ponds, and reservoirs. One-foot-square white cards placed under each spray would confirm the size and distribution of the Malathion bait droplets reaching the ground. Department of Fish and Game biologists would monitor and record any impacts on aquatic species. State university entomologists would survey populations of non-target insects and animals for any evidence of loss.

Although it was uncertain that we would be able to get the helicopters in the air on Monday night, Secretary Block and USDA staff in Los Gatos were satisfied that California was doing everything humanly possible to begin the spraying program on time and prevent the medfly from spreading. To calm the fears of California farmers that USDA might still quarantine the whole state, Block announced that he was working closely with California officials in deciding "jointly if there is a need to expand the quarantine area." Block also knew that the southern states were again threatening to institute their own quarantines of all medfly-host produce grown in California. In our unique national political landscape, we are a nation of semi-sovereign states. Each has governmental powers, including quarantine authority within its own borders. Government programs from highways to pollution to pest prevention require comity and cooperation. For this reason, Block intended his announcement to also be an unmistakable reminder to the southern states that USDA's national quarantine authority was paramount and that he would not tolerate individual state quarantines in conflict with USDA's authority. His clear warning was ignored by the 11 Southern states, all members of the former Confederate States of America.

Late Sunday, the aerial spraying opponents served me with a subpoena to personally appear in court at 8 a.m. Monday morning, in the Santa Clara Superior courtroom of Judge Bruce Allen, who would be hearing the request for a restraining order. Meanwhile, Judge Allen publicly announced that with respect to the hearing on Monday, "There's not going to be any aerial spraying until I am satisfied…there will be no health hazards." He set no deadline for his decision.

Chapter 11 (Aerial Spraying—The Legal Battle)

On Monday morning, July 13th, the *San Francisco Chronicle's* front page featured a giant picture of National Guard military tents above the paper's masthead. The headline, "C0PTERS AT SECRET BASE," overshadowed multiple articles on page one, covering every detail of the planned air assault, including the locations of Red Cross shelters. A last-minute judicial stay of execution offered the only hope there could be a reprieve from what some called the inevitable aerial bombardment. We refused to discuss where the helicopters were because of the persistent threats to disable them on the ground or shoot them down. The secrecy, reminiscent of the actual D-Day in 1944, only heightened the anxiety I had felt as I went to bed Sunday night with no idea of what the day on Monday would bring. Would the court allow us to proceed? If they did, would we have a base from which to fly? If we were able to start the spraying, would the helicopters be fired on or fail mechanically and crash? There was no limit to what could go wrong.

After an early Monday morning breakfast with staff, I reported to Judge Bruce Allen's San Jose courtroom. The mood in the courtroom was somber, as expected. When the bailiff intoned, "All rise," Judge Allen entered, his expression as grim as his black robe. The atmosphere in the courtroom felt like the beginning of a criminal sentencing hearing you knew would be bad. According to the paper, Judge Allen was known as "a very strict…very conservative" judge with a no-nonsense demeanor. He often handed down stiff sentences, including to some not even charged with a crime. He reportedly had jailed a spectator for ten days for talking in court and more than one attorney for contempt.

Everyone in the courtroom knew I was the director of a project seeking to spray a million men, women, and children with Malathion. As I sat next to the attorneys at the counsel table, I felt like a criminal defendant on trial. I remembered the time years before when, as a legal aid attorney in a difficult case, an angry judge told me he was going to send me to jail. After refusing to allow me to withdraw from the case and denying my motion for a continuance, the judge abruptly put the case over for a week and delayed jailing me. Instead, he said, "come back with your toothbrush because you will probably be going to jail." A week later, he had cooled off. I did not end up behind bars after all.

Looking directly at me and the lawyers defending the case, Judge Allen said he was very concerned about the health risks of aerial spraying, and he was not setting any deadline for completing the hearing. It might last more than one day. "As far as I'm concerned," he said, "there is no rush." My anxiety went up another notch. A 24-hour delay was manageable. I had been quoted saying we might not be able to spray until Tuesday night. Secretary Block had also signaled that USDA wasn't worried about a one-day delay. Even with no delay, we were already two or three weeks behind the medflies. Every day meant more flies and larvae in more places. The area to be sprayed had already expanded by 20 miles over the weekend. How much more would it expand while Judge Allen was making up his mind? What if he took the matter under submission for days, or worse, said no? Or said yes with conditions? We could not afford more delay. Deputy Attorney General Charlie Getz, appearing for the project along with Rod Walston, told reporters during a break in testimony that he hoped the proceedings would be completed and a decision rendered soon.

During the day, while I was in court, cars and pickups idled in long lines at the local dumps as the five o'clock deadline for fruit removal neared. Residents planning to flee packed up, while those staying covered their cars and toys and buttoned up their homes, not knowing whether the spraying would go forward or not.

It had been impossible to strip the 680 square miles of lush orchards and backyards between Wednesday afternoon and Monday. In July, nearly every tree was loaded, and it was hot in San Jose. The high on Thursday had been 96. Monday, it was over 90. It would hit 100 on Tuesday the 14th. People had no way of reaching fruit that medflies could reach easily, like loquats 60 or more feet off the ground. Not everyone was home in July or off work. Despite the super-human effort by many, trees with ripening fruit could be found everywhere. The Governor's renewed ground attack based on stripping fruit had been thrown together by advisors in Sacramento who didn't fully understand the enemy and the logistics involved. The drama of the last five days had helped awaken the public to the reality that the medfly was a big problem. At the same time, it exposed how embarrassingly porous and ineffective the quarantine was. The CHP had stopped 119,000 vehicles, resulting in seizures of fruit from more than 6,800. Quarantine inspectors at the airports continued to collect an average of 20 pounds of fruit daily from travelers leaving San Jose by air. It had become clearer over the weekend that given the size of the infestation, the speed with which it was growing, and the mid-summer weather, defeating the medfly on the ground had little chance of success.

In Judge Allen's courtroom, the opponents' argued that no aerial spraying could take place until after the preparation and completion of an adequate environmental impact review under either state law, federal law, or both. We argued that the emergency justified an exception to those requirements. Judge Allen said he was not convinced that an emergency trumped concerns about human health and safety. He said he would stop the spraying if he didn't feel it was safe. Whether there was an emergency and when it began was central to the opponents' case. They called me to the stand. My testimony was limited to how and when the decision to use aerial spraying had been made. I testified that the decision to move to aerial spraying at my level arose at the earliest in late June when the larvae appeared. Before that, with the help of the Governor's emergency declaration in December 1980, my decision had been to try to eradicate the medfly without aerial spraying. I further testified that the official state government decision to aerially spray occurred on July 10th when Governor Brown ordered it.

After I testified, Judge Allen instructed counsel to move on to the issue of whether the spraying would be safe. To prove it would not be, Walter Hays, the attorney for three cities and Santa Clara County, called to the witness stand Dr. Sumner Kalman, the Stanford University Pharmacology professor. Kalman testified, as expected, that malathion was a nerve poison and that, if present in substantial quantities in the human body, it could block the transmission of communications from the brain to muscles. Therefore, it was unreasonably dangerous to spray it on humans. The keywords and fundamental weakness in his argument turned on whether the spraying would result in substantial quantities of the pesticide in human bodies. Substantial quantities had been consumed by humans in suicide attempts. Several such attempts involved a person drinking an eight-ounce bottle of malathion. Some of these attempts had succeeded in causing the death being sought. Others had not, with the individual suffering no long-term effects. Dr. Kalman was forced to admit that he knew of no acute toxic reaction having occurred in any human in situations involving the small quantities proposed by the project, nor in any of the earlier Malathion spraying programs for mosquito control and medfly eradication. Particularly damaging to his argument was evidence that powder containing Malathion was routinely used by doctors to control head and body lice on children.

Dr. Kalman's other concern was the possibility of unknown health consequences from any exposure at all, consequences he said might not show up until years later. He testified that he believed Malathion had not been researched enough by the EPA and others to completely rule out all possibility it could be carcinogenic or mutagenic. The problem he had was the lack of evidence that Malathion caused either. His testimony, and that of other witnesses who opposed the use of Malathion, ran counter to the results of extensive testing in mammals, mainly rats, that had been given high doses of Malathion over long periods of time. Those tests had shown neither carcinogenicity nor mutagenesis. Those charged with protecting the public, including the EPA, had relied on this large body of research before issuing the specific approval to USDA to use Malathion as proposed. So had the California Department of Health in reaching its decision that the spraying would be safe. These research findings were summarized in the reports and approvals that the state's lawyers introduced into evidence. This, coupled with Malathion having been sprayed from the air over other human populations without a single reported case of adverse health consequences, outweighed Kalman's unsupported speculation that more studies might show evidence of harm.

Hays then called another doctor, an allergist practicing in Los Gatos. He testified to having treated two patients who presented with allergy-type symptoms that he believed were related to them having been exposed to Malathion from the ground spraying program. His testimony was weakened, if not entirely disregarded, when on cross-examination, he admitted that he could not be sure it was Malathion that caused the symptoms. To be certain, he said, he would need to expose the patients to a skin test using Malathion, something he said would be unethical.

Hays also called Dr. Kenneth P. Hagen, the esteemed University of California Berkeley entomologist, in support of the argument that aerial spraying was unnecessary because ground spraying could work. However, under cross-examination by Getz, Dr. Hagen was forced to admit that aerial spraying was the quickest and most efficient approach under existing circumstances. "I wish I could say something else, he said to Getz, "But I have to agree with you (on aerial spraying)."

When it was the defense's turn, Getz called Dr. Isi Siddiqui, who testified that the ground program could not succeed with the resources we had. He said at least 600 ground spray rigs and 5,000 employees would be needed.

In his closing argument, Rod Walston noted that no evidence whatsoever had been presented proving any danger to anyone from the aerial spraying. To the contrary, the evidence showed that Malathion had been extensively studied for years, had been used widely by home gardeners, and aerially sprayed over cities to control mosquitoes and medflies, all with no evidence of harm. There was likewise nothing in the extensive literature on Malathion that supported the argument that at 2.4 ounces per acre, Malathion would pose any risk of significant exposure, let alone risk of harm to anyone. Finally, he argued, everyone knows this is an emergency. In a declared emergency like this one, neither state nor federal law requires the lengthy environmental decision-making and review process the opponents claim is legally required before any action can be taken. He concluded by pointing out that the evidence had clearly shown aerial spraying was now the "only effective means" available to deal with it, adding, "This infestation is spreading like a prairie fire across the state of California. The plaintiffs are asking us to put it out with a garden hose."

After final arguments, Judge Allen left the bench and retired to his chambers to consider the matter. The lawyers stayed behind in the courtroom for further word of a decision. We knew he could take his time deciding or could rule against us. Even if he ruled in our favor, spraying might still be delayed by an appeal to the State Supreme Court. They could delay the spraying while they decided, or they could reverse a ruling in our favor by Judge Allen. There was nothing to do but wait. I had been waiting for a decision ever since the red telephone rang on my desk a week earlier. It seemed a lifetime ago. Sometime after midnight, aerial spraying would either start or it wouldn't. I left the courthouse and drove to the Los Gatos office. After being briefed on what I had missed while in the courtroom, I slipped away from the chaos and went to my motel a few blocks away and took a shower. I remember leaning against the wall of the shower letting the water run and run. I was completely exhausted.

When I returned to the project office, the scene rivaled that of a political campaign on election night. The phones were ringing continuously. One worker said: "You can't even take your hand off the phone. As soon as you put it down, it rings, and you pick it up again."

So far, nothing had been heard from the court. I stood outside, taking questions from half a dozen reporters asking if we were going to spray or postpone the spraying for 24 hours. I told them I didn't know. At that moment, someone from inside the office squeezed through the crowd and said loudly, "The judge ruled in our favor!" "There's your answer," I said to the reporters. "It sounds like we're on."

Judge Allen's prompt and favorable decision was electrifying. Suddenly, the door swung open, or almost open. The opponents, as promised, rushed to the California Supreme Court for a rare night session, presided over by my former boss, Secretary Rose Elizabeth Bird, now the Supreme Court's Chief Justice. She also happened to be a long-time resident of the Santa Clara Valley. She was no doubt personally familiar with the controversy. I knew her views on pesticides matched the Governor's, and for that matter, mine too. Except in this instance, I believed the law and necessity were on our side. I believed she would rule in our favor. Around 8 p.m., we received word that the Supreme Court had debated the matter for several hours before sending their clerk out to waiting reporters with a one-sentence decision, which the clerk read out loud. "The application [for a restraining order] is herewith denied," he intoned. Chief Justice Bird was rumored to be the only dissenting vote. It was nearing midnight in Washington, D.C., where the White House and USDA anxiously awaited word of the court's decision. A USDA official on duty told reporters the day had been "total chaos." I knew Congressman Norman Mineta, who had opposed the spraying earlier, was still urging Weinberger to allow us to use Moffett. In response to a reporter's question about whether we would be able to get off the ground, I said, "We've had cooperation from every level (of government) short of the White House." I meant it to be a hopeful statement that we might soon have Moffett. Instead, it came across as part of the sparring between Brown and Reagan.

After word of the decision came, a dozen different problems still needed attention. A reporter wrote, "Scribner keeps ducking into his office to talk to various officials. To a woman who insists on talking only to him, he says– 'I've been on the phone with the Governor four times in the last fifteen minutes and I've had to interrupt a meeting all four times, can't anyone else help you"? The reporter apparently checked his watch and wrote, "It's 9:37 p.m. and the phones continue to ring, one after the other, in a solid line of shrill announcement." Someone tugged my arm and whispered that Arnie Morrison had gotten through and wanted me to meet him at the Reid-Hillview Airport in San Jose as soon as possible. Trailed by reporters, I drove to the airport, which was mainly used by small planes. It did not appear to be the rumored secret base, at least not yet, as there were no helicopters in sight.

Arnie and I conducted a short briefing with the reporters. We told them the spraying would begin after midnight now that the court had allowed it. As I continued visiting with the reporters, Arnie disappeared. A few minutes later, a staff member pulled me aside and led me to an unmarked car. I squeezed in next to a project press officer, a pool reporter from the *San Jose Mercury*, and a photographer, all of whom had been sworn to secrecy. With me sandwiched in the middle of the back seat, we sped away, taking a circuitous route to shake any cars attempting to follow. After 15 minutes of turns, I had no idea where we were. We slowed to a stop in front of an opening in a chain link fence illuminated by the car's dimmed headlights. Two police officers appeared at the side of the car, demanding identification. I produced my project name badge, and the car was waived forward. Two hundred yards farther in, a lone helicopter sat bathed in the red glow of night-vision lighting while being fueled by a nearby truck. Both were parked on what appeared to be a grassy meadow. I later learned we were in the Gates of Heaven Catholic Cemetery in the foothills west of San Jose. Arnie and Jim Josephson were both Catholics. Josephson had been raised in San Jose, after which he played fullback and linebacker for Oregon State and served in the army in Germany. He learned to fly on the G.I. bill, then formed San Joaquin Helicopter Service with a partner. Arnie and Josephson had somehow secured permission to use this site, and with the help of Caltrans, they created a temporary secret base for the helicopters. Arnie appeared out of the dark. He greeted me with a big grin and wrapped his arms around me in a bear hug. "We did it, Scrib!" he said.

The helicopter, a civilian version of the UH-1 "Huey" flown in Vietnam, had been fitted with 46-foot booms extending out each side, on which four to six nozzles were mounted. This allowed it to spray a 200-foot swath from about 300 feet up. It looked like a giant bug. I watched as the refueling was completed, and a trailer holding the Malathion bait mixture was moved forward to fill a huge white tank that took up the center of the helicopter behind the cockpit. I learned only one ship was operational. The second helicopter had been left behind with a mechanical problem that couldn't be resolved in time for the first night. I thought to myself, one is better than none.

While the helicopter was being readied, we all stood around with the two pilots, who joked about the threats of being shot down. One said, "If we see some muzzle flashes, then the lights are going off." No one laughed. Mike Stancil, a Vietnam vet who flew helicopters there for three years and was wounded when his chopper was downed, said he was not concerned. "I've flown these things back with 50 holes in them," he said. As I stood in the meadow, I knew a crash was the biggest risk

166

we faced. For now, my goal was to get through this first night without an incident.

Before lift-off, I left the base to observe the spraying at ground level. Demonstrators and reporters had assembled at a major intersection on the flight path of the first pass. A line of lights extended in a straight line into the distance. The lights were held aloft by giant kytoon balloons erected by Caltrans ground crews. When I arrived, one person had already been arrested for trying to slash the line holding the balloon and strobe light. He missed, cutting the arm of a Caltrans worker. Another protestor recognized me in the crowd and yelled: "You son-of-a-bitch. You should be ashamed of yourself." Another asked in a loud voice if I planned to napalm the area next. Soon, the wop, wop, wop of a helicopter could be heard, becoming louder and louder until it swept into view, drowning out further taunts. It passed directly overhead a few hundred feet above us. Some of those present covered themselves with plastic sheeting. Then it was gone.

I was surprised not to see or feel any visible spray or a light rain of droplets. Little, if any, spray landed on us. One person claimed to smell the malathion. A young woman announced she was going to be sick. The helicopter's twinkling lights receded in the distance until disappearing in the glare of the city lights. No one knew when or where the next pass would be. The show was over, disappointing both the opponents and the media. As the press and protestors melted away, the Caltrans team, their work completed, began packing up. It was early morning now, and it had been a long day. I headed for the motel, a little surprised at how minimal the spray had turned out to be. I had expected it to be more noticeable.

Governor Brown had told a crowd On Sunday, "I may just come here and be with you." He had added, "To the extent I can share in all of this, I will." To make good on his commitment to stay overnight in the spray zone, he accepted a telephone invitation from Jim and Delphine Winstead, a young family with a child of four living in a two-bedroom home in the City of Los Altos. He stayed with them on Monday night, sleeping in their bedroom while they slept in the other bedroom with their son. They also offered their driveway to the *NBC Today* show the morning after for a live interview with Brown. I was scheduled to appear at the Winstead's' home at 7 a.m. to brief the Governor on the first night's spraying.

Before settling down on Monday night, the Governor visited the CCC encampment at Agnews State Hospital and spoke to the Mountain View City Council. He reportedly told the Council members and attendees they were "the people that have to take the burden of this, while the rest of the state gets the benefit." I wished he had pointed out they were benefitting, too. Without eradication, they would soon have tired of seeing their fruit ruined every year by medflies or alternatively having to spray pesticides themselves every week all summer. The theme that spraying would benefit only big agriculture was part of the false and self-serving parochial mindset I had fought unsuccessfully since December.

Chapter 12 (Another Night in the Cemetery)

I awoke Tuesday morning feeling like a condemned man who had been given a new life. Judge Allen's decision had burst the bubble of hysteria, and a single helicopter pass had erased the apocalyptic vision of death and destruction imagined for months. Luck had been with us. As the sun rose, so did my hopes for this new day. It would take me another day to fully appreciate what a magnificent job Judge Allen had done with a difficult case. All eyes were on him. His demeanor and thoroughness before and after the hearing, like Assemblyman Thurman's intervention in early December, marked a critical turning point in the public perception of both the problem and the solution. A picture of Judge Allen on the bench hearing the case appeared on the front page of multiple newspapers. The *San Francisco Chronicle* and *San Francisco Examiner* each ran a different statement below the picture. The *Examiner* wrote, "Public Health, not emergency powers, is the issue, he says." In each, their coverage was peppered with pithy quotes from his decision. Television talking heads and other papers like the *Sacramento Bee* and the *San Diego Union* also reported the Judge's observations that "a lot of hysteria" has been built up, and "ground spraying is not going to control the Medfly…aerial spraying is the only thing that can do that."

His willingness to thoroughly consider the matter and to explain his decision simultaneously buried both the Governor's claim that ground spraying could have done the job and that aerial spraying would cause harm to the health of pregnant women and others. Judge Allen tried to put to rest the unsupported claims of health risks trumpeted in the media for months by stating that the documents he reviewed showed a person would have to swallow a large quantity of malathion "like a cup of coffee" to become ill and that more potent spraying for mosquitoes had caused no harm. In addition, he said anyone "can buy it in any grocery store" and "I've personally used it for years." His decision became the independent review the public needed and opponents had called for. Yet, nothing he said changed the minds of those who believed intuitively that any chemical sprayed from the air could never be safe or guaranteed not to cause harm to human health in ways not yet known.

I called Arnie and requested an update on how things had gone after I left the cemetery. I learned that he, Hans Van Nes, and the pilots had decided to scale back the first night to a trial run of the navigation system and other operational issues and to cut the spraying short. The helicopter had made only six passes covering one square mile instead of the planned 17 square miles in Zone 1. I found the news disappointing but did not fault their decision-making. When I reported, those of us below had experienced only a light mist when the helicopter reached us. Arnie said this could have been because the pumps and spray nozzles had repeatedly clogged due to the thick bait mixture. I could only imagine what it would have been like if the pumps had jammed open and those of us below had been pelted with sticky globs of bait. Or if the helicopter had never left the ground or been hit by gunfire or crashed due to a mechanical failure. The pilots reported hearing what could have been gunshots or firecrackers during the six spray runs, though no evidence surfaced that anyone had fired on them. Considering what could have happened and what didn't, I was grateful we had gotten into the air and started. I counted the first night as a success.

When I arrived at the Winstead's home to brief the Governor, I found TV crews in their driveway. I couldn't tell if they had already filmed the segment for that morning's *NBC Today* show or if they were waiting for the Governor to come out. Mr. Winstead met me outside and ushered me to the Governor's bedroom. I took a nearby chair as he got up and dressed while I reported what I knew. He was aware that the spraying had been limited and not reached the Winsteads. I promised him we would have two helicopters in the air on Tuesday night. The Governor seemed upbeat when I left 15 minutes later.

At the office, I learned the predicted mass flight of residents had been as limited and uneventful as the spraying. Although hundreds of people had called the Red Cross during the day inquiring about shelter locations, by evening, most had decided to stay home and ride it out. Only a few of the 4,500 beds available in Red Cross shelters had been used. The Santa Cruz location, capable of accommodating a thousand people, had sheltered 13. The one in Fremont closed when no one showed up. In Milpitas, with cots and blankets available for another thousand refugees, the staff of nurses and volunteers outnumbered the 37 people who arrived. A special bus parked outside to transport senior citizens sat empty all night while two nurses sipped coffee and volunteers with ham radios chatted with other shelters having a similar experience. The Red Cross chalked up the night to disaster preparedness since only 90 people came to the shelters. The low turnout may have been because there was no reason to leave unless you lived in Zone 1. The more affluent who chose to leave likely chose to go to a motel out of the area. The main reason people stayed home was probably the detailed information in the media all weekend downplaying the risk. For those in Zone 1, deciding to shelter in the comfort of a home with the windows closed appeared more sensible and less hassle than sleeping on a cot in a shelter.

An article a day or two later parodied the relative risk of the Malathion with the health risk of smoking and drinking. The piece described an imaginary group of worried residents coping with their fear of the first night of spraying by getting together indoors for what amounted to a doomsday party. As with New Year's Eve parties, this one started well before the scheduled midnight spraying. The attendees chatted and drank to pass the time. As the evening progressed, they became more and more intoxicated and periodically would venture outside to see if the helicopters were coming and escape the thick cigarette smoke inside. As midnight approached, no one cared anymore about the spraying.

Another larval find on Tuesday in a place well beyond both our spray zones and the quarantine boundary increased the total since June 26th to 142, an unimaginable number three weeks earlier. The new find required a significant expansion of spraying to the northeast toward the city of Oakland. The next day, more larvae would be found on the opposite side of the valley 15 miles north of the current spray boundary in San Mateo County. The infested area now stretched north, almost to the San Francisco International Airport. We expanded both the aerial spraying zones and quarantine boundaries accordingly. We also had to add more inspectors to check outgoing passengers at the San Francisco and Oakland airports.

Continuing to turn up larvae everywhere while still not catching any wild flies was maddening. Where were the flies? I still believed that a release of non-sterile flies from the Peru lab had to be the most likely explanation for the blow-up. However, finding larvae in locations far from the Mountain View Gap undermined that theory. The possibility we had failed to detect significant breeding occurring under our noses began to look more and more likely as the cause. It didn't matter. We were here now. Our biggest problem was still not having a regular airport from which to operate.

Later Tuesday morning, the 14th we learned Reagan Brown in Texas was still threatening to impose a blockade of California produce shipments beginning July 20th. He said he intended to again stop trucks heading east from California at the Texas border and turn them back if they carried any unfumigated medfly host fruit. Texas and its southern state allies adamantly refused requests from USDA and California to back down. We alerted our team of lawyers in the Attorney General's office. They prepared new motions for restraining orders to be filed in the district court in Dallas and the Supreme Court in Washington, D.C. The California Grape and Tree Fruit League and Avocado Commission said they planned to file in Dallas, too.

We had one more hurdle before we could spray again. Although Judge Allen allowed the spraying to begin, his approval was limited and tentative. It applied only to the first night. He made it clear that he still had not ruled out issuing a restraining order if he felt it necessary. He said he would not hesitate to stop the second night of Malathion flights "if one person gets ill." He had, therefore, scheduled a further hearing at 1:30 Tuesday to hear a report on the first night's spraying. We were ordered to produce a lab report at the hearing proving that the Malathion used was pure and had been properly stored before use. The opponents had argued that Malathion, if improperly stored, could become more toxic and threaten health because of its breakdown of products. Given the hysteria, even though few people had been sprayed, I believed at least some would appear at emergency rooms with symptoms they believed might be Malathion-related.

In San Jose, at 1:30, Judge Allen gaveled the follow-up hearing into being. He began by repeating that there would be no further aerial spraying if there were any evidence of adverse health effects. Dr. David Disher, the chair of the 24-member Medfly Health Advisory Committee, appointed by Governor Brown the previous Saturday, took the stand on our behalf. He testified the committee had checked emergency room admissions and surveyed the medical community for any reports of illness related to spraying. No one had gone to the emergency room claiming any Malathion-related health problems. Nor was there any indication from the medical community that anyone had suffered any ill health effects. Project witnesses testified further that they had performed a final purity test before they mixed the Malathion with the bait and loaded it into the helicopter's tanks. These widely reported findings helped further calm the waters about aerial spraying. There was no renewed request for a restraining order. We were a go for Tuesday night's spraying.

While our lawyers were in court, I worked on securing a permanent airport, either Moffett or the San Jose County airport, and on finding more helicopters. Our best hope for more helicopters was Evergreen Helicopter Services, based in McMinnville, Oregon, the largest such company in the United States. I did not know that the USDA had approached them as part of its contingency planning. However, I learned their contract talks had stalled when Evergreen demanded USDA agree to indemnify them for liability. USDA refused, claiming they lacked legal authority to do so. When I learned all this from Arnie Morrison, I told him that I agreed with Evergreen. If I were their lawyer, I would be taking the same position, especially with people threatening to shoot down the helicopters. My solution was to have them contract with us instead of USDA. I telephoned the Director of California's General Services Department and requested that they have their top contract lawyer contact Evergreen and see what we could do. Amanda Behe, a skilled General Services lawyer, called me back within hours to report she and Evergreen's lawyer had agreed to meet the next day. I requested that they do so in my office in Los Gatos.

As the clock ticked toward midnight, all efforts to open an airport to our use failed. Neither the County nor the Feds would budge. Amazingly, the location of the temporary base stayed a secret. Finding it remained a high priority for the press and opponents. To keep it secret, Caltrans, before dawn Tuesday morning, had erased all evidence of our presence at the Gates of Heaven. People going to the cemetery to put flowers on graves or for funerals had no idea this was where the base was. Neither did reporters. Their guesses as to the location spanned sites in three counties.

Although the last six days had been hellish, each day had been better than the one before. A dedicated core staff continued to work tirelessly and cooperatively with the new state arrivals and with the experienced eradication professionals on the project. All were fitting in and doing good work throughout the project. In the heat of battle, we had become a smoothly functioning team despite the helicopter shortage and the lack of an airport. Rich Rominger had quietly recognized before I did that I was being overwhelmed trying to manage a vast 24-hour-a-day operation. Late on Friday the 10th, he had called Hans Van Nes, another department deputy director, and told him to report to Los Gatos as soon as possible. Hans packed a bag and arrived Saturday morning. He wordlessly integrated himself into the program. By Monday night, he had become the de facto manager of the night-time aerial spraying while I ran the day shift. Van Nes and Morrison joined me at the end of each day at the 5 p.m. management meeting.

Secretary Block at USDA deserves much of the credit for resolving the impasse between the need to spray and Governor Brown's initial resistance. Especially helpful was the fact that Block and Rich Rominger knew and trusted each other. Block, before becoming USDA's secretary, had been the state's ag director in Illinois. He and Rominger stayed in close touch. Block downplayed our early start-up problems, emphasizing that he was pleased we had started on time. He also expressed confidence the problems would soon be ironed out, as they were. Block helpfully sent USDA's chief pilot to the project along with other critical USDA personnel. In addition, he provided a steadying influence in Washington, D.C., as did Dr. Harry Mussman, the career professional administrator of USDA's Animal and Plant Health Inspection Service. As soon as Brown ordered aerial spraying, Block resisted pressure to quarantine all of California, hinting instead that a county-based quarantine appeared sufficient and more appropriate. Immediately after Monday night's start, he formally announced that the federal quarantine would be limited to the same three infested counties of Santa Clara, Alameda, and San Mateo, established by California. By using county lines, the infested area was easy for foreign countries and other U.S. states to understand and see on a map. Fruits and vegetables grown hundreds of miles away in other counties in California, such as Fresno in the Central Valley, remained outside of the area under quarantine.

After dark Tuesday night, we re-assembled the base in time for the two helicopters to fly from their National Guard base in Hayward, south of Oakland, across the Bay to the cemetery. Again, only one helicopter arrived. The other remained grounded with unresolved mechanical problems. We then lost another hour getting going because one of the ground light crews got lost trying to get into the proper position with the guidance lights. The rest of the night went better than the first, with spraying continuing until daylight. However, with only one helicopter, the results were underwhelming. Now, two days behind schedule, we had managed to cover only a third of Zone 1.

The news coverage Wednesday morning painted an embarrassing picture of our ineptitude, ranging from having only one serviceable helicopter and no airport to the Keystone cop description of the hapless guidance crew unable to find their way. The rocky start also destroyed the usefulness of the notices we had distributed, alerting residents to when their areas would be sprayed. The public had taken the first night's failures in stride, if not relief. To a lesser extent, they forgave the second night's problems, given we had been refused access to both local airports. They could also see we had our hands full maintaining the roadblocks, stripping fruit, going door to door with ground spraying rigs, and continuing to rear and release millions of sterile flies. Our problems, however, did not lessen their frustration with the slow pace of aerial spraying. By the end of week one, we would overcome the aerial program's shortcomings and successfully spray all the zones. But for now, we continued to stumble as both the Governor and I separately made dumb announcements that each generated additional criticism and public doubt about the management of the eradication effort.

On Wednesday morning, July 15th, to the dismay of everyone except his Republican opponents, Governor Brown issued a press release and letter asking the federal government to declare the medfly area a disaster. The letter addressed to President Reagan stated, "the infestation constitutes a disaster which is now beyond the control of the services, personnel, equipment, and facilities of the counties of Alameda, Santa Clara, and San Mateo." No one on the Governor's staff, including, apparently, the Governor himself, recognized the unintended consequences of declaring the situation a disaster. It played in the media as a shocking admission by Brown that the medfly was out of control and beyond the capabilities of the project to manage. A disaster requiring federal intervention and a USDA takeover was exactly what Republican operatives and their farmer allies had been calling for. If the project was a disaster, it was one Brown himself had helped to create.

The announcement grew out of a well-meaning attempt to help local farmers qualify for low-cost federal loans available in a declared disaster area. Whatever the intent of the request, the optics, as they say in politics, were terrible. They reminded everyone of Brown's obstruction, then flip-flop, and now two nights of feeble aerial spraying. It reinforced Brown's reputation for shamelessly tacking with the political winds. To those who believed his refusal had been driven by trying to please his liberal base, this looked like an effort to balance that with a handout to farmers hurt by the quarantine. A less cynical explanation would be that the misstep arose from the usual source, the bureaucratic anthill of governmental decision-making. The farmers in the quarantine area had clearly suffered losses. To trigger federal disaster assistance such as low-cost loans, a routine federal form generated in the state office of emergency services requesting the disaster designation may well have been sent up the ladder for approval. Why no one recognized the glaring negative political implications of doing this remains a mystery. Certainly, none of us on the project had anything to do with it. We all believed that with aerial spraying now underway, it would only be a matter of time before we eradicated the flies as they had in Florida in 1956 when half the state was overrun before aerial bait sprays eliminated the infestation.

Brown's disaster request led to another round of public criticism by pundits and Reagan officials. The next day, Richard Lyng, the undersecretary at USDA, visited Los Gatos. Lyng had been the Department of Food and Agriculture director in California when Reagan was Governor. Now, he was the number two in the nation. He blasted Brown for claiming the infestation was "now beyond the control of the state." Lyng said, "I wish he had worked more closely with his people at the (state) Department of Agriculture," and then he added, "I think everything may be served better for a few days if the governor wouldn't make so many statements." Lyng's remarks were widely quoted.

Like the Governor, I also made an announcement that set off a firestorm of criticism. I said that once the helicopters passed overhead, coating everything below with Malathion bait, people no longer needed to strip their trees and tear up their gardens. I thought the public would recognize that stripping fruit after we had sprayed it was no longer useful, and it would require people to come in direct contact with the Malathion bait spray. My announcement set off an explosion of local anger and recrimination, particularly from those who had already stripped. They had been forced to sacrifice their vegetables and a summer's crop of fruit, and now, their neighbors who hadn't lifted a finger were being given a pass. It wasn't fair. That the Governor's order to strip nearly 700 square miles had been unachievable and of marginal benefit mattered little to the tens of thousands of loyal residents who had worked feverishly to strip their fruit. They believed doing so might avoid the aerial spraying, and, in any event, it they believed it was a critical element of the eradication fight since we had promoted it back in January and February. They had answered the call and worked their hearts out then and again in July.

One newspaper described the experience of a resident with a large yard who worked full-time and took care of his elderly parents. His yard, part of a former orchard, now had other trees as well. Stripping his orange tree took three hours. The fig tree next to it was over 60 feet tall. In some cases, branches had to be sawed off, and the fruit picked from the branches once they were on the ground. He had called around for help but found none. After working to exhaustion both Saturday and Sunday, he had not been able to get to some trees, and those he had stripped still had fruit here and there that he had missed or been unable to reach. Out of time, he had to be back at work Monday morning. Another resident spoke for him and most when he said: "I don't feel as a taxpayer I got a fair shake. People who stripped are…in shock while people who didn't are sitting back saying, 'I told you so.'" Reading these stories was heartbreaking. I understood the frustration and anger. But making people roll up their sleeves and handle fruit dripping with Malathion for no purpose other than to equalize the suffering seemed as senseless as sending out the police to levy fines or make arrests of non-strippers.

The Governor said nothing publicly about my announcement, though he clearly disagreed with it. So did some of my own employees. The headline in the local paper was, "Switch raises; new furor, confuses Medfly warriors." The article accurately reported what I had said—"No stripping required after a property had been aerially sprayed." However, the rest of the article made it sound like I had ordered the prisons emptied of dangerous offenders. I was stunned by the venom directed at me and the non-strippers. Earlier, people had so feared Malathion that some were washing the ground spray off sidewalks and grass immediately after our truck crews had applied it to their yards. Now, they wanted us to arrest their neighbors if they did not go out and immerse themselves in handling fruits and vegetables covered with Malathion. By the next day, the unfairness of some getting away with not having stripped their fruit had eclipsed any concern about the safety of Malathion. I regretted not having discussed the announcement more thoroughly with staff ahead of time, but not the decision itself.

As the controversy raged, my primary attention continued to be on our immediate need for an airport and more helicopters. Governor Brown helpfully issued Emergency Order #3 authorizing us to use any airport in the area. His order, backed by threats from the Attorney

General to sue the city of San Jose, led to an agreement on Wednesday under which we would henceforth have full use of the San Jose airport in return for state reimbursement of their extra security costs and possible liability. Also, on Wednesday, Amanda Behe, our Department of General Services lawyer, and Evergreen's lawyer were in my office putting the finishing touches on a contract committing Evergreen to fly in at least three more helicopters that would begin spraying by Friday. Three more, for a total of six, would be delivered with crews in time to participate in the second application of bait. California agreed to indemnify Evergreen for all claims connected with the spraying. Behe helpfully rewrote the contract with San Joaquin to match the one with Evergreen. Later, at the afternoon press conference, I reported we would begin flying out of the San Jose airport that night and that additional helicopters would arrive Friday and next week.

Wednesday night turned out to be our best night so far, as we finally had two San Joaquin helicopters in service. The next morning, Reagan's Defense Secretary, Casper Weinberger, changed his mind and allowed us to use Moffett Naval Air Station. We quickly shifted San Joaquin's operations to Moffett beginning on Thursday night. Evergreen agreed to use the Hayward National Guard Base for their rest and refitting and the San Jose airport for their nightly operations.

The next day, a story appeared in the press claiming Evergreen had been a contractor for the CIA during the Vietnam War, implying an unsavory connection between the project's aerial spraying and the CIA's involvement in Vietnam. A little research established that Evergreen had bought the assets of a company that had once worked for the CIA but had no contracts with the CIA then or now. I reported these facts and said I considered the controversy irrelevant, adding that Evergreen was fine with me "as long as they get the bait on." The controversy quickly died.

A straw poll of readers in Thursday morning's edition of the *San Francisco Chronicle* had more good news. The poll found that 73% of those responding said they now favored aerial spraying. In the same article, opponents conceded the medfly posed a grave threat to the state and was spreading faster than any ground program could possibly have kept up with. The executive director of the Coordinating Committee on Pesticides, an organization of 62 environmental, labor, and health groups that had opposed the spraying, said, "Everyone is sort of ducking these days. We don't want to be responsible for potential massive damage to agriculture." Another group, Citizens for a Better Environment, one of the named plaintiffs in the litigation to block aerial spraying, claimed their group neither supported nor opposed the spraying of Malathion. I found their statement disingenuous and irritating since they had vigorously fought the aerial spraying beginning in December. The spokesperson for Friends of the Earth candidly admitted the truth. "We are between a rock and a hard place," he said. "We want to eradicate the Medfly too (but) we wanted to keep it on the ground."

Governor Brown's ground program with three hundred spray rigs, together with the CCC's involvement in the fruit stripping, continued in full swing along with the highway inspections. I had been the architect of the ground strategy in January and had defended the Governor's second program at his initial press conference. Now that aerial spraying had started, it was largely unneeded, but we could not afford to publicly appear to be relaxing our effort in any major way. We did need to continue the ground spraying around larval finds and focused on that. However, the stripping had taken on a life of its own, and I could not publicly disavow it as unneeded since Brown had ordered it. We, therefore, struggled forward, continuing what he had ordered.

After we started aerial spraying, continuing to release sterile flies, like stripping fruit, was no longer needed or helpful. When I announced at the morning press conference on Thursday that we would no longer be releasing sterile flies, it made sense to the public. We explained that another benefit of doing so would be making it easier to detect the wild ones. Gary Agosta, the manager of the detection program, explained, "…our vision is so clouded by the sterile flies, we can't be sure where any new wild flies are still present." By ending the release of sterile flies, "we'll know exactly what we're dealing with," Agosta said. The change also allowed us to shift people who had been rearing and releasing sterile flies to other programs, such as putting out more traps.

Friday morning, July 17th, Governor Brown appeared on the *ABC Good Morning America* show. He told a national television audience the spraying was going well. He reported that about half the area had been sprayed and that completion of the first application was expected any day. I told the press and public that morning that we would complete the first round of spraying "either Saturday at 6 a.m., or if not, then Sunday at 6 a.m., and if still not done, then by 6 a.m. Monday." Over the weekend, we succeeded in spraying the rest of the infested area except for one small final piece in the hilly area of Los Altos hills that was too dangerous to spray safely at night. We scheduled this area for daylight spraying on Monday morning. On Sunday, we notified residents door-to-door that the spraying would start at 6 a.m. and end at 11. Finishing this last piece on Monday morning would enable us to announce to other states and countries that we had started aerial spraying on the date initially recommended by the advisory committee and had finished the first application of bait spray on the entire known infested area within seven days. I believed that being able to say this was critical and that it would also forestall the Texas quarantine threat.

As luck would have it, at daybreak on Monday, the hills were socked in by fog, delaying the start. A few minutes before 11, an urgent call came in from Arnie. "We are running behind schedule," he said. "I need another hour. What should I do?" Without hesitation, I said, "Finish the job." They finished at 12:30. By then, outraged residents were flooding our phone bank and the city phone bank. The calls that started at 11:01 were still coming in at noon when Rich Hammond stormed into my office and demanded to know, "Who's responsible for the continued spraying in Los Altos Hills"? Without hesitation, I said, "You're talking to him." Stunned, he turned on his heel and left. I did not see him again for a week. I expected a call from the Governor's office, but one never came.

The angry calls and letters continued for the next week. I personally returned those from community leaders, including one from the mayor of Los Altos Hills. In each case, I admitted that I was the one who personally made the decision to continue the spraying. I was contrite and quoted in the press agreeing "that people were angry and that this didn't help our credibility" and "It is not the way to do it." I also wrote letters of apology for not living up to our commitment to spray in accordance with the notice. In both my calls and letters, I promised in the future, we would continue to give as much pre-notice as we could. In addition, I agreed that we would provide hourly reports to local police departments during daylight spraying so that residents could call 911 and find out for sure when spraying had been completed and when it was all clear. My apologies were sincere. But I believed then and now that, under the circumstances, I made the right decision. We were fighting the biological equivalent of a raging fire. No one was harmed, and the potential consequences of further delay in rescheduling and re-notice at a later date would have been substantial.

A study done a week later showed that the first week of spraying killed close to 100% of the medflies present in the areas sprayed. Trap catches dropped to near zero. The few flies we caught were almost all sterile survivors. Our first week of start-up problems had been ugly and painful, but the tide had been turned. As we got ready to start week two, foreign countries and other states could see we were on the right track.

Chapter 13 (The Man Who Drank the Malathion)

The first question people ask me when they hear I directed the medfly program is, "Are you the guy who drank the Malathion?" I tell them it was not me but B.T. Collins, the head of the California Conservation Corps. His widely publicized demonstration occurred in the chaotic first week of trying to carry out both the Governor's new ground program and initiate aerial spraying at the same time. A scheduling mix-up sent a group of CCC young people into a yard to strip fruit off trees only hours after a ground spraying crew had soaked the trees with Malathion bait. Five of the CCC members were briefly hospitalized after falling ill with nausea and stomach cramps, symptoms consistent with Malathion poisoning. Soon, word of the incident, no doubt embellished with phrases like "they almost died" or "they could have died," had raced through the tent city encampment of over a thousand Corps members. The following night, Collins ordered his troops to assemble in front of a makeshift stage in the main dining hall. The press, alerted to the incident and the meeting, appeared in force. During the day, Collins had called me and proposed our doctors mix up a cocktail containing Malathion in the exact concentration we were spraying as he planned to drink it to show his members it was safe. I referred him to Dr. Peter Kurtz, our on-site toxicologist. Kurtz told him not to do it.

That night, a standing-room-only crowd of young, uniformed Corps members and National Guard troops assembled as ordered. The presence of television trucks and a bank of TV, radio, and press reporters confirmed something big was coming down. Rumors flew that the ground spraying program might be canceled because of the danger. The makeshift stage was bare except for a large sign ominously labeled "MALATHION" placed next to a single glass of water on a table. In full uniform, BT Collins mounted the stage like George C. Scott in the movie *Patton.* He strode confidently to center stage and stood next to the table. A hush settled over the crowd. He told those assembled it was true that there had been a mix-up, but he said the stories of Corps members nearly dying were grossly exaggerated. He said those involved were now fine. He told the audience the glass of water on the table contained Malathion in the same concentration as that being sprayed on the ground and in the air. To prove it was safe and barely enough to kill a fly, he was now going to drink it. As the TV lights snapped on, and a thousand necks craned forward, Collins dramatically raised the glass to his lips, hesitated briefly, like a magician in Las Vegas, then slowly drained the glass. As he set it back down on the table, the audience burst into applause.

As word spread of his don't-do-this-at-home stunt, it helped dispel the hysteria about Malathion. In a newspaper interview, Collins was pictured feigning severe distress above a story in which he admitted he had felt a little queasy. "It tasted horrible, like kerosene," he said. "No wonder the medflies hate it." He then said, "I drank it because you don't ask your troops to do anything you wouldn't do." I wholeheartedly supported his style of leading from the front.

Neither the incident nor Collins' demonstration had any impact on the drubbing I was getting for not making homeowners strip Malathion-covered trees after our helicopters had sprayed them. Angry calls continued to pour into our hotlines, to city halls, and to talk radio. All demanded answers for why I was not fully enforcing the fruit stripping mandate everywhere, whether already sprayed or not. Assemblyman Byron Sher, a Democrat in Palo Alto, said, "Residents have been needlessly terrified over this, and it's time to get some answers." No answer from me short of recommending the arrest and prosecution of those who had not stripped would satisfy those who had. The Campbell City Council called a special meeting to rescind the stripping ordinance they had adopted the previous Saturday. They also called for the immediate dismissal of those responsible for ordering the stripping. That the stripping had been ordered by Governor Brown, at the request of environmentalists opposed to aerial spraying, seemed to have escaped their notice.

Once aerial spraying got underway, enforcing the stripping became the number one concern of most residents. The *Mercury* published an editorial on July 15th, demanding that the stripping be strictly enforced. They suggested that if local law enforcement wouldn't act, then maybe the National Guard should. If not the Guard, the editorial board wrote, "we don't see why California Highway patrolmen from other parts of the state couldn't be pulled into this area to help enforce the fruit-stripping order."

We tried to ignore the insistence on punitive actions for failing to do something that, in most cases, did not help eradicate the flies. Instead, we focused enforcement on stripping where it still mattered. This was within a three-block radius of properties where larvae had been found. In another editorial on July 16th, the *Mercury* demanded again that all those who had failed to strip be prosecuted. The editors said they didn't care who needed to be mobilized to "comb neighborhoods and report violators." The demand for enforcement came to a head at a meeting on Monday afternoon, July 20th. I was among those present, along with the Governor and local officials, including Joseph McNamara, the San Jose Chief of Police. McNamara, a nationally recognized progressive law enforcement leader, had now become a primary target of local ire because he flatly refused to make enforcement of the stripping mandate a local police priority. County law enforcement leaders took the same position. Local politicians aired their frustration at the lack of enforcement. McNamara stuck to his position that enforcing the stripping requirement did not warrant sacrificing other, more important law enforcement obligations. I agreed but could not publicly side with Chief McNamara without putting Governor Brown on the spot since it was his order. I explained that we were enforcing the stripping requirement in the three block areas where larvae had been found but not otherwise. The Governor limited himself to sympathizing with the frustration but chose not to become any more entangled in the controversy than he already was. Nothing was resolved.

Back at the office, I learned that Reagan Brown, the flamboyant Texas Ag Commissioner, had made good his threat to impose a blockade. Once again Texas said it planned to stop California trucks carrying produce at El Paso on the Texas border with New Mexico beginning on Tuesday. Florida and South Carolina announced they, too, would bar trucks carrying produce grown anywhere in California from entering or crossing their states. Now that aerial spraying had been implemented, the southern states offered a new rationale for the need for their quarantines. Now, they claimed the problem was that California did not have enough insect traps deployed statewide to ensure there were no medflies elsewhere in the state outside the three quarantined counties. Thus, unless the load had been fumigated or the driver carried papers showing it came from a county deploying not less than five traps per square mile, the truck could not pass. Some counties had thousands of square miles of forested mountains or barren deserts. In addition, the shipments were from farming districts hundreds of miles from the area currently infested.

We had already filed requests for a restraining order and permanent injunction in anticipation of the blockade, and federal Judge Patrick Higginbotham in Dallas, the same judge who had heard the case in March, granted California's request Monday night. Texas accepted the court's ruling. However, Commissioner Reagan Brown said his road inspection crews would continue stopping and inspecting trucks, allowing through only those that had not originated in one of the quarantined counties. In a parting shot, he told his Texas political base, "This crisis is not over.... Our growers and citizens are very concerned that this most insidious insect may spread." California's lawyers in the Attorney General's office convinced all the other states except Florida to back off. Their Governor, Bob Graham, claimed, "Despite recommendations of technical experts, nothing has (been) done." He knew better, of course, since his expert, Charlie Poucher, served on the advisory committee and was fully aware the known infested area had been sprayed, and we were moving into the second week. In Florida, U.S. District Court Judge Lynn C. Higby dissolved their embargo after Deputy Attorney General Greg Wilkerson pointed out that "Only one percent of California's produce comes from the three infested counties," and the federal government's quarantine authority pre-empted Florida's action.

In August, when wild flies were found over the hills from San Jose in the Central Valley, Texas, went back to Judge Higgenbotham and tried to get the restraining order lifted. At the hearing, Commissioner Brown showed his true colors while being cross-examined by California Deputy Attorney General Rod Walston. When Walston noted he had failed to answer a question, Commissioner Brown retorted, "You'll have to speak up, son; I don't hear Yankees too well." Walston, in an article about the litigation, wrote that the judge "chuckled but refused to vacate the TRO."

On Tuesday morning, the 21st, at the executive staff breakfast, I felt for the first time in a week that we had our feet under us. We had two airports and plenty of helicopters, Texas had been restrained, and USDA was pleased with our progress. Best of all, we completed the first round of spraying on time, something that had looked like an impossibility a week ago. Later, at the morning press conference, the press wanted better answers than I could give for the late spraying the day before and the public anger over my decision to let those who had not stripped go unpunished. I had expected it to be painful, and it was, but I had come to genuinely like and admire each of the reporters for their excellent work starting with the day I arrived in January. Their questions were fair, my answers were as honest as I could make them, and we had an unspoken commitment to the truth. Their presence helped remind me that I worked for the public, and their body language, questions, and stories told me where we were succeeding and where we were failing.

I started as usual with a cheerful "Good morning" as a staff person distributed the *Daily Medfly*. I then made a series of announcements before taking questions. First, I noted we had completed the first round of aerial spraying in one week. I then apologized for Monday morning's late finish, promising it wouldn't happen again. I emphasized that in the future, we would be notifying the local police and city offices when we started and stopped so the public would have a place to call to confirm the all-clear when we were done.

After a brief mention of the judge's favorable ruling in Dallas, which had been on the wire late Monday, I moved on to the discovery of more larvae. I ended by announcing that week two of spraying would begin at midnight on Wednesday and cover 227 square miles, an increase of 66 square miles from the first week's total. As expected, the reporters' questions focused on fruit stripping, and Chief McNamara's description of the meeting as confusing. One reporter said, "The governor was saying one thing, and you [meaning me] another." I agreed it was confusing, then praised the stripping that had been done and reiterated that fruit needed to be stripped within a three-block radius of larval finds. With respect to enforcement, I made it clear that our enforcement priority would be on those few individuals who harbored larvae in their own yards but were adamantly refusing to strip and refusing to let us do it. I knew this restatement of our position didn't fully answer the question, but given the Governor's continued support for stripping everywhere, it was the best I could do. The next question related to why we failed to finish the hill area by 11 a.m., as promised. Here, I took full responsibility for the decision, apologized, and said it wouldn't happen again.

While I was meeting with reporters in Los Gatos, the Grape and Tree Fruit League was holding a press conference in Los Angeles at which they portrayed the successful court action in Texas as solely a Republican triumph by growers and California's Republican Attorney General, George Deukmejian. In their telling, their lawyers had stepped in and saved California from the hapless and misguided environmentalism of Jerry Brown, who had blocked aerial spraying from the day the first medflies were discovered in June 1980. Neither assertion was true. Aerial spraying, as used in Florida and Texas, was never seriously considered in June 1980. The decision not to aerial spray was made by the eradication professionals at USDA, CDFA, and the respective local county agricultural commissioners. It had been fourteen years since aerial spraying had been used in Texas, and in the meantime, the new approach—SIT had been proven to be effective and uncontroversial. It worked successfully in L.A. in 1975-76 and again in 1980, successfully wiping out the medflies both times.

The Tree Fruit League ignored the fact that California's civil service lawyers in Deukmejian's office were officially representing Brown as Governor at his request and had done most of the work on the recent case as well as the U.S. Supreme Court case, which settled the issue of federal supremacy in setting quarantines, back in March. Thus, this new decision that the Texas quarantine was illegal reconfirmed what everyone already knew and had nothing whatsoever to do with Governor Brown or his decision to spray or not to spray.

Their taking credit for this favorable and entirely predictable outcome was especially galling given that our staff on the project had provided the factual background and USDA and the state's attorneys the legal arguments supporting the growers' case. The truth was accurately reported by two northern California reporters, Rick Carroll, and Paul Liberatore, in the *San Francisco Chronicle*. They noted that the Judge's ruling came after he "met with lawyers from California, Texas, and the U.S. Department of Agriculture".

To their credit, the reporters in L.A. skeptically questioned the creativity of the new narrative, especially the notion that farmers and Republicans led by Deukmejian had singlehandedly saved the day. The *Los Angeles Times* article observed that Bruce Obbink, the head of the Grape and Tree Fruit League, candidly admitted the real purpose of their press conference was to "remind the public" that "this Medfly disaster would never have happened if Brown had listened to us [growers] in the first place."

Tuesday afternoon, Governor Brown called his own press conference in Los Gatos to blast the claim he had created the medfly problem. He said, "Nobody recommended I approve aerial spraying before the technical committee met two weeks ago. This situation is laced with politics. It's simple. The Republicans want control of the U.S. Senate." He pointed out that the aerial spraying began on July 13th, "in the time we specified," adding, "I am proud of it." I was not proud of our chaotic first week of aerial spraying, but it was true that we did start on the date initially planned, as he said, despite his initial rejection of the committee's recommendation.

Everyone also knew that Republican senator S.I. Hayakawa's term would end in December 1982, and at the same time, so would Brown's second term as Governor. Polls showed Hayakawa was unpopular and vulnerable. Brown had run for President in the Democratic primary in 1980 and obviously had his eye on a Senate run for Hayakawa's seat.

Following the press conference in Los Angeles, the medfly-themed Republican attacks on Governor Brown continued and expanded. Next, seven Republican State legislators called for me to be fired, and the Tehama County Board of Supervisors wanted Jerry Brown to be removed from office. Assemblymember Carol Hallett, who represented Monterey County and served as the Republican minority leader of the Assembly, led the main attack. She and her farm constituents, in league with senior USDA officials in Washington, D.C., described the medfly as now out of control and claimed it was only a matter of time before the fly spread across California and beyond. She proposed expanding the spraying out 25 miles beyond the current quarantine boundaries to provide a buffer and switching to USDA's preference for fixed-winged planes instead of helicopters. Thankfully, Secretary Block continued to dampen the political hype, saying that the aerial spraying underway would succeed in eradicating the medfly. In an appearance the previous Sunday morning on *Face the Nation*, Block said he was "convinced right now that we're on schedule with the aerial spraying. We really are getting hold of the situation."

The controversy surrounding Governor Brown's refusal to order aerial spraying until forced to by USDA and the litigation overturning the southern states' blockades turned the medfly into a national political story. However, on the project, things quieted down. The federal and state employees, including the environmentalists from the Resources Agency, had coalesced into a team confident we would succeed. Claudia Luther of the *Los Angeles Times* wrote, "The chaos of Day 1 had given way to simple busyness." The *Sacramento Bee* reported, "Now that the first round of aerial spraying had been completed, the mood has really shifted. The general feeling on the project and off is that eradication is inevitable."

In the third week of July, we expanded the number of traps and tightened quarantine enforcement. The aerial team realigned what had been spray zones into long, numbered corridors. This allowed the helicopters to fly four to six abreast and cover the total area faster. We also changed the guidance system from a row of lights on the ground to a system based on electronic mapping guidance in each cockpit, and we formalized the agreement for daylight spraying in Corridor 8 in the foothills. None of these changes, however, solved the persistent problem of helicopters spraying beyond the end line of an assigned corridor. A particularly egregious example occurred during Monday's daylight spraying in the foothills. A helicopter allegedly sprayed Malathion bait on part of Stanford University's Jasper Ridge Biological Preserve, an area we had promised to be especially careful to avoid. Pesticides applied there could destroy or disrupt years of important insect research. Our flight plan had called for the helicopters to fly parallel to the western end of the preserve. When fog made spraying parallel too dangerous, the pilot instead chose to approach the end line head-on. As a result, on one run, the spray fell short, while on another, it continued for as much as 600 feet into the preserve. White cardboard markers placed to measure the amount of bait reaching the ground suggested the overspray was minimal if it indeed did occur. Thus, possible damage was limited to a tiny area of the preserve. Nevertheless, the overspray generated a headline suggesting that years of research might have been compromised. We promised it wouldn't happen again, and I don't believe it did.

Residents continued to complain of similar overspray along the edges and at the end of other less critical spray zones. At the Tuesday afternoon press conference on July 21st, I publicly criticized Evergreen Helicopters, saying that we needed them to do a better job not only with the boundaries but also with a string of faulty pump and nozzle problems. I said, "Their last night of operations will be Wednesday unless they follow our orders and [refit]…their choppers with spray nozzles that are consistent with our requirements." They made the changes requested. I also summoned San Joaquin's owner, Jim Josephson, to my office and told him they, too, had to do a better job of cutting off the spraying so that no bait landed outside the officially declared zone. I suggested the solution might be for the pilots to cut the spray a little earlier so that none landed where it wasn't supposed to. After a little back and forth, Josephson suggested I go up with him in his personal helicopter, which was parked on the school playground only a hundred yards away. He told me this would help us better assess how to solve the problem. We walked out of my office, and I climbed into the passenger seat of his bubble-front open-cockpit three-seater parked next to the larger CHP helicopter. We lifted off and, within minutes, were whirling over the low foothills of corridor 8. Josephson abruptly rolled right and down like a navy dive bomber. As the ground rushed up, my seatbelt was the only thing preventing me from plummeting out of the open cockpit. I tightened it a notch as Josephson rolled left in another dive before leveling off and pulling up in a steep climb, barely clearing the power lines at the end of our hypothetical spray corridor. After several more such passes, I conceded the pin-point perfection the public and I were demanding might not be achievable. Josephson promised he and the pilots would try harder, and I agreed to back off. Later in the program, when an emergency arose requiring my presence, I asked a CHP pilot at the office if he could take me up in Josephson's three-seater with Josephson's telephoned permission since the CHP copter was unavailable. The pilot rolled his eyes and said: "There's no way I would get near that bucket of bolts!"

On Wednesday night, three helicopters completed their 22-square mile corridor in three hours. That would be the story every night as the week was completed on schedule. The spraying had now become routine. The political war continued. The headline in the *San Francisco Chronicle* Thursday morning screeched, "U.S. Won't Give State Medfly Disaster Aid Brown Smells Politics." A similar front page headline and story ran in the *Los Angeles Times*. The Federal Emergency Management Agency (FEMA) based its denial of a disaster designation on the federal government's observation that "the situation has stabilized with the eradication measures underway." They said, "There is no sign the infestation is spreading out of control." They further explained that "The act does not permit assistance for the purpose of budgetary relief."

It would have been better to leave the matter there. However, Brown chose to argue that FEMA had granted a similar request in 1973 when frost killed eucalyptus trees in the Berkeley hills, creating a fire hazard. He said his request was nothing more than that. While technically accurate, the back and forth only kept the words "medfly" and "disaster" linked in the news cycle and furthered the claim that if there was a disaster, it was of Brown's own making. Not surprisingly, the federal government weighed in, saying that the situation "should have been solved a long time ago on a state level."

On Thursday, I spoke to the Rotary Club in Sacramento, an engagement I had originally accepted back in June when people wanted to hear how we had won the war on the ground. The Rotarians knew all that had changed. Accordingly, I focused my talk on the current success of the second week of spraying and my optimism that we were now succeeding in the air.

Governor Brown re-ignited the fruit stripping controversy by recording a special radio announcement regarding stripping's vital importance. The spot ran regularly on major radio stations in the Bay area. I had no choice but to again try to bridge the gap between my position and the Governor's. Therefore, that weekend, we announced we were creating a new stripping enforcement unit. The unit would vigorously enforce the fruit stripping requirement on properties within three blocks of a larval find. We said that residents in these three block areas would be given a 48-hour printed warning. That would be followed by a citation that carried a maximum penalty of $500 or six months in jail. In addition, the notice warned that if they did not comply, we would strip the property ourselves and bill them for the cost. We were as light-handed as possible in enforcing these orders, limiting our inspections to drive-by observations and issuing citations only to flagrant violators. In the first week of the new program, we issued over 40 notices. That resulted in close to 100% compliance. We further limited what had to be stripped to prime hosts. This still left a long list of fruits and vegetables in many of the yards, all of which were suitable egg sites for fertile medflies. Examples of fruits still on the list included all varieties of citrus, plus apple, apricot, avocado, bell pepper, cherry, fig, grape, guava, kiwi, kumquat, loquat, mango, nectarine, papaya, peach, pear, persimmon, plum, pomegranate, prickly pear, prune, quince, and tomatoes. We continued to be bitterly criticized for not arresting all non-strippers, regardless of whether they were anywhere near a larval find. Thankfully, three weeks later, in early August, the advisory committee formally recommended an end to all fruit stripping other than around larval finds.

Our quarantine enforcement efforts at the airports and the roadblocks on major highways sent a strong signal to both locals and to other states and countries that California was doing all that was humanly possible to keep the medfly confined to the currently infested counties. Yet, unbelievably, people continued to carry fruit out and, when caught, claimed not to have heard of either the medfly or the quarantine. It was embarrassingly obvious that the well-publicized roadblocks had fallen far short of what was required to keep the medfly corralled in the quarantine area. B.J. Lewis, a veteran USDA inspector, described to a reporter the frustration he and other inspectors experienced when, despite the innumerable warnings and the issuance of citations requiring a court appearance, the "constant flow of confiscations" from motorists continued day after day. Lewis described one example that particularly exasperated him. A woman had dutifully stripped her fruit trees, then, in direct violation of the non-removal orders, loaded them in her car and headed for her summer home in Santa Cruz, a neighboring county not yet infested. When she was stopped, "She just seemed not to understand," Lewis said.

To toughen up our enforcement, Frank Stegmiller, who headed up the project's quarantine section, warned the public in a front-page story in the San Jose News on July 22nd that inspectors would no longer ask, "Do you have any fruit?" and if the answer was "No" then allow the motorist to proceed. The new approach, he said, would begin with asking the motorist to "step out of the car." After that, they would be asked "to open their trunk." The new policy resulted in more citations, as well as more incidental arrests for drunk driving, drug possession, and other violations of law discovered at the stops. Despite stricter enforcement, the tide of fruit flowing out of the quarantine area continued.

On July 29th, after the final night of spraying in week two, I received a disturbing call from the director of a dialysis clinic in Mountain View reporting that a patient receiving dialysis had died that morning. Another six patients on dialysis in the clinic had experienced breathing problems, changes in heart rate, sweating, and shortness of breath but had survived. A doctor suspected the cause was organophosphate poisoning attributable to the overnight spraying in the area. I hung up, knowing this would be a front-page story the next morning. I telephoned the State Department of Public Health in Berkeley and luckily reached Dr. Jim Stratton. He told me to have a member of our monitoring crew rush to the hospital and take water samples from the dialysis machines and the main water supply and get them to Public Health's lab in Berkeley as soon as possible. We did that. As expected, details of a patient dying and the others mysteriously sickened appeared prominently in the morning paper. Fortunately, the headline "Kidney Unit Closed After Patient Mysteriously Dies" made no mention of the word Malathion. Dr. Stratton met me early the next morning at the hospital with the results of the overnight lab tests. At my regular morning press conference, I reported that the lab test results ruled out pesticide contamination of the water as a possible cause. Further support soon came from Dr David Discher, the chair of the Medfly Health Advisory committee. Dr. Discher, a toxicologist, told the press that while there were some symptoms of organophosphate poisoning, inconsistencies in the symptoms "make that a very, very, unlikely presumption." The story that afternoon ruled out Malathion as a possible cause. So did a long article, the next day headed "Malathion Didn't Cause Dialysis Death." The death and other symptoms were later determined to have been caused by an error at the clinic. Formaldehyde used to clean the lines had not been adequately flushed from the lines before patients were hooked up.

These last two days reinforced the feeling of living daily on the edge of disaster. So did a second incident that apparently occurred during the last night of spraying in week two. Early Sunday morning, a bullet hole was discovered in the tail boom of a helicopter owned by Evergreen. Fortunately, the bullet had not hit anything vital. The unknown shooter was never identified or caught. The incident generated another front-page story. We tightened security by having an airborne highway patrol helicopter during operations. It maintained direct communication with local law enforcement ground units, who were prepared to respond quickly to any similar incident in the future. When later another medfly helicopter pilot reported what appeared to be light flashes from a gun muzzle or mirror as he flew over Palo Alto, Police responded to the location. Witnesses reported kids had been playing with a pellet gun on the overpass. The bullet hole and periodic flashes from the ground were a grim reminder of the danger the pilots faced every night, not only from fog, powerlines, and other flying hazards but also from those who anonymously continued to threaten to shoot them down.

On Wednesday, July 30th, with the second round of spraying completed, the *San Jose Mercury News* gave us a front-page nod of encouragement. After cataloging the various controversies of the previous weeks, such as the slow start, the mixed messaging on fruit stripping, and the overspray complaints, the paper wrote that "after a ragged start, the Medfly war was smoothing out." The most recent overspray had occurred two days earlier on Monday in Cupertino. I was quoted admitting: "It was very ragged the first week…. better the second, and I think the third week will be better yet."

BOOK

FOUR

AUGUST 1981

Chapter 14 (A New Fight Looms)

As July turned into August, success at last seemed possible. As near as could be known, there were no more wild medflies in the areas being sprayed. On Monday, we released a map of the new corridors and the schedule for week three. The third round of four nights of aerial spraying would begin on August 3rd and end on August 6th. Both the *Mercury* and the *Chronicle* printed maps showing the new boundaries. With the changes, we could cover the total area of more than 230 square miles in four days instead of six.

Around the state, the fear of economic disaster began to ease as the summer harvesting peaked. Canneries moved to three shifts. Double tractor-trailers started hauling seven million tons of tomatoes to canneries. Long-haul trucks rolled out of packing houses loaded with freshly picked boxes of strawberries, peaches, nectarines, peppers, and other host fruits and vegetables bound for Chicago, New York, and other fresh produce markets across the country. Oranges, grapefruit, and lemons filled refrigerated ships bound for Japan and Asia.

Still, the fear of a shutdown hung in the air. "Growers in the San Joaquin Valley Praying Extra Hard," read the headline in the *San Francisco Chronicle* on July 27th. Each day brought the possibility that new fly or larval finds outside the current boundaries could suddenly bring down the quarantine curtain at the worst possible time. A statewide quarantine would trigger staggering economic losses, and not only to growers. Up to 90% of California's half a billion dollars in host fruit would be affected. At the project, both we and our federal partners believed we had a handle on the infestation now. We had not found a wild fly since July 14th. Harvey Ford, the deputy administrator of USDA-APHIS, scheduled a public hearing in Los Gatos on August 13th to hear comments from the public in the three counties under quarantine. He said, "Provided the current infestation does not change before then, the U.S. Department of Agriculture will not propose any changes in the current quarantine."

With aerial spraying on track, we turned our attention at the end of July to dramatically increasing the number of insect traps deployed in the project area and throughout northern California. In the core area, we hung 50 traps per square mile, then 25 per square mile stretching out to the quarantine boundary. Beyond that, with the help of the county agricultural commissioners, we placed ten traps per square mile, extending out 100 miles. In the rest of the state, five traps per square mile became standard. There had never been anything close to this level of trapping in the past, anywhere. Five per square mile had been sufficient in Los Angeles in both 1975 and 1980. In addition to more traps, federal and state personnel fanned out to every county to train local staff in the proper placement, baiting, and servicing of traps. The greater surveillance ensured any emerging wild flies would be quickly caught, and the area added to the aerial eradication effort. At the same time, this level of trapping would reassure other states and countries that no other areas of the state harbored the pest. Gary Agosta, the head of the trapping unit, reported that we now had 20,000 traps deployed in the three infested counties, and his 68 trappers were each checking more than 50 traps a day. What he didn't tell me was that some of the existing traps in outlying areas had not been checked at all after the first week of spraying. Agosta promised me that by August 6th, all 20,000 would be checked every seven days. We knew we might find a few wild flies outside the spray area but still within the quarantine line. We were not expecting to find wild flies turning up outside the quarantine boundary.

The advisory committee's first meeting since July 7th was set for August 6th. We planned an upbeat report like the one we had given to a visiting Japanese citrus industry delegation the day before. The Japanese told us how pleased they were with what they were seeing. High on the public's agenda would be the committee's recommendation on the total number of bait treatments needed. From the beginning, the understanding was that between six and 12 rounds would be necessary. By the time they arrived, the third application of bait had gone off flawlessly. I hoped, and the public hoped, that given the encouraging developments, only three more for a total of six would be needed.

Rumors that at the August 6th meeting the committee might vote to increase both the amount of Malathion per acre and the number of sprays appeared in local papers on August 1st. The *Chronicle's* reporter,

Rick Carroll, wrote, "A new fight looms in the Medfly war next week between scientists who call for increased aerial spraying and medfly Project leaders who resist the idea." Carroll based his article on knowing the committee had expressed a preference for 12 sprays at their November 1980 meeting. Since December, I had said at least six. Carroll wrote that he had interviewed Dr. Roy Cunningham, who told Carroll he expected the panel to discuss increasing the dosage. I had heard nothing about raising the dosage level. I could not recall that being discussed by anyone on or off the project.

Starting with my first meeting with the committee on December 30th, their recommendations had guided the project. I respected their scientific knowledge. I knew of no reason for changing the dosage. Ed Pope penned a similar article the same day in the *Mercury* with an even more provocative headline, "Spraying may be doubled," referring to 12 versus six. Our trap catch data showed that almost no flies had survived the first two sprays, and the final report, released later, would show zero wild flies were found in traps after three applications of the bait. I hoped that the committee would recommend fewer than 12 applications, at a minimum. In any case, I was not looking for a fight on either the dosage or the number of sprays.

The Republican opponents of Governor Brown said regardless of the number of sprays, we should extend the spraying farther out to get ahead of the flies. We were spraying in accordance with the committee's recommendations to treat either one and a half square miles in all directions from where a fly had been caught or three miles in all directions from where larvae were found. One politician suggested spraying out as far as a hundred-mile radius, while another liked the idea of spraying the entire state to be sure. I was accurately quoted stating, "I'm a strong believer in using pesticides judiciously," adding, "I'm "disturbed by the extremes, those who don't want to spray at all and those who want us to spray to the maximum." This quote would come back to haunt me when I resisted spraying areas where no wild flies had been caught.

Opponents argued we were spraying too much. They suggested in a front-page story that the amount of malathion reaching the ground far exceeded the 2.4 ounces advertised, and some areas were being overlapped and double and triple sprayed. In an excellent article by Mercury's Tom Harris, readers learned that the volume of malathion bait reaching the ground was calculated in two different ways. Both debunked the claim of excess spraying. One measure compared the total volume used to the number of acres sprayed. The second technique involved measuring the total volume as well as droplet size and distribution by analyzing the amount deposited on 1-foot square drop cards on the ground below the spray. This second analysis was performed by Dr. Norman Akesson at the University of California at Davis. It required measuring under a microscope the droplet number and size and calculating the total volume of spray on the card. According to Harris, what Professor Akesson found was that the volume of malathion on the cards added up to less than 2 ounces per acre. The total volume of malathion being released by air divided by the number of acres covered also confirmed that no more than 2.4 ounces was being released. Based on his calculations, there was no need to increase the dosage since the flies were finding the bait and being killed.

Human health remained a concern for some in the community despite Judge Allen's decision on July 13th. The medical committee created by Brown continued to review emergency room visits and other indicia of adverse health effects. In addition, the State Health Department conducted a survey of residents in the spray zones on their general health before and after spraying. Both found no evidence whatsoever of serious or even minor health consequences related to Malathion. The Health Department found that people in the spray zones reported feeling better after the Malathion spraying started. There had been a noticeable decline in headaches, difficulty sleeping, aching muscles, and watery eyes. The report by Dr. Richard Jackson surprised legislators and more than 100 attendees at a joint hearing of the Assembly Health and Agriculture committees in Sacramento. In response to questions, Dr. Jackson said he could not say what caused the results except that they might relate to relief from the incredible stress created earlier by fears of severe health consequences from the spraying.

On August 3rd, an inflammatory article appeared in *People Magazine.* The article "Politics and Pests Don't Mix, The Medfly Is a Case in Point, Experts Say" showcased the views of Dr. Frank Gilstrap of Texas A&M University. Gilstrap favored aerial spraying even before he was appointed to the committee to appease Texas and end the blockade of California truck exports. He was also the committee member who had been the most upset with Governor Brown. I believe the article played a significant role in both the residual anger members of the advisory committee harbored over how they had been treated at the previous meeting and in the anti-Brown narrative being pushed by Republicans. In a question-and-answer format splashed across three pages of pictures and text, the article's author interviewed Dr. Gilstrap and his boss, Texas A&M University's deputy chancellor for agriculture. Together, they bluntly blamed Governor Jerry Brown for California's having "mishandled the fruit fly problem from the beginning." The State's biggest mistake, they said, was that "they did not immediately go to aerial spraying." As I have noted here, the problem with the "from the beginning" argument is that Jerry Brown was not involved with the medfly from the beginning. California's eradication professionals and the scientists who opined the medfly would not survive the winter in northern California were running the program without political interference. There was no recommendation from the advisory committee to aerially spray in 1980. Brown did refuse to order aerial spraying on July 8th,1981 when Rominger and I and the advisory committee all recommended it. However, this article nationalized the blame Brown meme.

Dr. Gilstrap's statement in the article that releasing millions of sterile flies "has never been shown to be an eradication tool anywhere in the world" was also obviously untrue. Releasing sterile flies for eradication had been successful in experimental trials and succeeded twice as an eradication tool in Los Angeles in 1975-76 and again in 1980. Surely, he knew that. Furthermore, sterile fly releases were the strategy chosen for the USDA/Mexico eradication program, and this effort was ongoing at the time the article was published. In fairness to Dr. Gilstrap, the authors of the piece may have overstated his position. On the other hand, I believe he spoke for the whole committee when he said, "I don't know why he (Governor Brown) even called the meeting. It was a charade."

The *People* magazine article, in addition to helping nationalize the false narrative invented by California Republicans at their L.A. press conference, perpetuated the ideological battle between the pesticide industry and those who saw all pesticides as inherently bad and believed that biological control strategies could be substituted for pesticide use in every possible situation. Most farmers and knowledgeable environmentalists in California in 1980, and especially since, have recognized that controlling pests requires combining a wide range of data-driven options with more limited use of pesticides to manage the damage pests cause. Throughout his four terms as governor, Brown advocated and strongly supported integrated pest management, or IPM, as this preferred approach is known.

IPM, though, was not the focus on August 5th, when the Sacramento lab identified another wild, unmated female medfly, this one well south of where we had sprayed. The trap, in rural southern Santa Clara County, in a cherry tree had not been checked for three weeks, nor had others, including a second trap in the city of Los Altos where a second wild fly was discovered. The latter was not a problem since we had sprayed Los Altos several times. However, the one in the south county, plus one more trapped near it, represented a big problem because the two new flies were seventeen miles south of the current spray zone in Santa Clara County. This was also near the San Benito County line farther south and beyond it, the lush Salinas Valley in Monterey County. A quarantine of the whole state might soon become unavoidable. The new finds renewed the specter of more satellite finds popping up elsewhere in California. Accordingly, on August 5th, we faxed a document titled "Contingency Plan for Eradicating Satellite Medfly Infestations" to each of the state's county agricultural commissioners.

On top of the unwelcome news of more trapped wild flies, we had yet another embarrassing overspray incident. A San Joaquin helicopter pilot forgot to turn off the spray while making a big sweeping turn, spraying homes about a half mile beyond the end line. I wrote a letter to the homeowner complainants telling them I shared their frustration with these repeated errors. I assured them deputy director Hans Van Nes would be on board one of our helicopters in the next few nights to try to improve our accuracy. Unfortunately, even with Hans aboard, a San Joaquin helicopter later that week over-sprayed again. After another angry meeting with Josephson, he promised his pilots would try harder. Meanwhile, there were more reports of gunshots, though fortunately, no hits. August 6th suddenly looked significantly less upbeat than our report to the visiting Japanese group only a week earlier.

On August 6th, the advisory committee convened in Los Gatos. The headline in the *Mercury* read, "Scientists brace for more Medfly abuse." In the story that followed, reporter Bernard Bauer wrote, "They came to talk science, they left vilified, slandered, and bewildered at the hostility vented against them." Things had quieted down despite our problems with stripping and roadblocks. The public had accepted the necessity of the spraying, and more importantly, there had been no significant health or environmental problems. I was not expecting this meeting to be as controversial as the one in July. However, the committee members flying in from Hawaii, Texas, and Florida had not experienced the changed atmosphere and the widespread acceptance of the need for the spraying. They assumed they were returning to a hostile war zone.

I knew the advisory committee members were angry after the July 7th meeting in the broiling sun outside the school, followed by the Governor's disingenuous request to hear their views in person. At the meeting in his office, It was obvious that he never intended to follow their advice. Having worked in the legislature for five years where political posturing, shifting positions, and broken alliances were the norm, my disappointment with the Governor's failure to take their advice and mine had dissipated. I naively believed the committee members would be pleased Brown's decision had been swiftly reversed and even more pleased to see how well things were going now. However, that was not to be. They were bitter at having been played.

As they gathered, news arrived that three wild Mediterranean fruit flies had been caught in Florida in a backyard trap near downtown Tampa. The Florida Ag Department issued a press release saying it was impossible to know if they came from California before describing our program in some detail and thus implying they probably did. The article did, though, mention that Central America and the Caribbean Islands were infested and had been the presumed source of earlier Florida invasions. Florida officials interviewed by the press later joked that all medflies spoke the same language—medfly, thus they could have come from anywhere. There was no way to know. I put out a memo of the news flash to all staff, including that the flies had been officially confirmed in the Washington, D.C. lab. Florida's inspectors deployed more traps and made ready to strip the citrus tree where the flies were trapped. They would soon spray the surrounding three-block area with malathion bait via ground application. They said their next step would be scheduling helicopter spraying of a nine-square-mile area around the find. Their aerial spraying effort would struggle with the same mechanical difficulties we had, resulting in a ten-day delay before the first aerial bait was applied. The infestation proved to be small and was wiped out in one of the shortest eradication efforts in Florida's storied history of multiple medfly invasions.

In Los Gatos, our meeting began with the introduction of the two newest members, Dr. E.F. Knipling and Dr. Darrell Chambers, both distinguished members of USDA's agricultural research service (ARS) and acknowledged experts on the medfly. The original six-member committee, originally known as the Technical Review Committee (TRC), had grown to nine members in the spring. The new members strengthened the scientific approach important to the project's success. Dr. Knipling, a legend within USDA, had pioneered much of the research on the Sterile Insect Technique. Dr. Chambers directed the USDA Insect Attractants Laboratory in Gainesville, Florida. Prior to that, he had served at both the Hawaiian Fruit Flies Laboratory in Honolulu and the Mexican Fruit Fly Laboratory in Mexico. I was thrilled to have them on the committee. Next, the chair acknowledged the presence of Director Rominger as well as the members of the State Board of Food and Agriculture. The Board, an advisory body that normally met monthly in Sacramento, had scheduled their August meeting in Los Gatos to coincide with the advisory committee meeting. Following the introductions, Don Henry and I updated the committee and State Board on the aerial spraying, including maps showing the areas covered in the first two full weeks of spraying plus the about-to-be-completed coverage in week three. Dr. Knipling asked what data had been gathered on the effectiveness of the spraying so far. What were the trap catches telling us? We answered that after two rounds of spraying, the flies caught per trap had dropped from hundreds to one, two, or none, adding that a final report in preparation would show no flies in traps in areas that had received the third round of spraying. These results told us the bait spray was working as it had in the previous campaigns in Florida and Texas.

The committee then discussed a recommendation on the number of weekly applications. In December, they had suggested as few as one knockdown spray, followed by continuing with SIT or alternatively abandoning SIT and spraying for a minimum of six to twelve rounds, seven to ten days apart. To the surprise of most, myself included, the committee voted for eight applications as an interim recommendation with a further review at the next meeting. So far, the meeting had gone better than the media had predicted.

The next question concerned what to do about the new fly finds in the sparsely populated southern half of Santa Clara County, where there were fewer houses and many commercial fields of host fruits and vegetables. Don Henry conceded our finding wild flies so far outside the spray zone was a troubling development. He said, "I'm not going to play that down." Like Florida, our protocol called for spraying a mile and a half around each new fly find. However, Henry noted that since the second fly was near a reservoir, the spraying there might need to be conducted from the ground as a precaution to protect fish and drinking water. Although technically correct, the precautions were exactly the overly cautious approach Dr. Gilstrap had criticized. He promptly made a motion to go big and expand the aerial spray area southward from the current line to encompass the entire southern half of the county. He then suggested the project also spray another thinly populated area of a hundred and thirty square miles on the west side of the county where no flies at all had been found. This foothill area extended southwest to the Santa Cruz County line. Had I kept my mouth shut, as I should have, the next two weeks of my life would have been much less stressful. But I didn't. His motion struck me as the shoot-first and ask-questions-later approach I opposed. Further, it lacked a rational basis in science and was inconsistent with the committee's recommended protocol of one and half square miles around finds that we had been following.

Dr. Gilstrap backed his motion by calling what we had been doing "a program of minimals (sic) from the beginning almost to the lack of regard of biology." Drs. Knipling and Chambers, who had not been on the committee in July and thus were not as angry over that experience, responded that the project's recommendation was consistent with the established protocol. They said the program should target the spraying to where flies were detected, not spray based on guesswork. As the project manager, I jumped in to support Drs. Knipling and Chambers. I urged, with more emotion than reason, that we stick to our protocol and continue to rely on science as suggested by Dr. Knipling and Dr. Chambers and spray only after detecting the presence of flies. The vote was called, and Dr. Gilstrap's motion was overwhelmingly approved to the satisfaction of everyone present except me and the two no votes by Chambers and Knipling. The debate answered the unspoken philosophical question underlying the politics of pesticide use in California. Should they be used cautiously or liberally to control pests? Liberally won in this case. That answer also reinforced the narrative that California under Brown and his project director was proceeding too timidly and that the state should have opted for aerial spraying, if not from the beginning, at least sooner than we did. Now it needed to be pursued more vigorously.

The rest of the meeting was non-controversial and helpful. The committee unanimously approved minor changes in our operational protocol with respect to trapping, quarantine policy, and aerial spraying.

I especially welcomed their recommendation to stop fruit stripping immediately, except around larval finds. They also recommended that the roadblocks be ended thirty-five days after spraying had reached the end of a period covering two medfly reproductive generations, i.e., about 60 days from mid-July.

Looking back, I regretted my tone-deaf emotional reaction to Dr. Gilstrap's motion. I should have listened respectfully instead of trying to control the committee's decision. There was nothing especially nefarious about the motion and much to commend it, including the fact that in March, Florida's Charlie Poucher had discovered dead medfly larvae in California Bay Laurel, which, though not a recognized host, grew throughout the foothills.. Trying to place traps in the foothills, even using helicopters to insert the trappers, had been extremely difficult. If later, we had found wild flies present in the foothills, my stand in favor of strict reliance on first trapping wild flies would have been indefensible.

Two days later, we added to the spraying an area seven miles wide and 28 miles long extending south. The new, mostly rural zone included 92,000 households. We also implemented Dr. Gillstrap's foothills recommendation. As to the latter, we went even further by expanding the aerial spraying to the foothills farther north as well, and we announced we would follow the recommendation for eight applications, making September 9th the last day for aerial spraying for those areas sprayed in the first week. However, my change of heart came too late to erase the negative impression my passionate and intemperate remarks at the meeting had left in the minds of the State Board of Agriculture members. They and the farm representatives present at the meeting decided I needed to be replaced.

After the meeting, Tom Hale of the Grape and Tree Fruit League, the same group that had held the press conference taking credit for the legal victory against Texas, called Don Dilley, the chair of the advisory committee, and recruited him as an ally in their scheme to replace me. Dilley and others in the department's control and eradication section and ancillary sections of the Division of Plant Industry had long viewed any direction from upper management as political interference. That attitude had put me at odds with Dilley and other managers even before Chief Deputy Dan Dooley left to open a private law office, and Rominger shifted responsibility for the Division to me. It was also why problems with the medfly battle in 1980 in Santa Clara failed to reach the director's office or, when they did, were sugar-coated with false assurances the problems had been fixed. Dilley epitomized the quintessential company man wedded to the leisurely pace of regular coffee breaks and office politics. After he had been assigned to form the original advisory committee, he selected himself as chair.

The imperial management of the department's control and eradication unit particularly frustrated those in the field, like Arnie Morrison, Don Henry, and Jim Rudig, men who spent their careers away from both home and headquarters on the front lines of various pest control projects, battling new invasions without the resources needed to do the job assigned. Advancement, in the department, like most bureaucracies, although theoretically competitive, provided those at headquarters with an inside track on promotions that too often depended more on friendship and seniority than competence.

Shortly after the August advisory committee meeting, Hale arranged a surreptitious meeting with Carol Hallett, the Republican minority leader in the State Assembly. Following that meeting, Dilley penned a memo, requested by Hallett and signed by several others in the department, claiming I had repeatedly refused to follow scientific advice. The memo urged I be replaced by the Republican Chief Deputy Director at CDFA, George Strathearn, a well-liked cattleman. Strathearn, if aware of the machinations behind Rominger's back, avoided them. The letter would surface later when Hallett and other Republican legislators held a press conference in Sacramento, attacking Jerry Brown and calling for my resignation and a USDA takeover of the medfly program.

Over the next week, a wave of new wild fly discoveries on the fringes rocked the project. The timing and locations of the new finds, each a step beyond the current lines, created the impression that an army of medflies was advancing in all directions. No army existed. The main body had been wiped out. However, more than a thousand new traps had been hung after we stopped releasing sterile flies. These new traps and a few old ones that had not been recently checked were where we began catching a fly here and a fly there on the outer edges or just beyond the quarantine boundary.

We jumped on each new fly, spraying most within 24 hours and then adding them to the nearest spray corridor. Florida's Poucher had warned more flies might be out there. But this did not prevent the media from reacting to each new find with shock and dismay, followed by another banner headline speculating that the spreading flies could soon reach California's fabled Central Valley. Fear of finding a wild fly in the Central Valley gripped the farm community because it would almost certainly trigger a Japanese quarantine of the entire state.

On Saturday, August 8th, the lab in Sacramento confirmed we had trapped a mated female in a backyard apple tree in the town of Boulder Creek, 21 miles southwest of the recent Santa Clara finds. Boulder Creek was in Santa Cruz County, bordering Santa Clara. The find meant we now had medflies in a fourth county. The Santa Cruz County Board of Supervisors called an immediate emergency session for the next day to discuss contingency plans for a large-scale mass evacuation in the event of aerial spraying. Rich Hammond cautioned the media that aerial spraying would be problematic. "It is in a difficult area," he said. "Bear Creek runs through the town." He recommended stripping the fruit trees and sampling fruit in the area since the fly was a mated female that might have already laid eggs. We opted to do both and in addition, to order aerial spraying.

Two days later, on August 10th, the lab in Sacramento confirmed another wild fly, this one trapped in an orange tree in the city of Livermore, in Alameda County, 33 miles northeast of San Jose. A more frightening location could hardly be imagined. Livermore sat astride Interstate 580, the main freeway between San Jose and the Central Valley. Thousands of commuters flowed in and out of San Jose daily to and from the Central Valley, only ten miles east of Livermore. The likelihood that medflies would soon be found in the Valley set off a crisis reminiscent of how Americans felt in 1968 when the Viet Cong launched the Tet Offensive. Overnight, impending disaster dominated the news. I tried to calm the situation by reminding everyone that the advisory committee had warned in July to expect at least eight satellite infestations in the state. I said: "We haven't lost the war, it's just a bigger battlefield." The *Sacramento Bee* wrote on August 11th that farmers "are frightened as the fruit fly marches steadily toward their fields." This story in the state capitol's newspaper, more than any other, furthered the image of an army of flies swarming over the hills into the Central Valley. No army was marching or swarming. Instead, we were belatedly checking traps beyond the previously defined infested area and thus identifying these satellite hotspots. Clark Biggs, the spokesperson for the California Farm Bureau, called for immediate spraying in Livermore. I issued the order to do so on the 12th. Spraying began at 9 p.m. on the 13th. Livermore became new Corridor 11. Boulder Creek in Santa Cruz County became new Corridor 12, with spraying there to start the following Monday.

Although I had opposed using multi-engine, fixed-wing planes over heavily populated areas, I now recognized we needed them in the large agricultural corridors. They could carry five times as much bait as a helicopter and flew faster, enabling them to cover large rural areas efficiently with minimal risk to those on the ground. They could only spray in daylight during early morning hours when the air was still. They also made wide sweeping turns and sprayed from a higher altitude, resulting in bait landing beyond the target zone. Neither of these disadvantages concerned the rural population. They supported the agriculture all around them. We contacted the two firms in Arizona that USDA worked with in the past, and they agreed to deliver a minimum of six planes on 48-hour notice. We signed a contract, and the Department of Defense agreed that we could base the fixed-wing planes at the Navy's airfield at Crows Landing alongside Interstate 5 in Stanislaus County.

On Wednesday, August 12th, less than a week after the advisory committee meeting, we trapped another mated female with eggs, this one in the city of Milpitas close to the south end of San Francisco Bay in northeast Santa Clara County. Although this fly find was inside the existing quarantine line, it was outside the current spray corridor. I wanted it sprayed that night. Doing so meant we could not afford to wait even 24 hours to allow door-to-door delivery of spraying notices to residents. The staff and I huddled around a map table where Jim Rudig, the noticing manager, insisted we honor our commitment to deliver individual written notices no matter how short the timeline. He said his people could do it that night. I delayed the start of spraying until midnight, and Rudig's teams managed to cover the nine-square-mile area before the spraying began. We coupled the ground noticing effort with requests to radio and TV stations to run alerts.

The same day as the Milpitas find, Republican Assembly member Carol Hallett, in league with USDA officials in Washington, D.C., launched her coordinated campaign to put USDA in charge of the medfly project. At a Capitol press conference, flanked by seven farm legislators, she demanded Brown fire me and turn the project over to USDA. To back up her demands, she distributed copies of Don Dilley's letter. The letter turned out to be a mishmash of hyperbole and untruths, misrepresenting what the advisory committee had recommended and falsely claiming I had not followed their advice. The next morning, my picture captioned "resignation asked" appeared on the front page of the *Sacramento Bee* next to the headline, "Final Try to Block Medfly from Valley." In her press conference, Hallett claimed Jerry Brown had blocked aerial spraying from the beginning and that I had ignored the advisory committee at every opportunity. She also bizarrely claimed Brown and I both favored using "backyard gardening techniques" to fight the medfly, a veiled reference to the fruit stripping.

Unknown to Rominger and those of us on the project, Hallett had cultivated a back-channel connection to Greg Rohwer and Bill Helms, assistant administrators under Harvey Ford at USDA headquarters. Rohwer, a key architect of the 1956 Florida medfly battle, had wanted the project to move to aerial spraying soon after it started. Hallet's choice of the words "backyard gardening techniques" likely originated with Rohwer. It had never been part of previous eradication projects beyond local fruit removal from the site of larval finds. I believed after it had been recommended by the advisory committee in November that it made sense in the winter. I did not support it in the summer except around larval finds. Jerry Brown ordering universal fruit stripping again in July no doubt infuriated Rohwer because it was not only unhelpful but worse, as it could lead to people taking the ripe stripped fruit to relatives outside the area.

Hallett's statement went on to detail multiple specific examples of how she claimed we had failed to follow the committee's advice and Florida's successful strategies in the past, as well as those used by Florida in Tampa the previous week. She called for turning over the program to USDA, using four-engine planes instead of helicopters, and expanding aerial spraying out another 25 miles in all directions. The latter would have put planes in the air over millions in the Cities of San Francisco and Oakland. Her claims of misfeasance were uniformly untrue. For example, she claimed our goal was pest control when it should have been eradication, that Florida had never allowed an infestation to grow to 2,000 square miles, and in Tampa, they had sprayed the next day, whereas we had ignored the advisory committee's advice to aerially spray in November and had refused to spray the Santa Clara hills as the committee recommended on August 6th.

In a three-page single-spaced memo, I rebutted each point, noting that eradication had always been the goal; the advisory committee had not recommended aerial spraying in November; only USDA had. Furthermore, the committee had recommended fruit stripping in November because aerial spraying would be ineffective in winter. The community had blocked the aerial spraying in December, not Governor Brown. Her claim that Florida would never allow a problem to grow to 2,000 square miles was palpably false as medflies there had twice spread over close to half the state; as for comparing Tampa's prompt action in August 1981 to our delay, that, too, was false. We had a helicopter in the air spraying over San Jose four days after obtaining permission to do so, and that was only six days after the advisory committee officially recommended it. In Tampa, it took ten days for their lone helicopter to get off the ground and make its first pass. The one point she made that was true was that I expressed opposition to spraying where we had not found any medflies. However, even there, I followed the committee's recommendation despite my disagreement with it. In sum, we followed scientific advice throughout the program except for the Governor's refusal to spray on July 8th, a decision he reversed under pressure two days later. I was amused that Hallett was unaware that Florida adopted our California protocol for their eradication effort in Tampa, including using a helicopter instead of a fixed-wing plane, as had been the case in their earlier programs. Finally, it was poetic justice that shortly after she left the podium, Florida discovered more medflies outside their quarantine and spray area, requiring them to expand their program like we were doing. None of my rebuttals changed the perception that my days as project director were numbered.

The next major story in the *Mercury* reminded their liberal readers that the farm community's antipathy toward Jerry Brown predated the medfly crisis. The headline read, "To farmers, Brown is the other pest." The article featured a litany of their complaints about Brown, especially his support of the grape boycott and the creation of the Agriculture Labor Relations Board (ALRB), which allowed farm workers to unionize. As the summer and the medfly battle continued, angry farmers, Republican legislators, and opinion writers continued to heap blame on Governor Brown. Everything but the original appearance of the medfly was all his fault, they claimed, either because he didn't order aerial spraying in June 1980 or because he blocked aerial spraying during the two-day hiatus in July '81.

Chapter 15 (Medflies Reach the Central Valley)

On Thursday, one day after the Hallett press conference, multiple medflies were discovered in traps a few miles over the hill from Livermore in the Central Valley. The traps had been placed in a commercial apricot orchard south of the town of Westley near where Interstate 580 crossed the hills from Livermore into the Central Valley and connected to I-5, the main Freeway running the length of the state from Oregon to San Diego.

Assemblywoman Carol Hallett immediately renewed her demand that Brown fire me and turn the project over to USDA. This time, she added that if he didn't, she would "initiate articles of impeachment" on Monday. She said the spread into the Central Valley was the result of "Scribner's reacting to the Medfly instead of taking the preventive measures called for long ago by the technical committee." Senator Ken Maddy, the Republican minority leader in California's 40-member Senate, joined Hallett in supporting my being fired and, failing that, impeaching Brown. He told reporters, "Disaster has struck the San Joaquin Valley. Our farmers are panicking right now." Without mentioning Dilley by name, they claimed Brown and I had "ignored every recommendation they [the committee] had ever made."

Rural Democrats, including Agriculture Chairman John Thurman, joined the chorus condemning Brown. Thurman represented Westley and Stanislaus County, where the new flies appeared. He happened to be meeting with farmers in a café in his district on the day the flies were discovered. There he signed a hastily drafted petition to impeach Brown written on the back of one of the restaurant's paper placemats. Willie Brown, the outspoken African American Speaker of the California Assembly, joked in the *Capitol News Scope*, a gossip column, that "What Thurman did is exactly what I would have done at a Ku Klux Klan rally." Thurman, however, defended me, saying, "Scribner should not be the fall guy here." He added that he has "too many people to answer to" and "If that isn't corrected, Jerry's got to get out of there." Thurman joined Democratic State Senator Rose Ann Vuich in recommending the aerial program be expanded to include spraying all along Interstate I-5 down the west side of the Central Valley.

Governor Brown was reportedly in meetings in Los Angeles. He did not respond publicly to the attacks. Inside the Governor's office in Sacramento, before the flies had been found in Westley, an aide admitted off the record that medflies in the Central Valley would be "very, very bad." Others, though, such as his press secretary, Cari Beauchamp, said she did not think the discovery would be "much bigger than any other day." Gray Davis, responding for the Governor, dismissed the impeachment threat as "pure political posturing." He said, "We have a great deal of confidence in Jerry Scribner and Richard Rominger." He also said that "Hallett knows full well that the federal government has been working closely with the state for eight months." A USDA official, Shannon Wilson, who had been involved since the fall of 1980, also weighed in to put the Westley flies in perspective. He said he had anticipated weeks earlier that the fly would get into the Valley unless California was very lucky. "We weren't lucky," he said.

Both Rominger and I took the position that the odds for eradication were still good. I was reported to be a little testy, which was true. I told the press that their inexorable march-of-the-medfly theme was creating a false impression. I said, "We have a problem but we're going to get rid of it." Friday afternoon, the lab, as expected, confirmed the Westly flies were wild. We immediately sent busloads of Rudig's noticing crews to Stanislaus County to distribute notices door-to-door in the towns of Westley and Patterson, warning residents we would be spraying immediately beginning at midnight. In addition, during the afternoon, the quarantine staff met and agreed on a new joint federal/state quarantine line in Stanislaus County. We also dispatched a team to Arizona to make sure the fixed-wing planes would be arriving to spray the agricultural areas. We were going to need them. In my Friday afternoon press conference covering what we were doing, I said, "I make no apologies for the effort we've made. We've worked day and night since December. I can't guarantee that we won't find another fly…but I can guarantee that we will eradicate them everywhere we find them."

216

As if on cue, Rohwer and Helms overnight, each sent individual letters to Rominger, repeating Hallett's claims and recommending an immediate change to federal management of the project. Their letters described the project as chaotic, with the helicopter spraying coverage being hit and miss or incomplete, and referenced other problems parroting Hallett's charges. Rohwer's complaint with our aerial program boiled down to his preference for using fixed-wing planes as they had done in Florida. Even as to that, we had already agreed to use their contractor, Globe Aviation, for the rural areas. In addition, we had sprayed Milpitas the same night the flies were identified and then Westley on Friday night, plus more than 70 square miles around it in Stanislaus County. The latter operation had used six helicopters flying with military precision. The Rohwer and Helms letters were wildly inaccurate and caused an uproar and near meltdown in the federal/state cooperative relationship with USDA. Rominger called Secretary Block and learned the letters had not been cleared with him, nor with Harvey Ford, nor Ford's boss, Dr. Harry Mussman, the head of APHIS. Nor did they reflect USDA's position with respect to the project. Ford left on the next flight to California to meet with Rominger and me to clear the air.

On Saturday morning, August 15th, every major paper in the state ran huge headlines reporting medflies had reached the Central Valley, sparking fears that a quarantine of the entire state might be next. The articles also noted that we had sent in a fleet of helicopters and sprayed a large area around the finds Friday night. The *Sacramento Union's* headline that morning, "Medfly bombers over Valley," was followed by two big stories, each with its own headlines. "Brown blamed," read the one on the left, while "Stanislaus invaded" filled the right half of page one. Speculation as to the source of the new flies centered on a homeowner carrying infected fruit who might have stopped at a roadside rest in the area. Alternatively, they could have come from the eggs of a mated female escaping from inside a vehicle traveling that route. Either way, the flies might have been breeding in Westley for weeks. It turned out that the Stanislaus agricultural commissioner's staff of 12 trappers had been so busy putting out new traps that they had not had time to check the traps in the orchard for weeks. The last check had been on July 29th, well before the August 6th advisory committee meeting. The most likely source was not a traveler but, instead, a breakdown in our quarantine procedures. In July, apricots grown in Westley were being picked and trucked to the processing facilities in Sunnyvale in the Mountain View Gap. The bins were supposed to be thoroughly cleaned before returning to the orchard. A mated female could have hitched a ride in one of the trucks shuttling between Sunnyvale and the orchard, or eggs in an apricot or part of one left in a bin could have been the source. Such a bin had been spotted during the harvest by one of our inspectors at a checkpoint and sent back for re-cleaning. Additional support for the quarantine failure theory came from the fact that no wild flies were ever found at the roadside rest or anywhere else in the County.

Whatever the source, the headlines continued as reporters interviewed individual farmers at length. The farmers expressed outrage that Governor Brown had not ordered aerial spraying a year earlier and predicted this latest development guaranteed that farmers would now experience enormous losses. Gene Bays, the farmer in whose orchard the medflies had been found, said, "It's out of control now. They'll have to spray the whole state." Rominger was quoted in the *Union* saying the situation was not "out of hand." The *Mercury* calmly noted the project's response to new finds, "Copters spray Central Valley, Response to new finds immediate."

Harvey Ford arrived in Los Gatos on Saturday afternoon to meet with Rich Rominger and me, as well as with the federal employees. At our meeting, Rich and I told Ford that nearly everything in the Rohwer and Helms letters was categorically untrue, as were Hallet's claims. The truth was that the chaos of the first week and a half had smoothed out, and federal and state employees were all working well together. We also told Ford we would welcome more help from USDA, including having a new full-time deputy project manager from USDA on site again. Wayne Granberry's six-month term had ended in June, and no one had replaced him. We asked that the new federal manager be Dick Jackson, a veteran USDA employee who had arrived on the project about two weeks earlier and impressed everyone. His easy manner belied a strong managerial background and encyclopedic knowledge of medfly entomology. Jackson was well-liked and admired for having invented the "Jackson" trap, tens of thousands of which were in use in the eradication area. Jackson had earlier shared with me how serendipitous his creation of the trap had been. It happened almost by accident as he and his wife were having breakfast. He looked at a waxed half-gallon milk carton on the table and realized a simple tent-shaped insect trap could easily be constructed of waxed cardboard open at both ends with a removable sticky floor insert. It would be cheap, waterproof, and easy to place and service in host fruit trees. A cotton wick soaked with a medfly attractant known as Trimedlure could be hung inside the roof of the trap and draw medflies who would become stuck when they landed on the removable floor. The traps were cheap, ingenious, and effective.

Harvey Ford readily agreed to our suggestion that Jackson be the new deputy project director. We also proposed that another USDA employee, Dr. James Brazzel, who had been assigned to the project in July, replace Dilley as chair of the advisory committee. In the short time he had been aboard, Dr. Brazzel had already organized and led a team of state personnel assessing the effectiveness of the first three weeks of aerial spraying. An incurable optimist, he had previously headed the entomology department at Mississippi State University and, more recently, had managed the successful cotton boll weevil eradication program for USDA. Harvey Ford was visibly pleased with the quality of our recommendations and our receptivity to more robust federal participation. Both Jackson and Brazzel proved to be terrific partners. After the meeting, Ford returned to Washington and Rominger to Sacramento satisfied that our joint project was again on firm footing.

Friday night, August 14th, we had responded to the confirmation of medflies first in Livermore and then in the Westley with a spraying blitzkrieg covering the finds in Livermore, Milpitas, Westley, and Patterson. This completed round four of spraying. While Rominger and I were meeting with Harvey Ford, on Saturday, trappers were finding another 50 wild medflies in traps in the Westley orchard. This, at first, appeared to put an exclamation point on the picture of the unfolding disaster. For the next 24 hours, we felt suspended on the edge of a cliff with no bottom in sight. The panic subsided, however, when it became clear on Sunday that this last batch of wild flies had been trapped before we sprayed. When all the traps were checked again on Sunday, only a single wild fly turned up, and it was also in the same small area already known to be infested. Over the next few days, the fact that medflies had reached the Central Valley proved less important than our quick reaction to it. In the next two weeks, only three more wild flies would be found in Westley. That was the end of it. There were never any more wild flies caught there or anywhere else in the Central Valley.

With the flies under control, we turned our attention to minimizing the impact of quarantine regulations on crops currently being harvested in the 300-square-mile quarantine zone in Stanislaus County. Federal and state quarantine inspectors and the County's Agricultural commissioner huddled with growers over the weekend. The much-ballyhooed predictions of massive financial losses fell apart. Fresh fruit had already been picked and sent to market. What little had not could easily be fumigated or even exported without fumigation using one of two alternative treatments. A newly approved treatment allowed farmers to spray malathion bait themselves weekly on a host crop and receive certification that the crop was medfly-free. Prolonged cold temperature storage, another permitted treatment, would take care of premium table grapes. According to Bruce Obbink of the Table Grape Commission. These were normally kept in cold storage anyway before and during export. The rest of the grapes would be going to wineries or juice, so again not a problem. The peaches were already destined for canneries to become fruit cocktail and canned peaches. Everything else that had not already been harvested was also usually frozen, packed, or canned. The largest unharvested crop, processing tomatoes, would soon be trucked to canneries to become tomato paste, sauce, or ketchup. Tarping loads on the way to canneries and bin sanitation for return trips would be the primary quarantine tools. The recalibrated economic outlook led to a dramatic downplaying of the crisis and headlines such as "Stanislaus Find Raises Hopes in Medfly War" and "Medfly Invasion Not Expected to Hurt Consumers This Year."

Round five of aerial spraying began Monday morning, August 17th. Over the weekend, we activated the fixed-wing contract. The planes arrived in time to take over the spraying in the large rural areas, including new corridor 14 covering Westley and the 70 square miles of Stanislaus County to the south along I-5. Fixed-wing planes would also take over spraying corridors 9 and 10 in southern Santa Clara County. They would also be used in the rural areas in Alameda County in the newly established Corridor 15. Helicopters would begin spraying the other corridors in round five starting on Monday with new Corridor 12 in Boulder Creek in Santa Cruz County. The rugged terrain there dictated daylight spraying. On Sunday night, a judge denied the request for a delay, and spraying started when the fog lifted. It was halted an hour later due to the receipt of a telephone threat to shoot down the helicopter. Deputy sheriffs traced the threatening call to a residence in Boulder Creek. They arrested the two adult male occupants for threatening a public official and drug possession, after which the spraying resumed and was completed on time.

While the spraying was taking place in Boulder Creek, Assemblymember Carol Hallett in Sacramento was formally announcing that articles to impeach Governor Brown had been drafted and would be heard in the Assembly on Thursday, August 20th. She claimed she had at least two Democrats willing to vote for impeachment. Gray Davis accused Hallett of the "basest form of political demagoguery" and "playing on the fears and anxieties of the farming community." He said USDA has been "a full partner since Day One...and will remain so." Hallett then suggested direct talks between her, and Brown aimed at having the medfly program taken over by USDA and run by an expert selected by either USDA or the advisory committee. Davis rejected her proposal out of hand and repeated, "We stand by Scribner and Rominger." However, as is the norm in politics, a compromise solution was already being discussed by intermediaries. John Thurman, aware of the USDA meeting the previous Saturday with Rich Rominger and me, hinted that a resolution involving a "co-manager type of supervision would be satisfactory." However, he wanted the staff from Huey Johnson's California Resources Agency removed from the project.

Thurman's swipe at them probably came from the turf-conscious CDFA staff, especially Dilley and Republican allies in the farm community.

The farm lobby opponents of Jerry Brown had initially backed Hallet's exaggerated claims of a disaster and attributed it to Governor Brown's delay in ordering aerial spraying. Now that it had become clear there was no disaster and hence no justification for the statewide quarantine being readied by Japan, they began frantically trying to rein her in. Over the weekend, USDA urged Japan not to quarantine California since the additional finds had been promptly sprayed, and there was no sign of further spread. USDA argued that a statewide quarantine would be unfair overreach and might set off a trade war. Hallett's inflammatory rhetoric undermined USDA's argument. Privately, the Japanese government asked USDA to impose the statewide quarantine order. Having USDA take the lead would head off the trade war talk and relieve the pressure Japanese officials were getting from their farmers. The Reagan administration resisted. Their position was that a statewide quarantine was unfair to California, a state larger than many countries. Furthermore, except for Westley, the infestation remained confined to urban neighborhoods far away from California's main farming areas. Trapping flies briefly in one commercial orchard in one corner of the huge valley simply did not warrant quarantining the entire state. USDA continued to insist that a statewide quarantine was unreasonable. USDA also pointed to the large numbers of traps placed throughout the state and the absence of any sign of infestation elsewhere.

The counteroffer to Japan was that USDA would expand the quarantine as Japan requested, but only if it was limited to the urban counties in the north, plus a large portion of Stanislaus County. Japan held firm. USDA did, too, repeatedly urging Japan to accept the more limited new quarantine as consistent with past practice. Round-the-clock negotiations continued in Washington D.C. between USDA and their Japanese agricultural counterparts, along with international trade representatives from both countries.

The tension on the project became unbearable Tuesday afternoon. Everyone could see the strain I was under. They were under it, too. We were holding our breath, not knowing where wild medflies might show up next. Would I be fired? Would Governor Brown be impeached? Would USDA take over? Would the entire state be quarantined at the peak of harvest season? How would this end?

I told the staff I needed to run an errand and to hold my calls. People understood. After slipping away from the office, I drove to the Los Gatos library, where I found a copy of the poem "IF" by Rudyard Kipling. As a teenager in high school, I had been moved by seeing Douglas Fairbanks, Jr., alone on a stage on the Ed Sullivan TV show, give a dramatic recital of the poem. The first line is: "If you can keep your head when all about you are losing theirs and blaming it on you." This perfectly captured what I and the whole staff were feeling. The poem continues with "doing that and much more" before ending with, "Yours is the Earth and everything that's in it, and—which is more— you'll be a Man, my son!"

The poem spoke to what we had faced since June, including the collapse of all we had fought for during the past six months. We had battled the medfly with honesty, integrity, and courage, values that had been my guiding star in scouting, sports, and life. Being prepared, doing my best, and keeping my head in the face of adversity was all I could ask of myself and others. It was all the public could ask of us. That afternoon at the five o'clock staff meeting, I passed out copies of the poem and told the team that no matter how things turned out, I knew we had all done our best. Then, I began the meeting.

Chapter 16 (Cooler Heads Prevail)

The domestic pressure on the Japanese government negotiators in Washington, D.C., made agreeing to USDA's limited quarantine impossible. Japan's farmers read the papers, too. So did U.S. farmers in Texas and other states. USDA's assurances that the medfly was under control and limited to the California counties already known to be infested ran counter to the dire predictions of total disaster from California farmers and state officials like Hallett. With Texas and other U.S. states urging USDA to impose a statewide quarantine, Japan's leaders could not justify to their own farmers doing any less. Japan had tens of thousands of small growers of mandarins and other medfly host crops. They faced ruin if the medfly arrived there.

Farmers in Japan had followed every detail of the medfly battle in California beginning in the summer of 1980. From the beginning, their government had requested and received a steady stream of reports and written assurances that we were succeeding. They backed that up with frequent U.S. visits by delegations of farmers and officials. One tour group after another arrived in Los Gatos all spring. Each time, they interviewed staff, met with federal officials, and toured the Central Valley by helicopter so that Rominger and USDA officials could help the Japanese appreciate the geographic immensity and diversity of California agriculture. The visitors poured over every aspect of our effort.

Yuji Kiyokawa, the commercial consul at Japan's consulate in San Francisco, regularly called me on my direct line for confirmation or clarification of every detail he read in the *San Francisco Chronicle* and other newspapers. On Monday morning, August 17th, after the tumultuous finds and overnight spraying in Livermore and Westley, Mr. Kiyokawa called me directly to go over what he was reading in the papers. I confirmed that the traps were being checked daily and that only one fly had been trapped in Westley after we sprayed, and none anywhere else in the Central Valley. I am sure he called other sources, as well, before reporting what he was hearing to Japan's negotiators in

Washington. Mr. Kiyokawa was quoted Tuesday morning in the *San Francisco Chronicle* stating, "no decision has been made yet."

Leaders in California's Ag community continued scrambling to undo the claims made earlier. They now said the medfly was not out of control after all, especially since Livermore and Westley had been promptly sprayed and no more flies were being found. Governor Brown weighed in, hinting that a Japanese overreaction could damage trade relations. Fred Herringer, the President of the California Farm Bureau, alarmed that Hallett's political campaign against Brown was doing more damage than the medfly, issued a formal statement bluntly aimed at Hallett. He wrote:

> The find (in one apricot orchard) was not unexpected, and it does not mean that the Medfly is out of control. The politics of the situation are creating much of the problem with many officeholders and seekers trying to grab headlines at the expense of our eradication efforts and at the expense of farmers by creating false fears among our trading partners.

On Tuesday morning, Governor Brown met with rural legislators over breakfast in Sacramento, promising better communication, including daily briefings, and assuring them that any new wild flies would be sprayed within 24 hours. He also telephoned Ambassador Mike Mansfield in Tokyo and sent a telegram to the Japanese Prime Minister urging Japan not to "unfairly quarantine California." Texas went to court in Dallas in an attempt to cancel the restraining order they were under. We dispatched our lawyers to keep it in place.

In Washington, Harvey Ford, on behalf of USDA, and William Clark, the deputy secretary of the State Department, continued to meet with Japanese representatives, urging restraint and requesting a final decision be delayed for two weeks. Japan refused. Late Tuesday morning, word came that a statewide embargo on shipments of medfly-host exports to Japan would begin on Wednesday, August 19th. The quarantine would bar all untreated exports of medfly host fresh fruit to Japan effective immediately, no matter where they were grown in

California. In 1980, fresh fruit exports like oranges, lemons, strawberries, and grapes from California had totaled more than 750 million dollars.

On Tuesday afternoon, in Sacramento, the makings of a political compromise between Hallett and Brown surfaced when John Thurman revealed a more significant role for USDA was under discussion. Gray Davis, on behalf of Brown, met with Hallett. Both knew a vote on impeachment would fail, but having such a vote would damage Brown. So would his acceding to a federal takeover. The compromise, originally floated by Thurman became the basis of a pull-back by Hallett. On paper, such a compromise looked reasonable. Especially since we had already agreed with USDA to make Dick Jackson the deputy director and Dr. Brazell the chair of the advisory committee, though neither change had been publicly announced. Hallett, believing Davis and Brown had agreed to co-leadership going forward in return for her withdrawing her motion, scheduled a press conference to announce an agreement had been reached and that she was calling off the impeachment hearing.

While the deal was being negotiated in Sacramento, Rominger and I were having lunch in Los Gatos. Rominger was called away from the table to take a telephone call. When he returned, he told me the call was from the Governor's office, and he had agreed that Dick Jackson and I would be "co-directors." I adamantly objected, telling Rich I would sooner resign and have Dick Jackson run the program without me than to see it compromised by an unworkable doubled-headed management structure. I reminded Rich that I had created the unitary command structure back in December to pull together a situation where state employees refused to answer to federal employees and vice versa. However, Rominger said he had already told Gray Davis yes, and Davis had told Hallett they had a deal. At that moment, she was in the middle of a press conference announcing the co-leadership deal. I refused to back down on my insistence that there be only one manager.

Something similar had occurred with the U.S. allies in WWII. Winston Churchill wanted Roosevelt, Marshall, and Eisenhower to agree that Mongomery would command all ground troops in the European theater, including the American army groups. Eisenhower flatly refused to operate under joint or divided leadership, angering both Churchill and Roosevelt. No such change occurred. Rominger agreed to call Davis back. We returned to the pay phone together and reached Davis. After Rich explained my position, Davis told him to put me on the phone. "Jerry," he said, "none of this is going to matter in the long run. All that people will remember is whether we won or lost." I said it did matter, adding, "Gray—how would Jerry Brown like to be co-governor"? That abruptly ended our conversation.

I later learned that Gray went back to Hallett in the middle of the press conference and publicly disputed her characterization of what had been agreed. He told the press I wasn't being demoted. The only change was that Rominger would be more directly involved. He went on to say that my decisions had always been subject to Rominger's approval, and I would continue to report to Rominger, as would Jackson. Hallett went ahead with a press conference and announced she was dropping the impeachment effort, leaving the new management structure unclear to the press.

In Sacramento, after the press conference, Assembly Speaker Willie Brown publicly ridiculed Hallett's impeachment effort. Later that day, Governor Brown blasted his legislative critics. That evening, in a long interview on KCBS radio in San Francisco, he repeated his concerns about pesticides and their environmental risks. Thurman tried damage control by telling the press it was a reorganization and not a shake-up. A state worker in Los Gatos requesting anonymity told a reporter that I had not been canned. "They can't 'can' Scrib," he said. "He's the only one who really knows what's going on." Arnie Morrison was the only person who ever called me Scrib. I appreciated his vote of confidence. The following day Rominger wrote a letter to Hallet stating he would be the medfly project director, consistent with his being the director of CDFA and thus of the medfly program as well. Dick Jackson's title would be deputy director. My title would be changed from project director to project manager.

On Thursday morning, August 20th, Japan sent a telegram to the White House announcing a temporary suspension of their statewide quarantine. They agreed to accept exports of produce from California, other than those from the federally quarantined counties, while the issue was studied further. This unexpected temporary pullback came about entirely because of the tenacious efforts by the Reagan administration negotiators to stave off the negative economic fallout to California's growers. After the initial curtain came down Wednesday, the negotiations continued between the U.S. Deputy Secretary of State and Japanese Ambassador Yoshio Okawara, leading to the compromise. A USDA scientific team left overnight immediately after the announcement to engage in more specific discussions with Japan's experts. California farmers breathed a huge sigh of relief. USDA and the Reagan administration came through for California. The reprieve dramatically lowered the political temperature in California, as did the new federal role in the

In Los Gatos, he press remained puzzled as to how the shuffling of chairs would work. Nor was it clear to me and Dick Jackson. On paper, it appeared USDA would be taking charge as Hallett wanted, but I would still be present on the project in some capacity reporting to Dick Jackson, the deputy director. USDA had stayed well away from the political turmoil in Sacramento. Prior to the announcement in Sacramento, the understanding had been that Dick Jackson would come aboard as the project deputy director reporting to me as Rominger and I had requested. There had been no time before Thursday morning's press conference for Rominger, Jackson, and me to discuss what, if any, change would take place. As Jackson and I sat side by side behind a table full of microphones, the press asked how the new management structure would work. Before I could answer, Dick Jackson smiled and said simply, "I report to Jerry." His answer ended any further discussion of the management turmoil and reset the program to what it had always been—a joint Federal-State cooperative effort, not a USDA takeover. To make light of the change, a staff member created a cardboard desk sign for me. It read PROJECT DIRECTOR with DIRECTOR crossed out and below that in the same sized type, "MANAGER."

The change in project management was described in the media as "State Juggles Medfly Staff." Notwithstanding Arnie Morrison's assessment that I hadn't been "canned," it was obvious that the price for Hallett dropping her impeachment motion was a substantial increase in the federal role and a quasi-demotion of me. Being a pawn in the public tug, a war between Brown and Hallet had been awkward but not as painful as the look on Rich's face when I let him down by insisting on unitary management. Governor Brown's legislative director, Diana Dooley, a close family friend, called me on August 20th to make sure I was all right. So did Rich. I appreciated their calls and support. I knew that Rich and the Governor had gone out of their way not to have me fired. I also knew keeping me in place had been key to denying Hallett and the Republicans the victory over Brown they wanted.

Gray Davis turned out to be correct. The management titles proved to be irrelevant. For the rest of the project, Dick Jackson and I worked together without a single instance of disagreement. We operated as interchangeable managers subject to Rominger's oversight. I took the lead when in Los Gatos, while Jackson, who was there seven days a week, managed the project when I wasn't. Rominger, on occasion, overruled both of us and the advisory committee as well. As the spraying became routine, I started each week in Sacramento on Monday by meeting with the directors of the divisions I supervised. Tuesday through Thursday, I lived and worked in Los Gatos. When we were both there, I usually handled the press, while Jackson managed everything else, coordinating with me as needed. We both kept Rominger advised of what we were doing. Most weeks, I returned to Sacramento on Thursday night or Friday morning then spent Friday at my office and weekends at home with family. Under Jackson's on-site leadership, the team of federal and state employees continued to work together seamlessly as one unitary organization. From August 20th until the end of the project, a year later, despite a few more wild flies turning up, California farmers felt confident eradication was only a matter of time. So did Japan's farmers.

At the end of August 1981, we suddenly faced a new round of unexpected wild fly discoveries. This time, though, the public and politicians were unfazed and confident the new finds, along with the existing ones, would soon be eliminated. A new wild medfly was trapped in Santa Cruz County on Friday, August 22nd, four miles from where the first one had been found two weeks earlier. That same day, the Sacramento lab identified two more, both of which had been trapped outside the spray boundaries. The first was in Mountain View, and the second was in the small town of Hollister in San Benito County, south of Santa Clara County. A helicopter sprayed the nine square miles around the Hollister fly that night, and we added San Benito County to the state and federal quarantine, making it the sixth northern California county subject to quarantine restrictions. More wild flies were trapped in San Jose on the 24^{th,} including one outside the spray zone. Officials in the State of Georgia promptly announced they were quarantining five additional counties near Stanislaus County. Our attorneys filed suit to block Georgia's action ending the threat.

On August 25^{th,} the advisory committee returned for a two-day meeting. Seven new members were added, bringing the total membership to 16. The new members included entomologists Dr. James Brazzel of USDA, Dr. Ken Hagen of U.C. Berkeley, and Dr. Richard Rice from U.C. Extension. The other four were non-academic members; Pat Patton, the head of the cooperative Mexico-USDA medfly program; Mickey George, a California farmer; Dick Nutter, the President of the California Agricultural Commissioners Association; and Greg Rohwer from USDA-APHIS headquarters. Dr. Brazzel was named the new Chairman, as Rominger and I had requested in our meeting with Harvey Ford on August 15th. The advisory committee's formal title was revised to Technical Advisory Committee (TAC) rather than the previous title of Technical Review Committee.

As the committee began their meeting, medflies were discovered again in Los Angeles County, and a wild medfly was trapped in downtown Oakland. A hundred thousand people lived in the nine square miles around the fly in Oakland. Eighty thousand people resided in the L.A. spray zone. Crews promptly began delivering notices of imminent aerial spraying in both cities. The following day, the committee, now fully controlled by USDA, completed its most substantive meeting ever.

Under Dr. Brazzel, the enlarged and renamed Technical Advisory Committee became the deliberative scientific advisory panel I had wanted all along. Dick Jackson and I also changed how we interacted with the committee. For this meeting, we prepared a formal three-page list of specific questions. The committee tackled them one by one. Their recommendations in response included increasing the number of traps per square mile and requiring the lure to be dyed a bright color. They also wanted the traps rebaited as often as weekly in hot areas and told us that trappers in the future needed to rotate the traps per a newly revised host list. With respect to the statewide trapping program, they wanted the training and supervision to be conducted and monitored by the project under Dick Jackson's overall supervision. They formally approved weekly Malathion spraying in commercial orchards as an alternative to fumigation, something farmers had already started doing. They specifically rejected the suggestions of various politicians to spray varying distances out from the project perimeter and alongside I-5. Instead, they called for spraying a 2.5-mile radius around a single fly find and a five-mile radius around multiple fly finds. This confirmed our existing protocol. Continuing to pull back from earlier overkill, they suggested the eighty square mile spray zone around Westley was excessive and should be substantially reduced, given that flies had been trapped only in a two-thousand-acre orchard and nowhere else in Stanislaus County. At their next meeting, they would recommend a similar reduction in the hundreds of square miles being sprayed in San Benito County in response to finding a single unmated fly in Hollister.

I could not take back my performance on August 6th but was pleased to see the committee revisiting the excesses that had occurred earlier. I was especially pleased with the committee's decision to bring back the use of sterile flies to treat the biologically sensitive Jasper Ridge area at Stanford University. For the rest of the project, the advisory committee would consistently provide solid, scientifically based advice and guidance on a broad range of issues. I was a little disappointed that one of the first things the committee changed was my open meeting policy. While I would have preferred they continue their entire meetings in public, they opted for a compromise approach under which the first part of the meeting was closed. After that, they opened the meeting to the public and reported on their recommendations and took further public input. Other public bodies in California similarly used executive sessions for some matters, followed by a public session. The new procedure by the reconstituted TAC seemed to meet everyone's needs.

In Los Angeles and Oakland, the new medfly discoveries garnered widespread press coverage. Both were sprayed within twenty-four hours, as the Governor had promised. That had now become routine, and so had the use of fixed-wing planes in the rural areas in the north. In Los Angeles, the public response was muted after the initial excitement. Their highly trained and experienced staff jumped on the new finds in a textbook counterattack as they had back on June 5th, 1980. By noon, the flies found at 10 a.m. were on a plane to Sacramento for formal identification as wild medflies. Without waiting for confirmation, inspectors began placing more traps. By the end of the first afternoon, a hundred traps had been hung in the immediate square mile around the find, and more were being deployed in the 9-square mile zone around where the first flies were found.

The County Ag Commissioner, Paul Engler, again took the lead in handling everything in Los Angeles except the aerial spraying. He also arranged radio announcements of when the spraying would take place and a promo urging residents not to take fruit out of the area. The enterprising homeowner where the flies were first trapped promptly put up a hand-lettered sign in her front yard announcing the location as a historic landmark. So many people stopped by that she soon took it down.

We managed the spraying in Los Angeles from San Jose. On the 26th, Darryl Ward, the head pilot and project manager for Evergreen, took off from San Jose, flew to Los Angeles, and sprayed the nine square miles, then flew back to the base in Hayward all in the same night. Ward called it one of the most challenging assignments of his flying career:

> We left at 3 p.m., flew down there, sprayed from 10:30 p.m. to 1:30 in the morning, and came straight back to our

group at Hayward Airport...21 hours on the job, 14 in the air—can't do that too often.

As Ward was spraying in Los Angeles, I was being interviewed by Ted Koppel on ABC's *Nightline*. I was described by a Sacramento reporter who watched the interview as "tired" and "puffy-faced ...after another fifteen-hour day that had begun warm and bright and ended in gloomy darkness with more bad news." I am sure the description fit, except that although tired, I remember feeling upbeat and optimistic. I recall admitting to Koppel that, "I do seem to be getting more blame at the moment," (however), "I think we're going to win in the end."

By Friday, the 28th of August, a total of 15 male medflies and nine maggots had been found on 14 properties in Los Angeles. All were within the spray zone. The area, located 30 miles from where the flies were discovered in June 1980, appeared to be no larger than two square blocks. However, given the road traffic patterns in and out of the area, L.A. officials made the quarantine 105 square miles and erected large signs on key roads warning against taking fruit out of the area. Because the roadblocks in the north had been dangerous, expensive to operate, and not especially effective, none were set up in Los Angeles. One official commented that if Governor Brown had sprayed earlier in the north, the medflies would not have reached Los Angeles. There was no evidence linking the new flies in the south to those in the north. The Los Angeles flies more than likely arrived the same way they probably arrived in 1975 and 1980—in fruit carried in by one of the thousands of travelers arriving daily from Hawaii, Mexico, Guatemala, or any of the many other countries coping with medflies.

On the project, morale remained high at the end of August as we transitioned to a more traditional USDA operation. Jackson and Brazzel assumed a central role in improving the detection and quarantine programs while the state staff continued to manage the aerial spraying, ground spraying, administration, and public outreach.

The last week in August was tumultuous with the expansion to Los Angeles and Oakland. Yet, a surprising and unexpected shift occurred in the project. Everything seemed saner now. I attributed the change to the successful August advisory committee meeting, the prompt response to the last few wild flies, and the day-to-day stability provided by a strong federal presence under the quiet leadership of Dick Jackson. The opponents of aerial spraying paid little attention to the August discoveries beyond the initial reports. People believed eradication was now inevitable because each of these new finds had been promptly sprayed. I had time on my hands for the first time since late June and could not resist wanting to revisit how our seeming success on the ground had failed so completely at the end of June. I remained convinced that the most logical explanation had to be an accidental release of 50,000 unsterilized fertile flies right at the time apricots, the medfly's favorite host, became plentiful and began to ripen. Others believed enough wild flies could have been breeding undetected for them to explode as they did. I knew we had released more than 5 billion sterile flies. It seemed impossible to me that this number of sterile flies could have been too few, too late, or that they had been simply not up to the task of mating with what should have been the relatively small number of wild flies surviving the winter.

After I reviewed the documentation related to the fly shipments from Peru, when they arrived, and where they were released in relation to where the first larval finds turned up, I wrote a memo concluding the release of fertile flies from Peru had been the principal cause of the outbreak. The starting point for my conclusion was the fact that irrefutable evidence existed that at least some unirradiated flies had been released. We knew that because we had caught two unirradiated yellow-dyed flies with eggs in the quadrants where the Peru flies were released. Dr. E. F. Knipling had argued persuasively on August 26th that the minimum release had to be at least 50,000 fertile flies. Further, in his view, this alone would more than explain the explosion of larvae in the quadrants where that shipment had been released. Further support for the cause being a fertile release was catching only four fertile flies anywhere on the project in June. Finally, if, as some thought, the Los Gatos identification lab had failed to identify all the wild flies being trapped, that error would have produced larvae randomly scattered throughout the project over time instead of only in the Gap and only close in time to when the Peru flies were released there. To me, there appeared to be no other reasonable explanation.

On August 31st, I released my five-page single-spaced memo addressed to Rich Rominger titled *The Cause of the 1981 Medfly Infestation*. The memo received wide play in the press. However, almost immediately, both USDA and Karen Corwin, the entomologist in charge of the CDFA ID lab in Sacramento, pushed back. Karen Corwin, whom I had great respect for, wrote a counter-memo dated September 2nd in which she suggested the two yellow-dyed Peruvian flies with eggs found in traps in the two heavily infested quadrants were alone, not conclusive. Although the pupae were irradiated in batches of 50,000, she noted that she had dissected more than 1300 additional yellow-dyed flies trapped in the same quadrants and found all of them sterile. In her view, the two fertile dyed flies could be attributable to contamination. Such contamination had occurred in shipments from other labs. She also pointed to reports in the literature of similar volatile, unsuspected outbreaks of large numbers of larvae in early summer in other places in the world. She specifically mentioned Dr. Nadel's visit in April when he said: "We should not be surprised to find our apricot crop 100% infested even though we had trapped no adult flies and discovered no larvae during the spring." She also took issue with the committee's opinion that trapping only female flies suggested the end of the infestation was near. She wrote that in Guatemala and elsewhere, trapping only females could signify one of two possibilities: either the end of an infestation or an incipient population explosion. Finally, she suggested the cause could have been a breakdown in correctly identifying all the wild flies caught during the spring. It was possible that more were caught but not recognized as such by the lab in Los Gatos.

On September 3rd, Peruvian officials denied there were any problems in their lab, pointing out that a federal official had monitored their procedures. Reporters then tracked down the federal official, Leonard Stishakoss, now working at another medfly laboratory in

Mexico. He was quoted in the *Sacramento Bee* admitting that there was a "slight possibility" that flies shipped from the Peru lab might have escaped sterilization. He went on to describe the procedure of loading canisters of pupae into the radiation chamber and then setting them aside to be dyed. He said there could have been a mix-up, but "someone would have to be pretty sleepy to do that." He mentioned the clumsiness of the one-at-a-time process of irradiating the canisters as another possibility for error. He said that if there was a brief oxygen shortage, more radiation might be needed to guarantee sterilization, especially at the ends of the canister, where the flies could get a lower dose of radiation and thus not be sterilized.

On September 4th, the *San Jose Mercury* led with a story describing the long-standing problems with the sterile flies from the Peru lab. Under the headline, "Early alarm was sounded on Peru flies." The article included an inflammatory quote in Isi Siddiqui's May 21st memo, the first sentence of which read, "A potentially explosive situation exists in the sterile Medfly shipments from Peru." The memo went on to detail a litany of problems, such as the death of 38 million sterile flies killed by poor packaging, as well as pupae arriving mixed in with other insects and foreign matter. The reference to an explosive situation was not to an accidental release of unsterilized flies but to the possibility that calling out the lab might so offend the Peruvian government that the USDA/Peru cooperative program might be ended.

A week after my memo and Karen Corwin's counter-memo, the USDA released its brief report. They admitted there probably was an accidental release of fertile flies but claimed, without evidence, that it had had only a minimal impact. Instead, they blamed the outbreak on mistakes occurring in what they described as the "state's I.D. lab" by state officials who "failed to identify the size of the problem early" and later "might have had trouble telling wild flies from sterile ones." The slanting of their report to place the blame on California disappointed me, particularly because identification problems if they occurred, would have been due to a federal scientist's decision to change the color of the dye on some of the sterile flies. In addition, the supervisor of the project's I.D. was a USDA employee.

The controversy faded because, at this point in the eradication effort, it did not matter what went wrong except perhaps to historians. The *Los Angeles Times* quoted me in an editorial in which I said, "It's our fault either way. We either goofed on Peru (by releasing the suspect shipment), or we goofed on not spraying sooner." Internally, we agreed to drop any further debate about the origin of the June blow-up. That is where it remained until further information came to light after eradication was declared.

BOOK

FIVE

FALL 1981-

DECEMBER 1982

Chapter 17 (The Beginning of the End)

By the time the advisory committee met on September 9th and 10th in Los Gatos, it was clear to everyone that the medfly would be eradicated, even though the infestation had grown to more than 1,300 square miles. The only question most residents cared about was when the spraying would end. Farmers and everyone else also wanted to know when eradication would be officially declared. The initial spray zones, now part of long corridors, had been sprayed seven times. The advisory committee had said eight applications would be required. The residents in the original zones were ready for it to be over.

At the September meeting, Dick Jackson and I presented the advisory committee with written questions requesting specific criteria for phasing down the spraying. They responded that the end date of spraying for each location would not be eight or any other set number of aerial applications. Instead, spraying would end when ground temperature data confirmed that two medfly life cycles had elapsed without any emergence of new medflies. Dr. Tassan, with computer help from John Pozzi, would deliver the temperature data gathered by the ground monitors to an advisory subcommittee headed by Director Rominger. Their recommendation for when to end treatment in specific corridors would then go to the full committee for approval. The temperature data so far meant corridors first sprayed the week of July 13th would continue to be sprayed another three to four weeks beyond the eight weeks set earlier. However, the committee, recognizing that additional new fly discoveries had changed corridors, suggested the project release those parts of corridors meeting the two life cycle criteria while continuing to treat a two-and-a-half-mile radius around any later fly finds until that area also qualified for release. These first reductions, now anticipated to occur in mid-October, would be partially offset by additions in other areas resulting from new wild finds in Alameda and San Mateo counties. The deletions and additions would require adjustments to corridor boundaries but otherwise caused no great concern.

The committee next took up the issue of how often the sprays should be applied during the approaching winter rain, fog, and cooler temperatures. They set winter applications at once every three weeks between November 15th and March 1st. The project could adjust that timing as needed based on the temperature in day-degrees in each corridor to determine the actual schedule. We had also asked for a recommendation on how often to spray new wild flies discovered during the fall; the committee suggested that new finds be sprayed at the same three-week interval until March.

In response to our request for guidance on when to end the roadblocks, the committee recommended ending them no later than mid-October. Rominger ended them on September 30th, two weeks early. By then, more than five million vehicles had been inspected, and thirteen hundred motorists had been cited for carrying fruit. The roadblocks had been dangerous, expensive to operate, and unpopular. Nevertheless, the committee defended their use, saying roadblocks had been significant in reminding the public the medfly could be spread by carry-outs of infested fruit.

The public acceptance of the need for aerial spraying did not prevent another sniper from hitting one of the helicopters spraying Santa Cruz County. The helicopter landed safely and resumed spraying after crews determined it had sustained only minor damage. Gunfire and muzzle flashes continued to be reported by pilots spraying Santa Clara County.

The aerial spraying spawned thousands of claims of auto paint damage. We referred claimants to their insurance companies and to the California State Board of Control. The Staley's company, alarmed by the number of such complaints, refused to supply more bait under their contract with USDA without a hold-harmless clause. No one could explain to me why the damage to automobiles had occurred in Florida and was occurring now in California—as far as I knew, neither Malathion nor corn syrup normally damaged paint. Later, I was told the cause was xylene, an additive mixed into the bait as a thinner. In any case, if we wanted the bait, we had no choice but to give them the requested liability protection. As had happened with the helicopter contract with Evergreen, USDA said they lacked legal authority to sign such a clause. Therefore, California again assumed the contract and provided the hold-harmless clause. By the end of the project, more than three million dollars in automobile damage claims had been filed. Where insurance companies had already paid the claims, they sued the state and me personally for reimbursement. Fortunately, the courts denied their claim on two grounds: first, my advice at a press conference in July recommending residents call their insurance companies was proper, and second, that the companies' demands for reimbursement by the state had not been timely filed.

When the advisory committee next met, on October 7th and 8th, they voted to end aerial spraying in corridors covering 400 square miles. The areas to be dropped included those we had sprayed that first week starting after midnight on July 13th, as well as portions of southern Santa Clara County and two hilly corridors, 8 and 18. On Monday, October 12th, we released new modified and renumbered corridors and announced that on November 15th, aerial spraying on an additional 937 square miles would also likely end. These reductions would leave the remaining area being sprayed over the winter at roughly 200 square miles. These remaining corridors would be Los Angeles plus and areas in the north with persistent low ground temperatures or more recent wild fly discoveries. After the advisory committee meeting in October, I slipped away for two weeks on a family vacation.

On October 22, 1981, the disaster I had hoped would never happen occurred. After midnight, blinded by fog, a spray helicopter crashed in flames into a residential neighborhood. I had returned from vacation and was home asleep in Sacramento. I awoke to hear my wife saying, "Yes, he's here," as she passed me the phone. The reporter said: "One of your medfly helicopters has crashed into a house. It's on fire.Do you have a comment"? I said I didn't, and thanked him for the call. After reaching the aerial staff and learning the location of the crash, I dressed and headed for Fremont, California. I drove in silence at first, not knowing the fate of the pilot or anything beyond the reporter's statements.

I had flown in the co-pilot's seat on a nighttime spraying mission and experienced first-hand the isolation and risk the pilots lived with night after night. The helicopters flew only a few hundred feet off the ground, over people's homes in the dead of night while watching out for power lines and other hazards. Flying at night hour after hour was dangerous and exhausting. It was made more so by the need to fly in a tight formation of as many as five other helicopters to cover each corridor. Repeated landings to refuel and reload bait spray were required, and those, too, added to the danger, as did the Bay Area's variable weather. When I had flown, the pilot and I wordlessly cataloged the family lives spread out below us. Each yard was different. One had the bicycles, swing set, and doghouse you would expect to see in the backyard of a home with young children. The next a boat or other recreational vehicle, a barbeque, a hot tub, and a pool. All experienced our clatter overhead and our uninvited viewing. All would wake up to the sticky spray covering everything. Seeing their helplessness and sacrifice, including having been required to strip their fruit and pull up their gardens, reminded me of all we had asked of them and how it must feel to worry not only about the safety of the pesticide we were spraying but the danger inherent in the low-level flights above them as well. After I landed that night, I knew the pilots, like the out-numbered fighter pilots who saved Britain in WWII, were our unsung heroes in this war. And as we neared the end, I hoped we could finish the job without the loss of a single one. It was not to be.

It was still pitch black and foggy as I came within range of the all-night Bay Area radio stations, KCBS and KGO, and learned the pilot had been killed in the crash and others on the ground had been injured and taken to hospitals. I arrived in Fremont to floodlights and the intermittent flashing red of dozens of police and fire vehicles reflecting off the wet pavement. The flames were out. Crowds of onlookers surrounded the charred house and burned-out helicopter wreckage. Arnie took me aside. Still shaken from having watched the pilot's body being pulled from the wreckage moments before I got there. He related his understanding of how the crash had occurred. It happened after the night's spraying over Livermore had been completed. The seven

242

Evergreen helicopters had lifted off from the San Jose airport to return to their base in Hayward. On the way back a fog bank rolled in off the San Francisco Bay, dropping visibility to zero. In the fog, they could not see each other or the lights below. Charles Faircloth radioed that he had lost sight of Darryl Ward, whom he had been following moments earlier. He could not see the ground. He dropped down to get below the fog to make an emergency landing. People on the ground in the residential neighborhood below reported they heard what sounded like an engine cutting in and out shortly before the crash. The tail rotor snagged a utility line, bringing the helicopter down. It exploded on impact next to a home, and the resulting fire destroyed about a quarter of the house and part of the roof. The resident, asleep on the couch, suffered minor injuries when a neighbor rushed into the house to rescue her but then fell, carrying her out.

The first responders had cleared two blocks around the crash site as a precaution in case the helicopter had been carrying Malathion. Thirteen people, including five residents, were taken to local hospitals and given precautionary treatment for Malathion poisoning. This turned out not to have been necessary as the tanks had been emptied at the airport. Police and firefighters received treatment for inhalation of fumes from the burning fuel, and one firefighter suffered a broken thumb. The other six pilots managed to land safely. One came down in a supermarket parking lot in Castro Valley, three landed at the Livermore airport, and two were able to return to San Jose and land there.

At the morning press conference, reporters wanted to know what caused the crash and whether the project planned to suspend the aerial program or switch to daytime spraying pending the National Transportation Safety Board's investigation. I told them what I knew and said we would not be suspending the spraying. I added that the pilots made all decisions related to flying safety, including whether to fly on any given night, and that fog had been something we had been working around since spraying started. As further evidence of the decision-making process, I pointed out that it had been clear in Livermore, while the Evergreen's helicopters were spraying, and clear at Moffett, where San Joaquin was based. The San Joaquin's pilots had opted not to take off and spray Oakland that night because of their concerns about fog due there later. Evergreen believed it would be clear in Livermore and San Jose, which it was, but then the fog that rolled in before they reached their base in Hayward was exceptionally dense. Something similar had happened before. Mike Stancil, San Joaquin's head pilot, had described this earlier incident to Tom Harris of the *Mercury* when Harris went up with the helicopters in September. Harris quoted Stancil as follows:

> one night...The whole valley was a blanket of fog when we headed home, and I found one little hole and dropped in under it. (my) wing mates followed in quick succession and the other helicopter team, Evergreen, converged on the same spot at the same time. That must have looked like quite a show from down below.

I had hoped we could get through the aerial spraying without a crash. Now, we had failed in that effort, too. I took little comfort in the fact that the consequences of this crash were far less than would have been the case if a large, fixed-wing plane had crashed during spraying in an urban area. The National Transportation Safety Board later concluded the primary cause of the accident had been the fog and the pilot's inability to land safely under the circumstances. During the fall and winter, we would continue to make frequent adjustments to the spraying schedule dictated by changeable weather. The pilots continued to have the final say on flying.

Following the press conference, I sat down and wrote a heartfelt note to the family of the pilot. Sadly, there had been other accidents and other deaths during the project. One employee died of a heart attack, another, suffering from stress, committed suicide in his motel room. There also had been another non-injury aircraft accident occurred on September 16th at Crows Landing. In that one, the engine on a PV-2 taking off on a fixed-wing spraying mission caught fire. Fortunately, the plane was not yet airborne. An engine and one wing burned, but no one was hurt. In October, thanks to an alert highway patrol officer, we avoided losing an agricultural inspector who was trapped standing on the tongue between a moving set of double trailers hauling tomatoes to the cannery in Modesto. The set of doubles had been halted at the agricultural inspection station on State Route 152 at Pacheco Pass. The inspector in front cleared the driver to pull out, not realizing her partner was still between the two trailers checking the backload. The driver pulled out and headed downhill at considerable speed. An alert CHP officer coming the other way uphill saw our man hanging on with one hand and waving frantically. After a brief chase, he caught the truck, rescued our inspector, and then drove him back to the inspection station.

Later in the program, Larry Russell, the USDA pilot on assignment to the medfly program, was seriously injured in a second helicopter crash. He and an instructor were on a night training flight at another northern California airport. The helicopter crashed, killing the instructor and badly injuring Russell. Like the captain of a ship, I felt responsible for the safety and well-being of everyone under my command as well as the citizens whose lives and property we damaged and disrupted. I managed the project. They happened on my watch. Fortunately, there were no more deaths.

Near the end of October, we caught three more wild flies: an unmated female in Santa Cruz County near the border with Santa Clara County and two males in the Mountain View Gap. We caught the last two on the same property on which we had trapped a wild male on August 20th. Our repeat catches in the Gap after five aerial sprays there reaffirmed the need to spray for two complete life cycles. However, by mid-November, we were optimistic eradication was just a matter of time. I reduced my time in Los Gatos to one day a week, and Dick Jackson became the on-site manager.

At about the same time, neighbors around the former Berry School had had enough of the noise caused by our two helicopters based on the school playground and the frequent coming and going of project vehicles in the surrounding residential neighborhood. The Los Gatos City Council declared the project a nuisance. Dick Jackson appeared before them and agreed that we would reduce the number of personnel at the site, move some of the vehicles, and eliminate the helicopter use at the school.

In Washington D.C., during the fall, the U.S. Senate amended the annual agriculture appropriations bill to address the funding and administration of pest eradication programs. At the request of California Senator S.I. Hayakawa, an amendment was passed empowering the Secretary of USDA to override state officials if necessary. Hayakawa did not call out Jerry Brown by name but noted that the lack of such a provision forced Secretary Block to threaten a statewide quarantine before California's governor agreed to order aerial spraying. The bill also earmarked another 50 million dollars to cover USDA's share of the hundred-million-dollar estimated cost of eradicating the medfly from California.

At the November 6th meeting, the advisory committee recommended ending spraying in all but 319 square miles in the remaining corridors. They based their decision on a combination of the absence of new fly finds, day-degree data, and winter environmental stress. Over the next week, spraying ended in all or parts of 27 cities and towns in Northern California, including Oakland, Fremont, Newark, and Union City in Alameda County; Hollister in San Benito County; Ben Lomond and Boulder Creek in Santa Cruz County; and Mountain View, Sunnyvale, Cupertino, Los Altos and Los Altos Hills plus most of San Jose in Santa Clara County. Half of the remaining area was in Livermore and Stanislaus County in the north and Los Angeles in the south. Further reductions in January would leave the total winter spray area at a little over 200 square miles. We also phased out ground spraying in most areas. The committee, however, rejected a proposal to switch to the SIT strategy in Los Angeles after the completion of the first life cycle.

The continuous monitoring of air and ground temperatures had firmly established the time required for medfly reproduction at each stage in dozens of different climatic conditions. However, many other unanswered questions remained. At a workshop held in November 1981 at the University of California in Davis, fruit fly researchers met for two days and issued three pages of recommendations for further research on everything from trap design and chemical attractants to further research on medfly behavior. In November, the Entomological Society of

America made the medfly program a central topic at their annual national convention held in San Diego.

The extensive environmental hazards assessment program that Governor Brown had ordered to be conducted during the spraying confirmed that Malathion in the air never exceeded parts per trillion. Nor did any buildup or persistence of any of the pesticides occur in the environment. All the studies concluded that the ground and aerial spraying had produced no significant disruption of the ecology. Nevertheless, the project funded $450,000 in additional biological studies to measure the extent to which the Malathion bait sprays impacted various non-target insects such as honeybees, lacewings, parasitic wasps, white flies, and aphids, and any of nine crops and two non-crop plants, Monterey pine, and laurel. The results of these studies also confirmed that the bait sprays produced no lasting adverse effects.

Toward the end of November, two strikingly different retrospectives on the project appeared in the media. On November 20th, the *San Francisco Chronicle-Examiner* published a scathing article in the Sunday edition predicting a second disastrous blow-up covering 4,000 square miles would occur in 1982. Under the headline, "Secret report: Medflies will be back stronger in '82," reporter Bill Mandel previewed an unreleased report by investigators for Republican Senator Daniel O'Keefe. Mandel relied primarily on interviews with two former employees I had removed from the project. The article preposterously claimed the secret report would show that none of the Malathion bait reached the ground during the first five applications and that Japan had never threatened or advocated a quarantine, embargo, or boycott of California produce. According to Mandel, the secret report would soon be the subject of a hearing by a special California Senate committee on legislative oversite.

Senator O'Keefe held a press conference on November 27th and followed that with a personal visit to the project. He claimed the purpose of his visit was to assist personnel from the State Controller's office who were due to arrive on the 30th to begin a preliminary audit of project expenditures. The hearing, scheduled for December 16th at O'Keefe's request, was canceled by Senator Alan Robbins, the Chairman of the Joint Legislative Oversight Committee. Nothing further came of Senator O'Keefe's posturing. Medflies did not come back stronger in 1982 nor spread to 4,000 square miles.

Before O'Keefe's November 27th press conference, Stephen Ferris, a *Fresno Bee* staff writer, wrote the first of a seven-part series of front-page stories in the *Fresno Bee*, explaining why SIT failed in northern California in 1980 and again in 1981. In the first two of his seven articles, Ferris interviewed Dr. E.F. Knipling, who told him bluntly that "in the case of the 1980 northern California Medfly outbreak, the population reached too high a level before it was discovered." Knipling further opined that there were never enough sterile flies to overflood the number of wild flies. Therefore, the 1980 project should have started with an aerial spray to bring down the population to a level where the available sterile flies could finish the job.

Knipling's views were consistent with a retrospective on why the project failed from June to December 1980, which appeared on Sunday, July 12, 1981, in the *Mercury News*. In this lengthy article titled "It's our agricultural Vietnam," Mark Saylor and Carl M. Cannon made the same case as Knipling and Ferris. They argued the infestation was too big and discovered too late to be eradicated by SIT. Their article goes on to describe a Vietnam-like unwillingness on the part of California management to recognize the failure in the making. "Looking back…the first and fundamental mistake was failing to recognize the fly had [already] become widespread and entrenched" when discovered.

In addition to Knipling, Ferris interviewed others, including Dr. Gilstrap from Texas. Gilstrap clarified his position on SIT, admitting that he did not dispute that it had worked on "some islands" and in L.A. However, he argued it was not an established eradication strategy as "there had been insufficient research data to guarantee it (worked)."

Bob Roberson, the Plant Industry division chief at CDFA during 1980, told Ferris that he agreed with Knipling's observation that the state lacked the number of sterile flies needed, but he defended the use of SIT since it had worked in L.A. in 1975. Roberson noted that Dr. Knipling's suggestion to reduce the wild flies to a level manageable with SIT assumed this was a viable option. Roberson said, "Obviously, [the] aerial spray would have been difficult to sell in June 1980." Finally, entomologist Don Henry, thrown into the battle in late June, told Ferris, "I think if there's a lesson I learned, it's not to try to bring in sterile flies until you know the size of the area you're dealing with."

In the third article, which appeared on November 24th, Ferris asked Don Dilley, the chair of the advisory committee, about the decisions they had made that may have contributed to the medfly program's failure. Don Dilley candidly admitted he had no medfly experience and that the USDA scientists, Dr. Cunningham and Dr. Ozaki, were "the real brains of the outfit." However, he defended the advisory committee's decisions not to recommend aerial spraying in October and November 1980 when USDA had urged it. Dilley said, "the weather was too cold, and the flies were in the larval stage." He also defended the committee's decision not to recommend aerial spraying in April 1981 when the number of wild flies caught had exceeded the criteria because he said, "there was yet no evidence to indicate that they were part of a spring breeding population." The remaining four articles reprised the public's fear of Malathion, the Governor's two-day flip-flop on permitting the spraying, and the political fallout in August. Ferris concluded the series by expressing optimism that we would eradicate the medfly in 1982, now that aerial spraying was winding down. I found all the articles accurate and consistent with what I knew about the June to December 1980 failure of SIT and broadly on target with one significant omission. In my view, the strategic failure was the failure in July to recognize the threat in San Jose had become far greater than the one in Los Angeles. The one person who seemed to recognize that San Jose, not Los Angeles, was the four-alarm fire was Karen Corwin in the lab. On June 19th, 1980, she opened the San Jose package that had been shipped in early June to discover two fertile medflies had been trapped there in a single trap. Yet, all the emphasis remained on the South. If Santa Clara County, even as late as June 20th, had been flooded with trappers putting out more traps as was occurring at the same time in Los Angeles, and if the program in the north had been run with the same vigor and quality as the one in the south, the results with SIT might have been different despite the initial failure to identify the first trapped flies more promptly. None of the articles addressed why SIT failed again in 1981 when, after winter, there were presumably fewer wild flies and more sterile ones, plus the addition of fruit stripping and ground spraying.

The answer to that came in a remarkable Ph.D. thesis by Dr. Hilary Lorraine at U.C. Berkeley, published in 1984. Dr. Lorraine was present for much of the project and conducted extensive interviews with project personnel during and after it ended. She documented an appalling number of fundamental errors in implementing SIT in the north in 1980 that continued in 1981. Dr. Knipling was more correct than he had even realized. He assumed the number of sterile flies released was too small for the size of the infestation. However, there was an even bigger problem. Later mating studies done in Hawaii in 1983 showed the bulk of the sterile flies we released were less competitive in mating with wild females than the sterile males used in Los Angeles in 1976 and 1980. Most of the sterile flies released in the north came from the Mexican lab in Metapa. They were noticeably smaller than the sterile flies reared in the USDA and State labs in Hawaii. Whether size alone explained their reduced competitiveness or some other unknown factor mattered less in Dr. Lorraine's analysis than the project's failure to recognize that mating was failing in both 1980 and 1981.

Dr. Lorraine further showed that the failure to recognize that the SIT was not working was due to a series of other errors. The first was the project's failure to create a usable list of medfly finds by date and address. Had we done that, as repeatedly recommended by Dr. Cunningham in 1980, the project would have quickly recognized that wild flies were being repeatedly caught on the same properties where they had been caught earlier despite the release of sterile flies on and around those same properties. In 1981, this pattern continued. Finding the first fly caught in 1981 on a property where fertile flies had been caught in 1980 should have been a blinking red light that SIT had not been working in 1981. Doing more, including stripping fruit and ground spraying, would not change the outcome if sterile flies were not mating with wild ones.

The second major error was a breakdown in the protocol by which flies caught in traps were sorted to identify the occasional fertile fly in a trap full of sterile flies. The lab process called for punching the heads of each fly under a black light to be sure the dye was present inside the head. This procedure was surreptitiously abandoned by the head-punching staff as early as September 1980. Their reason was that the process was so tedious that the volume of sterile flies brought in for sorting overwhelmed them. They defaulted to a visual hand sort of colored vs. wild flies except when a supervisor or outsider appeared. Only flies lacking any color were punched, and not all of them. This eyeball sorting became even more unreliable after the technical advisory committee approved a change in the dye color identifying sterile flies reared in the USDA lab in Hawaii. In the summer of 1980, these pupae arrived dyed a vibrant cobalt blue. Based on a hypothetical concern that the blue dye on sterile flies could rub off on an undyed fertile fly in the same trap, one of the USDA scientific members on the advisory committee recommended a switch in dye from blue to green. Thereafter, it became impossible for the ID lab personnel to reliably recognize by vision alone a green-dyed sterile fly from the naturally green hue of a wild medfly.

The errors being made in the project's ID lab went completely undiscovered until July 8th, 1981. In a touch of irony, all the advisory committee members and Rominger and I were in Governor Brown's office in Sacramento when the secret test results were tallied by the two people who conducted it. Gary Agosta, the trapping supervisor, in cooperation with a federal scientist on the project, clipped the wings of 100 sterile flies and placed them in groups of ten in traps sent to the ID lab. After the sort, they asked to see the written report on each trap sort. Less than 10% of the wild flies sorted in the ID lab at the project were being accurately identified as such. I did not learn of the test or the results until I read Hillary Lorraine's thesis. However, the July 8th results were privately shared with USDA officials. The lab supervisor throughout the project was a USDA employee. The undisclosed (at least to me at the time) test results were the basis for USDA's September 1981 hypothesis that errors in the identification lab had been the primary cause of the blow-up, not the release of unsterilized flies from Peru.

The test also explained why no adult male wild flies were detected during the spring emergence. They were being caught. Perhaps even in large numbers. But the male flies, both sterile and fertile, were smaller than females, and most of the flies being caught—tens of thousands a day—were expected to be sterile. Therefore, the technicians in their visual hand sort first pushed the smaller flies aside, counting them as sterile. The larger females, both wild and sterile, were eyeballed, and those that lacked dye or were questionable were sent to Sacramento for dissection. Since most turned out to be sterile or unmated, the assumption was the I.D. lab was working as intended.

Looking back, the errors in the ID lab could and should have been caught in the fall of 1980. But, nearly every aspect of the project in the north was under-resourced from the beginning. The repeated catches of wild flies in the same locations should also have led to a recognition that SIT was not working in Santa Clara like it was in Los Angeles. The errors could have been caught as late as the spring of 1981 had I listened to Cherryl Denny, the manager of the rearing and quality control lab on the project. She warned me privately that the I.D. lab might not be up to par. She also expressed concerns to me about the mating effectiveness of the Mexican sterile flies, and Isi Siddiqui warned me the Peru lab's deliveries were of poor quality. The failure to conduct the secret quality control test on the identification lab earlier was an obvious management failure. I knew what the protocol was supposed to be, and despite not being an entomologist, I should have recognized that punching the heads of 90,000 flies a day was physically impossible with the limited staff of technicians in the lab.

I didn't because, from the beginning, I resisted looking for signs of failure. In January, I committed whole-heartedly to the new ground program as an all-or-nothing gamble, a long shot that would either work or we would have to go to aerial spraying. Those who claimed the medflies would not survive winter in the north were either right, or they weren't. I believed that winter dieback would give us a second chance to succeed with SIT, especially with help in the form of ground spraying. Beyond that, the sterile flies were the backstop to everything we were doing. I recognized we were flying blind, given that the medfly was an elusive insect in a new environment. It was a high-stakes poker game. I believed winter, plus ground spraying, gave us a strong hand despite not knowing where and in what numbers the enemy was. From January to June, I was loathe to tinker with what had worked twice in Los Angeles.

By May, the spring emergence had been mostly good news, but we were at the point where the number of wild flies caught in different locations had technically been met. Yet, the opposition to aerial spraying remained fierce. What I feared most and believed was entirely possible in May and June was an inconclusive situation where we had tripped the criteria with a minimal number of flies or larvae. That would leave agriculture and the public again polarized between whether aerial spraying was required or believing that continuing the ground program could finish the job. I feared in this situation we would likely face the legal argument that an environmental assessment was needed before any aerial spraying could take place. Accelerating the planning for aerial spraying in May would strengthen the legal challenges already filed. Suggesting there were more wild flies being caught than the ID lab was identifying would have frightened both agriculture and the public opposed to aerial spraying. I decided not to do either but to ride it out and hope for the best. I deliberately ignored Cherryl Denny's warning, telling myself that my job was to keep the project moving forward and leave the entomology and management of the ID lab to the experts on the project and the advisory committee. If we failed, I hoped the failure would be clear and unambiguous and so obvious to everyone that there could be no argument this time that we had to do what Florida and Texas had safely done. We simply could not let a foreign insect ruin California.

Chapter 18 (Mission to Japan)

At their meeting on January 12-13, 1982, the advisory committee suggested aerial spraying in Los Angeles every 14 days instead of weekly and reducing the area to be sprayed to a 1.5-mile radius around infested properties. However, Rominger rejected any change. Spraying in Los Angeles would continue weekly until April 28, 1982. By that date, aerial spraying had taken place in California for a total of 43 weeks.

I never imagined that aerial spraying would continue this long, especially after the August 1981 data showed most flies died after two weeks of spraying and with two exceptions within six weeks. Trapping a wild medfly in October after five weeks of spraying and another one in November on a property sprayed six times reminded us again of how little we could be sure of with respect to medfly behavior in the cool micro-climates still considered infested. Nevertheless, it appeared to me all but certain that California's medflies had been eradicated by the end of 1981. All known infested areas in the state had been sprayed six or more times. The one fly, trapped in November, had arguably survived six sprays. However, this find was very suspicious, and it was believed that it and several other flies had been planted. A subsequent investigation was inconclusive, and therefore, because the fly had been trapped in a cold, foggy corridor, that area would continue to be sprayed for another six months to complete two full life cycles of spraying.

By late February, California's farmers and shippers had had enough. Led by the President of the Western Growers Association, they began pressing for an early end to Japan's quarantine restrictions. At their request, Rich Rominger, on behalf of CDFA, and Floyd Mori, California's Director of the Office of International Trade, wrote to the U.S. Ambassador to Japan, Mike Mansfield, requesting his assistance in facilitating a visit to Japan by a California delegation of state officials, legislators, and farmers. The trip's purpose would be to present arguments for why it was time for the Japanese government to end its restrictions on exports from California. Led by Rominger, the team visited Japan the week of March 13-20. California presented its case in a series of meetings with Japanese officials, farm organizations, and newspaper editors. The case rested on the fact that since November, no fertile flies had been detected anywhere in California despite intensive statewide trapping, and at least one life cycle would have been completed in all the infested areas, including Los Angeles, by April 1982. Under these circumstances, California argued it would be unfair to delay the lifting of sanctions until another two life cycles of monitoring had occurred. This would put off official eradication until mid-September, meaning the Japanese quarantine would impact another entire growing season. The Japanese responded by agreeing to send a delegation of experts from their Ministry of Agriculture, Forestry and Fisheries (MAFF) to California in April. They would evaluate firsthand the progress that had been made.

On March 21, 1982, *the San Francisco Examiner* published a front-page story on the backlog of $28 million in claims against the State of California related to the eradication effort. None had been paid. The total of 11,706 claims was "the largest ever for a single program and more than the state normally received in a year for all state operations combined." Almost all the claims were for automobile paint damage. These totaled $9.4 million. The other $19 million were exaggerated claims of health impairments like nausea and headaches caused by the malathion. All the claims were now at the State Board of Control for processing.

Beginning in January, CDFA met with the Attorney General's Office, Department of Finance, and Board of Control. In June, legislation was signed appropriating 4 million dollars to pay medfly claims approved by the Board. Reimbursement for automobile paint damage was limited to the lesser of $689 or 20% of the car's value. I was a named defendant in some of the personal health injury claims and testified both in court and in depositions for years following the end of the project. To the best of my knowledge, none of the claims of personal health injuries from the malathion spraying were found to be meritorious or successful at trial.

In early April, as they had in November, the San Francisco Examiner published another lengthy article on the medfly. They described it as an "incredible revenant." And predicted that "No one in the state Medfly Eradication Project will be surprised to see [it in 1982]." We did not expect to see it in 1982, nor did the Japanese. Their four-member team arrived on April 6th. They reviewed all program activities in Los Gatos in depth before joining USDA and CDFA officials on a helicopter tour of California's major agricultural producing areas. They visited in person the citrus groves in Ventura County, where most of the lemons exported to Japan were grown, and met with officials in Los Angeles to review the program there. At the end of their California tour, the team flew to Washington, D.C., for further negotiations with USDA. Though pleased with the tour and what they saw, Japan's official position remained a preference for waiting until all spraying had been completed and, ideally, until the official final eradication announcement.

Meanwhile, on April 15, 1982, Dr. David Discher, M.D. sent Governor Brown the 23-page comprehensive report of the special medical advisory committee that Brown had ordered established on July 11, 1981. The Blue Ribbon, a community-based committee, evaluated every health complaint received during the project. In addition, to address potential future health impacts, the committee had arranged for California's birth defects monitoring program to compare future birth defects in the counties where spraying occurred against unsprayed counties. The San Francisco Bay Area cancer registry agreed to similarly expand their normal review to compare cancer incidence over time in the sprayed versus unsprayed counties. The committee also recommended a special in-depth study to see if there was any increased fetal wastage in the spray area.

The April 15, 1982, report concluded that:

"The Medfly eradication project has been conducted with exemplary regard for the protection of public health. Medically diagnosed instances of health effects have been very few, and these all appear to be cases of non-disabling or temporarily disabling hypersensitivity reaction, not of malathion poisoning. About 150 instances of injury have been claimed. These have not been validated by timely medical observation".

All three post-report studies were funded, completed, and later published with negative results. Those of us on the project had naively believed this sort of data would put to rest health fears related to aerial spraying. This proved to be wishful thinking. When the next medfly aerial spraying program took place in 1989, again in Los Angeles, opponents raised all the same arguments about unknown environmental risks and human health risks made by opponents in 1980-82. The 1989 program was as controversial as ours had been. and would lead to major changes in how to fight future infestations in California.

After we completed the second life cycle of aerial spraying in L.A. on April 28th, the Japanese suggested they would welcome a return visit to Tokyo by U.S. and California officials to continue the discussions. On April 26th Rominger wrote again to Ambassador Mike Mansfield requesting he arrange visits in Japan by California officials for mid-May. Rich indicated he and I would attend for California and Greg Rohwer and Harvey Ford for USDA. Rich closed the letter by stating: "Our purpose is to assist in reestablishing as soon as possible good feelings and good trading relationships between California, the U.S., and Japan as we get the Medfly issue behind us." On May 19th, Rominger and I left for Japan via Honolulu. Ford and Rohwer joined us in Hawaii for three days of intense meetings with the current and former Directors of Agriculture for the State of Hawaii. The meetings included our staff at the rearing laboratory and entomologists doing research for us at the University of Hawaii. We also met with airport management and representatives of the major airlines at the Honolulu airport to discuss tightening quarantine inspection there and baggage inspection on arrival in California.

As our plane circled to land at Narita outside Tokyo, I was overcome by a flood of memories from my time in Japan 22 years earlier. While I lived there as a senior in high school, I climbed Mount Fujiyama, now visible out the plane's window. I also traveled by train as an Explorer Scout to the south of Japan to attend an all-Asia Scout jamboree. In 1960, at age 17, I graduated from high school in Tachikawa, a Tokyo suburb, and said goodbye to my family and Japan to fly to the U.S. and enter college in Florida. I could never have predicted the changes in my life in the more than 20 years since then, nor that I would now be returning to Japan as a deputy director of California's Department of Food and Agriculture.

Our hosts took us by bullet train two hours south of Tokyo to tour an important Japanese mandarin orange and strawberry farming district in Shizuoka Prefecture. We had meetings during the other days, followed each evening by elaborate ceremonial Japanese dinners, complete with toasts to our success. The Japanese officials made it clear from the outset that they were satisfied the medfly no longer presented a danger to their farmers and further that it was time to resume normal trade relations. One free afternoon I visited Tokyo's Ginza district and bought gifts to take home. Then I took the same train between Tokyo and Tachikawa I had ridden years before. Although the train was familiar, I barely recognized Tachikawa. The main gate to what had been an American Air Force base was still there, but now it was a Japanese self-defense force installation.

Upon returning home, we were able to declare the medfly eradicated from Los Angeles, Stanislaus, and San Benito Counties and to eliminate the quarantines in those counties effective June 1st. Japan responded by eliminating special import requirements on medfly hosts from all of California except those remaining in Northern California counties still being treated.

On June 11th, the advisory committee met. Dick Jackson reported to the advisory committee that no new Medfly life stages had been recovered since November 1981, despite more than 100,000 traps deployed throughout the state. The committee recommended all spraying in the remaining corridors end within three weeks. They also recommended that the trapping be scaled back to five traps per square mile in urban and high-risk rural areas. This was a return to the standard in 1980 in Los Angeles and other high-risk Southern California counties. With respect to the rest of the state, on July 1st, the standard would be lowered to one trap per square mile outside a one-hundred-mile radius of the Northern California program area. A month later, the same standard of one trap per square mile would be phased in within the project area in the north and become permanent with the onset of winter. This standard in the north reflected that the cooler weather on which the original studies (since replicated) were based had been mostly correct. Ironically, after spending 100 million dollars eradicating a medfly infestation where scientists said there would never be one, we had come full circle, with the prevailing scientific wisdom again stating that a viable medfly infestation was highly unlikely in Northern California.

Unfortunately, our fight wasn't quite over. On June 24th, 1982, almost a year to the day from when the first larvae appeared in June 1981, a male medfly was trapped in Stockton, California, 30 miles north of Westley. The area was sprayed within 24 hours. The quick reaction recalled what had happened in San Benito County at the height of the panic over finds around the edges the previous summer. There, we sprayed hundreds of square miles for weeks before the advisory committee eventually cut the spray zone down to the immediate area of the fly find. No other flies were ever found in San Benito County. Now, with the single fly in Stockton, we should have first done more trapping to see if an infestation truly existed. Instead, we pounced by setting up a quarantine and commencing spraying. Three days after the first bait spray in Stockton, USDA announced a complete review had concluded the fly was not a carryout from the infestation 30 miles away but more probably a possible new introduction. Nevertheless, the spraying continued for eight weeks, ending on August 12th. No more flies were ever trapped in Stockton. At the advisory committee meeting on July 13-14, the committee voted to recommend that in the future, the response to a single fly should be limited to more extensive trapping. Treatment should take place only if warranted by finding more flies or larvae. To legitimize our immediate jump on the fly in Stockton, the committee retroactively supplied a fig leaf of approval by noting the decision to spray was based on it being "close to previous satellite infestations and in [a] major farming area."

The Stockton fly, however, turned out not to be the last trapped wild medfly of the 1980-82 program. On July 21st, 1982, another wild fly was discovered in a peach tree in Los Angeles. This time, consistent with the advisory committee recommendation, we did not immediately spray it. Instead, we put out fifty traps in the immediate area and adopted a wait-and-see approach to see if any treatment was called for. No more flies were caught. The Stockton spraying ended in mid-August. By that time, aerial spraying in California had spanned a total of 55 weeks from July 14, 1981, to August 12, 1982. The Stockton and Los Angeles medflies were the only wild medflies found anywhere in California in 1982. The completion of aerial spraying in Stockton finally ended a program that lasted more than two full years and, at its peak, had employed 4,000 people. Less than 300 employees remained in August 1982. Two-thirds of these were laid off or returned to their civil service positions. The rest stayed to monitor the required trapping of the uncompleted final life cycles and to close the facility.

On September 21st, the advisory committee held its final meeting in Los Gatos, after which we held a press conference to declare the medfly had been eradicated. That night, we celebrated at a party in the same local Los Gatos hotel where Rominger and I had called Gray Davis at lunch a year earlier, at the height of the crisis. It was finally over except for decommissioning the school, inventorying and storing accumulated equipment and vehicles, and preparing detailed reports to the legislature on the program expenditures. The expenditures totaled 100 million dollars, split approximately equally between California and USDA.

In November, Governor Brown was defeated in the U.S. Senate race against Pete Wilson. As there are in all elections, there were multiple reasons people voted the way they did. Medfly was not the only or even the most important reason Brown failed to win the Senate race. But, as my father would say, it didn't help. In November 1982, Governor Brown readily acknowledged the uphill fight he was facing in the following excerpt from a pre-election interview:

I believe there is a negative residue of the controversies and problems I had running for president last time—the skepticism, derision, and controversy that came out of that—the fighting with the legislature a couple of years ago, the Medfly. These are not so much substantive issues as just a negative impact that has been left.

The history of California and the United States might have been much different if Brown had been elected to the U.S. Senate in 1982 instead of Pete Wilson. Wilson would serve in the Senate until 1991 as California's 36th Governor from 1991 until 1999. Had Brown, in July 1981, disappointed his supporters in the Bay area and reluctantly approved the overwhelmingly unpopular aerial spraying as unavoidable, necessary, and environmentally safe, it might not have changed the outcome in November 1982. Like politicians everywhere, he was a captive of events over which he had little control.

In early December 1982, Dick Jackson and I made a joint presentation at the Annual Meeting of the Entomological Society of America in Toronto, Canada. I went first and compared our experience to that of Columbus on his first voyage, noting that he did not know where he was going or where he had been when he got back. We could say that at least we knew where we had been. We covered the political and entomological challenges we overcame in successfully eradicating the medfly from a new environment, covering 44 cities in eight counties inhabited by over two million residents fearful of pesticides.

Later that month in Sacramento, after a warm send-off at the department's going away party for Rich Rominger and his deputy directors, we each formally submitted our letters of resignation to make way for the new appointments of the incoming Republican Governor, Attorney General George Deukmejian, who had been elected Governor in November.

Epilogue

After losing his race for the U.S. Senate in November, Jerry Brown's first two terms as Governor ended in December 1982. Agriculture's vendetta continued in 1984. With the help of pro-law enforcement conservatives, Republicans funded a successful campaign that ended the judicial careers of Chief Justice Rose Bird and two other liberal Brown appointees on the California Supreme Court. Governor George Deukmejian then appointed three conservatives to take their place, dramatically altering the previous liberal cast of the court.

After a hiatus from politics, Brown returned in 1989 to head the Democratic Party in California. In 1998, he was elected mayor of the City of Oakland and re-elected in 2002. In 2006, he became California's 31st Attorney General, and in 2010, he returned to the Governor's office for a third term. He was re-elected for a fourth term in 2014. His commitment to the environment and better government never wavered.

In January 1983, I opened a general law practice in Sacramento. When asked about my practice, I told friends I hoped to specialize in "paying clients." For the first few years, though, I had time to take on many pro-bono and court-appointed cases and time to teach a course on "Legislative Policy Making" as a visiting lecturer at the Graduate School of Policy at the University of California in Berkeley. Beginning in 2000, I became a registered lobbyist with a Sacramento legislative advocacy firm whose clients included multiple Southern California public entities plus two unions and a variety of business clients. I also continued to handle a few legal cases for the firm. In 2009, I retired.

Then, in January 2011, after Jerry Brown was elected Governor again, I returned to government service. In June 2011, at the request of Secretary Diana Dooley, the Governor appointed me to be the general counsel of the California Health and Human Services Agency. I retired again at the end of September 2015. In April 2018, my replacement at the Agency left, and Secretary Dooley asked me to return and serve again as general counsel until January 1919, the end of Brown's 4th term as Governor. I have been retired since.

Rich Rominger left government service at the end of 1982 and returned to the family farm. Ten years later, in 1993, newly elected President Bill Clinton appointed Rominger as the Undersecretary at USDA. Rich and his wife Evelyne moved to Washington, D.C., and Rich served with distinction for all eight years of the Clinton administration. My wife Penny and I remained personal friends with Rich and Evelyne and Diana and her husband Dan through the years. We visited the Romingers in Washington, at their farm in Winters, California, and at the Dooley's in Sacramento. The Romingers and Dooleys attended our 50th anniversary; Both couples attended the Romngers 50th, and Penny and I attended their 60th. Rich died at 93 on December 21st, 2020, a few days short of what would have been Rich and Evelyne's 70th anniversary. Jerry Brown and I were among those asked to speak briefly at the Celebration of Life held later.

Before the ceremony, Governor Brown and I briefly revisited our experience with the medfly. I told the Governor I believed he acted primarily on his personal conviction that, if it could be avoided, spraying an urban population with a pesticide was unacceptable. He insisted it came down to more of a political decision than one about pesticides. I persisted, including changing the subject several times. At one point, I mentioned to him that we had both attended Berkeley, had both been involved with civil rights, and had been at the same San Quentin death penalty vigil when Aaron Mitchell was executed. When we returned to his motivation for not spraying, he said, "Politics is simply who gets the most votes, and repeated that his supporters in the Bay Area were united in their opposition, which was true. I then offered that my biggest regret was that both Rich and I had failed to impress upon him more forcefully the fact that USDA was poised to impose the quarantine if he balked, as they said they would, and did. Brown nodded in agreement that we could have made that clearer. He then repeated that his decision was based on political calculation, adding that it was the wrong decision.

Later, when he spoke, he focused his brief remarks to a small audience of mostly local farm families and lifelong Rominger friends and family on a humorous and self-deprecating admission that he had been wrong on the medfly. He recounted how when he first ran for

Governor, his support of farm workers and the environment had left him few friends in agriculture. He said Rich Rominger had supported him when almost no one else in agriculture did. On the medfly, he said, "I should have listened to Rich," who I always liked. Instead, he said, "I listened to the wrong people."

When I got up to speak, I turned toward Evelyne and spoke of how her warmth and wit, along with Rich's kindness, had meant so much to our family. I recounted the many times we had visited the farm, where Rich and their son Charlie had helped me load hay for our horses while Evelyne fixed us lunch. I ended my remarks with a horseback rider expression, noting that Rich and Charlie (who died earlier of cancer) "had ridden on ahead, and we would all catch up with them later."

After 1982, I believed the medfly would continue to be a problem, but in the future, the fear of spraying a small amount of malathion to eliminate it would be less controversial. I was wrong about the Malathion, but I was correct in predicting the medfly would return repeatedly. Entomologists believe it is either continuously present at a low level or continuously introduced. Since 1982, there have been multiple emergency medfly eradication programs in the state. Two were again in the Santa Clara Valley in 1989-90 and 2007. Medflies were eradicated again in Los Angeles in 2023 and are present again in 2024.

Aerial Malathion spraying remains controversial. In September 1999, Mayor Rudy Guiliani of New York City stood before a battery of TV cameras and radio reporters trying to calm the public outcry over fears of Malathion being sprayed by a helicopter over parts of the city to end a mosquito-borne encephalitis outbreak that was killing people. At the time he spoke, three people had died, and 65 new cases were being investigated, one of which became a fourth death. He said the spraying to kill the mosquitoes was necessary to prevent more deaths and called for calm, saying, "There is absolutely no danger to anyone from this spray." Dr. Roger Nasci, a research entomologist at the Federal Centers for Disease Control and Prevention, also spoke. According to the *New York Times*, Dr. Nasci said, "To put new fears into the public eye when they're unwarranted, I feel is inappropriate. This is a very safe chemical with a very good track record." As happened in California, neither the press nor the public believed Malathion was a "very safe chemical." Radio call-in shows were overwhelmed by callers more concerned about the Malathion than the encephalitis that might kill them. According to one of the show's producers quoted in the *Times* article, the callers wanted information they could trust. "They don't feel they're being told the truth of the long-term effects of Malathion."

California recognized in 1996 that frequent aerial spraying and SIT programs were unsustainable. Instead, California instituted a new program known as the Preventative Release Program (Medfly PRP), which aims to prevent new infestations in the Los Angeles basin by continuously releasing sterilized male medflies in parts of four Southern California counties, Los Angeles, Riverside, San Bernardino, and Orange. The program includes a sterile fly-rearing facility in Los Alamitos that raises the sterile flies. So far, this approach has worked. Sterile flies remain the treatment of choice, where outbreaks of medfly and other destructive fruit flies occur.

Nationally and internationally, USDA and researchers around the world, including at the IAEA in Vienna, are continuing to support and improve medfly control and eradication using an Integrated Pest Management (IPM) approach. The components of this approach include quarantines, high-density trapping, host larval surveys, chemical control with bait sprays, and biological control, including the sterile male technique. Multiple detailed Environmental Impact Statements (EIS) have been prepared by APHIS since 1984, including EIS1 in 2001, EIS2 in 2008, and an EIS in 2016 (Los Angeles).

Mediterranean Fruit Fly.

Medflies spread out
of Africa to Europe.

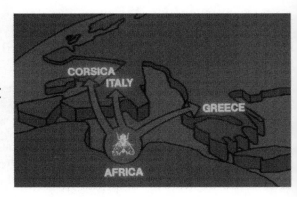

Medflies invaded Hawaii, Which is still infested.
Then appeared repeatedly in Florida, Texas,
and California.

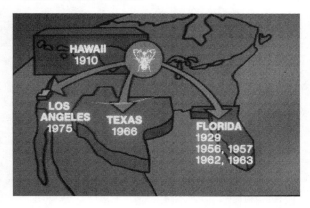

Ovipositor used by females to puncture the skin of hosts and deposit eggs. The punctures allow in pathogens, causing rot.

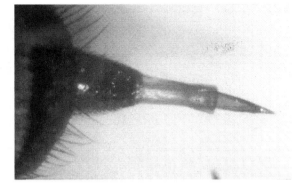

Apricot with medfly larvae (maggots).

After a few days, the larvae drop to the ground to pupate and emerge as a new generation of egg-laying adults.

In 1956, aerially spraying Malathion mixed with fly bait is used for the first time to eradicate medflies in Miami and elsewhere in Florida. No human health problems are reported.

In 1966, aerially spraying Malathion bait was used successfully in Brownsville, Texas, to end an infestation of medflies there.

In 1975, the first ever Medfly infestation in California. Release of Sterile flies used instead of aerial spraying. A new approach called the Sterile Fly Technique (SIT). Millions of sterilized medflies are released by ground and air to mate with the invaders, producing only sterile offspring and ending further reproduction.

In June 1980, wild medflies were trapped again in Los Angeles and in Northern California in San Jose.

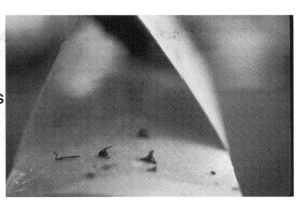

Los Angeles declared eradicated

by December of 1980

Medflies not expected to survive winter in cool weather in the north.

By December in San Jose, the infested area had grown to be 100 square miles of suburbia.

Aerial Malathion bait spraying was proposed but blocked by local government entities.
Spraying postponed.

The legislature urges a new manager at the highest level to be assigned to take charge of the eradication project and find a new way to eradicate the flies.

Fruit Stripping
Quarantine
Ground Spraying
Sterile Flies

A new plan was proposed, including Fruit stripping, Ground Spraying, and more sterile flies.

On December 24, 1980, Governor Brown issues a Declaration of Emergency, ordering the National Guard, Cal Trans, CCC, and other agencies into the battle against the Medfly.

National Guardsmen begin arriving to provide support services to hundreds of other state employees, including members of the California Conservation Corps (CCC).

National Guard Truck with ladders for fruit stipping.

The first 400 members of the
California Conservation Corps arrive.

CCC members
stripping fruit.

photo byJerry Clark

CCC members are housed at the Santa Clara County
Fair Exhibit Hall. Food and Laundry Services are
provided by the National Guard.

Employees go door to door with notices of mandatory stripping of fruit to be followed by ground spraying.

Core infested area of 50 square miles defined.

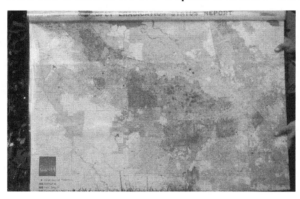

Residents in the entire 100 square mile area help in the fruit removal campaign by stripping their yards and trees and bagging fruit.

Twelve cities appoint stripping coordinators.

One of many
citizen helpers.

One hundred spraying rigs follow stripping crews.
68,000 yards are sprayed six times.

Sterile flies ready to be released by ground trucks.

Fleet of ground sterile fly release trucks loaded and dispatched daily.

Additional flies released by air.

> "The major health problem . . . . . .
> is the possibility of excessive
> wide spread anxiety and
> over-reaction based upon fear
> and lack of appropriate information"
>
> Santa Clara County Medical Society
> Maurice Rappaport M.D.
> President

Medfly becomes a national story as other states and countries push for aerial spraying.

Texas and 10 other southern states block trucks carrying fruits and vegetables from anywhere in California. Federal Courts intervene to end blockades.

Debate rages all spring over fear of aerial spraying of Malathion.
Some doctors claim aerial spraying will

cause severe health consequences. State and County Health Departments say anxiety is the biggest problem.

A new Sterile fly-rearing laboratory inHawaii producing 100 million sterile flies a week comes online in April.

Few wild flies are caught in May and June.
Then suddenly on June 26, homeowners begin calling in complaining of "worms" in the apricots.

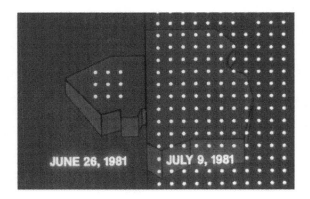

JUNE 26, 1981   JULY 9, 1981

By the first week of July, dozens of properties are reporting infested fruit. Aerial Spraying is now the only way to stop the flies.

California Director of Food and Agriculture Richard Rominger and Deputy Director Jerry Scribner confer prior to meeting with Governor Jerry Brown to recommend aerial spraying.

July 7th, 1981: The Advisory committee meets at the Berry School to discuss aerial spraying. 600-800 residents attend. All strongly opposed.

Press coverage of the meeting.

Governor Brown orders a new massive ground spraying and stripping program instead of aerial spraying.

California National Guard mobilized again.

National Guard erects tent city to house CCC on grounds of Agnews State Hospital.

In July 1981, CHP Freeway Roadblocks and inspections were established on all major freeways.

photo byJerry Clark

photo byJerry Clark

Inspections operate 24 hours a day for 3 months until mid-September.

Fruit seized.

On July 10th, Governor Brown orders helicopters to begin aerial spraying at midnight beginning on July 13th after a federal threat to quarantine all California fruit and vegetable shipments unless spraying is ordered.

Local communities deny the use of airports, spraying gets off to a slow start the first week

By the end of week one of spraying: two contractors are each using six helicopters a night.

Hilly areas are sprayed in daylight.

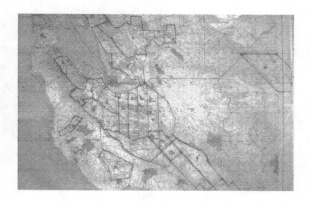

Helicopters spray long corridors up to 10 or more times.

Beginning in mid-August 1981 until the end of the project, Dick Jackson and the author acted as interchangeable managers of the Medfly project under Rich Rominger, the Director.

photo by author

In October 1981, the author and family were able to get away for two weeks on a Panama Canal vacation cruise, during which they won the passenger costume party posing as Mediterranean Fruit flies.

By the end of November 1981 aerial spraying has been completed in most areas of Northern California.

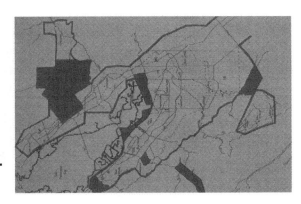

photo courtesy Japan MAFF

In May 1982, the author and Rich Rominger traveled to Tokyo, Japan, with federal officials to formalize the Japanese agreement to end their restrictions on California fruit exports.

In September 1982, the Medfly was officially declared eradicated. We celebrated with champagne in Los Gatos.

photo byJerry Clark

The 1980-82 Medfly Eradication Project spanned eight counties in California. Before it ended, 44 cities had been sprayed with

Malathion bait multiple times over a period of 13 months.

Wild Medflies have been trapped every year in California since 1982, and there have been multiple infestations requiring eradication. However, since the 1990's, California has maintained a program of continuous sterile Medfly releases in vulnerable southern California. This strategy has worked to end the cycle of Medfly detections, necessitating expensive and unpopular eradication programs. California and the rest of the continental U.S. remain Medfly free. Hawaii continues to be infested.

ACKNOWLEDGMENTS

I could not have written this book without the help and support of more people than I can thank. Before, during, and after the project, and in writing this book, my wife, Penny, has been my biggest supporter. It would never have been started or completed without her insistence the story be told.

Mara Wildfeuer, Don Henry, Rich Rominger, and Ken Malovos reviewed drafts as did my sister, Jeanne Domuret. Verla Vierra's editing suggestions and proofreading were invaluable.

Rich Rominger, was an extraordinary human being. He saw strengths in me I did not know I had. His vision, kindness, and patience were admired by everyone. Working for him and the friendship with Evelyne and the Rominger family enriched my life far beyond the medfly battle.

The men and women who fought the medfly were as devoted to me as I was to them. Before, during, and after the 1980-82 battle, they continued to serve California Agriculture with distinction. I miss those who have since died, including Dick Jackson, whose outstanding leadership from the time he joined the project to its successful conclusion was the highlight of his exceptional career with USDA. We would not have eradicated the medfly without his expertise and that of other federal scientists and employees, including Dr. Roy Cunningham, Dr. James Brazzel, Charles Overmiller, Wayne Granberry, Gordon Tween, Ed Stubbs, Scot Campbell, Haywood Cox, Shannon Wilson, Roger Pollard, and especially Harvey Ford, and USDA Secretary John Block.

CDFA management staff who shared this incredible journey include Dick Knoll, Norma Cox, Mimi Khan, Betty Taylor, and Donna Bardaro in Sacramento and in Los Gatos, Jean Walker, Marilyn Bonin, Tom Palmer, Marci Breisacher, Rich Hammond, and his staff from the Resources Agency. Arnie Morrison, Don Bowman, and Hans Van Nes were tireless and indispensable, leading the aerial program with help from Marie Balboni. Richard Steffen, George Farnham, Roger Blake,

Annie Zeller, and Jackie Montague-Wynne were outstanding in public relations. Gina Kaklikian and her team in the phone bank kept the public and media informed night and day. Cherryl Denny, Russ Stanland, and Karen Corwin worked around the clock in fly identification from the beginning until the end of the program. Others in Sacramento included George Buxton, Ron Oshima, Olaf Leifson, and Rex Magee. Dr. Robert Dowell coordinated medfly research projects during and for many years after the 1980-82 battle. Deputy Attorneys General Charlie Getz, Greg Wilkerson, and Rod Walston in the Attorney General's Office won every case up to and including those in the California and U.S. Supreme Courts and U.S. District Courts from Texas to Florida. Joe Barnett, Assistant Chief of the California Highway Patrol, and Bob Graham at Cal Trans were with us every step of the way. Dr. Richard Jackson and Dr. Jim Stratton at the Department of Health were invaluable help. Remembering these and many other employees who helped win the battle kept me writing. This story is theirs, too.

I also want to acknowledge and thank Don Henry, Dr. Isi Siddiqui, Gary Agosta, Jim Rudig, Dr. Peter Kurtz, and Pat Minyard, who each contributed invaluable insight and support during the project and after it by meeting with me and being interviewed for the book. Both Dr. Siddiqui and Don Henry went on to distinguished careers at CDFA, heading the Division of Plant Industry. Dr. Siddiqui was the U.S. Foreign Trade Representative in Washington, D.C.

I owe a particular debt to Dr. Hillary Lorraine. Her PhD thesis and interviews during and after the project, combined with her masterful analysis of the interplay of politics, personalities, and science, supplied much of the missing information that explains why the project failed in 1980 and 81. I relied heavily on her work in reconstructing and understanding the events around me at the time.

Finally, as is evident in the NOTES, this story has been preserved by the exceptional writing of the dozens of reporters who covered the Medfly project day by day. I remember them all with great fondness. We shared a unique experience as they covered the inside and outside of a drama with all the elements of a mystery and war, the outcome of which hung in the balance for more than a year. Tom Harris of the *San Jose Mercury* did an excellent job covering the science. He flew with the helicopter pilots and praised the men and women of the CCC for their work in support of the environment. Sam Chu Lin, a legendary television reporter who lived in the area during the medfly battle, did several long pieces that aired on KRON TV, including one on the medfly pilots with whom he flew. His piece captured not only their skill and dedication but the loneliness of being away from family in what was, in every sense of the word, a war. Over a dozen reporters covered the Medfly project for the *San Jose Mercury's* morning and afternoon editions. Bernard Bauer was with me at the secret airfield. I remember Ed Pope and Steve Johnson and the others who covered innumerable press briefings. I may have bristled at some of Rick Carroll's articles in the *Chronicle*, but he, like the other reporters, recorded history with unflinching professionalism and a commitment to accuracy that I admired. I will be forever grateful to Susan Sward at the *San Francisco Chronicle* and John Johnson at the *Sacramento Bee,* each of whom wrote compassionately and honestly about the political turmoil and stress I was under. Tracy Wood of the *Los Angeles Times* lived at the project for weeks at a time and provided excellent on-the-ground reporting for the *Times* as well as insightful inside background on the project in her interview with Hillary Lorraine.

NOTES

Chapter 1. (The Medfly and Malathion)

1. CDFA's Mediterranean Fruit Fly FACT SHEET, 10/23/08
2. "1000 eggs in her lifetime of 60 days" Hagen, K.S., W.W. Allen, and R.L. Tassan, "Mediterranean fruit fly: The worst may be yet to come," *California Agriculture*, 1981, 35:5-7 at page 5.
3. Mediterranean Fruit Fly, Ceratitis Capitata (Wiedemann) (Insecta: Diptera: Tephritidae. University of Florida Extension. Original publication date July 2001. EENY-2141.
4. "the Med fruit fly will be on the islands as long as they are above water." Henry Weinland, *The Flying Invaders*, Naturegraph Publishers, 25-26
5. "Sixty-eight cases of pears" *San Francisco Examiner*, January 6, 1912
6. It makes little difference what Marcuse & Co. think" Ibid
7. "It has been found impossible thus far, to legally prohibit passengers from carrying with them on their voyage delicacies in the nature of fruits," Weinland, *Invaders*, 31
8. G.G. Rohwer, *The Mediterranean Fruit Fly in Florida—Past, Present, and Future*, presented at the 40th Annual Meeting of the Florida Entomological Society, September 11, 1957
8. 1929, "The Saga of the Mediterranean Fruit Fly, Part 1": 1929-1950 Posted 3-19-2013
9. Ed L. Ayers, "The Two Medfly Eradications Programs in Florida" *Florida Agricultural Experiment Station Journal* Serie No. 680
10. Florida medfly fight in 1956, Al Messerschmidt, "How Florida beat the Medfly," *San Jose Mercury*, July 13, 1981, A1,4
11. How Florida Erased Medfly, by Carolyn Susman Special to The *Chronicle*, July 14, 1981
12. A Florida homeowner in Miami reported worms in his grapefruit. Florida medfly fight

13. 29 Counties: The Saga of the Mediterranean Fruit Fly, Part II: 1950 to Present, Fla. *Dept of Agriculture* March 26, 2013
14. The second major group of insecticides, Rachel Carson, *Silent Spring*, Fortieth Anniversary Edition, published in 2002, by Houghton Mifflin Company, page 28
15. Malathion's "alleged safety." Rachel Carson, Silent Spring, 30-31
16. John Johnson, "Continental US Has Repulsed Medfly So Far." The *Sacramento Bee*, July 10, 1981, A3
17. Mississippi, Miriam Pawel, *The Browns of California*, Bloomsbury Publishing, 154
18. Free Speech Movement, Mario Savio Pawel, 158-161
19. Fellow Legislators praise Departing Senator Beilenson
20. San Quentin, Pawel, 215
21. Miles Corwin, "Last Man Executed in California: Furor Over Mitchell Case Resounds 18 Years Later*,"* *Los Angeles Times*, 8/23/1985
22. Miles Corwin, "Jerry Scribner, the activist who became a target," *San Jose Mercury*, July 24, 1981, A6
23. Jerry Brown, Tom Hayden "The Mystic and the Machine," *Rolling Stone Magazine*, Dec. 19, 1974
.
Chapter 2. (Chief Counsel to Deputy Director of Agriculture)

1. Rominger is "a high-class individual," Al Pryor, interview with Paul Ames," The State of California vs. Agriculture." *California Farmer*, August 12, 1978, p56-59
2. "Scribner was our problem in Rose Bird's Office," Ibid,
3. Rominger. "The Quiet Man," Bert Clinkston, *California Business*, April 1977, PP 36-51

Chapter 3 (Medflies in Los Angeles and San Jose)

1. *TRC Minutes*, November 20, 1980
2. N. E. Messenger, and R.E. Flitters, "Effect of Variable Temperature Environments on Egg Development of Three Species of Fruit Flies," *Annals of the Entomological Society of America*, Volume 52, Issue 2, 1 March 1959, Pages 191–204, https://doi.org/10.1093/aesa/52.2.191,

3. Hillary Lorraine, "The California 1980 Medfly Crisis: An Analysis of Uncertainty Management under Conditions of Non-routine Problem Solving, Ph.D." *Thesis* University of California. Nov. 1984, 29

4. Frank Sweeney, and Susan Youchum, "Fruit fly spraying plan may end up in court," *San Jose News,* December 3, 1980, A1

5. "All things considered, there doesn't seem to be a persuasive scientific case for spraying now." 'Editorial,' "Let Sleeping Fruit Flies Lie" *San Jose Mercury* December 4, 1980, p.

6. "We can't live with it," Ibid.

7. Biological control strategies had been tried in Hawaii as early as 1915, Weinland, p. 50

7. Carey, James R., "The Mediterranean fruit fly in California: Taking Stock," (Biological control not eradication) *California Agriculture,* January-February 1992, p, 13-

8. Kenneth S. Hagen, William W. Allen, Richard L. Tassan, "Mediterranean fruit fly: The worst may be yet to come," *California Agriculture,* March-April 1981

9. Bill Workman, "Santa Clara Fly Spray Postponed," *San Francisco Chronicle,* December 11, 1981

10. Fagan seeks help from Thurman, Dennis E. Raglin, *Rain of Controversy: The 1981 California Medfly Crisis,* Student paper for a class at the Center for California Studies, *California State University,* Sacramento May 1996

11. Beverlee A. Myers, *Memorandum, Health Hazard Assessment of Aerial Application of Malathion in Santa Clara County,* December 16, 1980

Chapter 4 (A Christmas Surprise)

1. On Eisenhower's judgment of Bradley and Patton, see: Stephen E. Ambrose, *Supreme Commander: The War Years of Dwight D. Eisenhower.* DOUBLEDAY & COMPANY, Garden City New York, 1970, page 189

2. Michael Doyle and David Strauss, *How to Make Meetings Work,* Playboy Paperbacks, publisher, 1976,

3. *State Work Plan*, (U.C. Davis, Special Collections Library. Richard Rominger papers)

4. "At this point, we do believe a declaration of emergency would assist us," Gary E. Swan, "Medfly emergency declaration urged," *San Jose Mercury*, December 23, 1981, Page 1B

5. "a grave situation... that could ruin state agriculture." Swan, "Medfly Emergency"

6. "every means at your disposal—including the National Guard," Gary E. Swan, "S.J. wants   National Guard to fight fruit flies," *San Jose Mercury*, December 24, 1980, page A1,8

7. "We're talking about a $12 billion-dollar industry," Swan, S.J wants National Guard

8. "hysterical" and "spineless," Editorial *California Farmer*, January 17, 1981

9. Governor Brown's *Proclamation of a State of Emergency* (Author's files)

10. John Spalding and Bob Schmidt, "Brown issues fruit fly state of emergency," *San Jose News*, December 24, 1981, Page A1

11. Rick Carroll, "The Secret Report on Fruit Flies," *San Francisco Chronicle*, December 24, 1981, Page A1

12."moved too slowly..." Carroll, "Secret Report."

13. three-car funeral, Peter Schrag, "The California Fruit Fly Wars," *The Nation*, October 10, 1981, 339

14. "It never should have gotten this bad as it is," Carroll, "Secret Report."

15. "Brown mobilizes fruit fly SWAT team", *Sacramento Union News Service*, December 25, 1980

16. "State to tackle fruit flies" *San Francisco Examiner* December 25, 1981, A1.

17. "Brown orders 1,000 workers to fight fruit fly," *Oakland Tribune*, December 25, 1981, A1.

18.. Rick Carroll, "Brown Declares an Emergency Over Fruit Flies" *San Francisco Chronicle*, December 25, 1981, A1.

Chapter 5. (The Medfly Technical Advisory Committee Meeting)

1. Eisenhower and unity of command. See Stephen E. Ambrose, *Supreme Commander: The War Years of Dwight D. Eisenhower*. DOUBLEDAY & COMPANY, Garden City, New York, 1970, pages 162-163

2. Hilary Lorraine, "The California 1980 Medfly Crisis: An Analysis of Uncertainty Management under Conditions of Non-routine Problem Solving," *Ph.D. Thesis* University of California. Nov. 1984, Pages 40-44

3. Steve Johnson," SWAT teams' open fruit fly war next week, *San Jose Mercury News*," December 31, 1980, p. 4A

4. "20 square miles wouldn't be enough," Steve Johnson, "Troops readied for fruit fly war," San Jose Mercury, December 31, 1980.

5. *Minutes* of Technical Review Committee, December 30, 1980

BOOK TWO   JANUARY – JUNE 1981

Chapter 6 (The First Month)

1. Gary E. Swan, "Fruit-fly campaign underway," *San Jose Mercury*, January 5, 1981, page B1

2. "We're not going to be the Gestapo," Ibid

3. "to employ every appropriate means at our disposal," Cari Beauchamp, (Press Secretary), Governor Brown's Press Release, 1-5-81 (Scribner Files)

4. "YOUR HELP IS NEEDED", Full Page Notice, *San Jose Mercury,* January 5, 1981, B8

5. Mark Saylor and Gary E. Swan, "Tree-Stripping starts today," *San Jose Mercury*, January 6, 1981, A1

6.. Mary Jo Moss, Photo, "State workers help National Guardsmen unload cots for Fruit-Fly fighters," Ibid

7.. "Governor Brown watches area fly war," *San Jose News*, January 6, 1981, A1, back page

8. "They have battled raging floods," CCC in its element: offbeat work," Tom Harris, Environment Writer, *San Jose Mercury*, January 6, 1981, A1, back page

9. "Battling the Medfly Logo, Saylor, and Swan, "Tree Stripping."

10.. The experts behind the fruit-fly war, Mark Saylor, *San Jose Mercury*, January 6, 1981, page 3B

11. Editorial, "Join the Medfly War," *San Jose Mercury*, January 6, 1981, page 6B

12. Rick Carroll, "Fruit-Fly Drive Moving Slowly", *San Francisco Chronicle*, January 8, 1981

13. YOUR HELP IS NEEDED, *San Jose Mercury*, January 9, 1981, page D10

14. "we have done everything possible to eradicate the medfly." Ed Pope, "400 added to Medfly task force, *San Jose Mercury News*, January 10, 1981, page A1.

15. Poucher identifies medfly larvae in California Laural, Ed Pope," New problems emerge in assault on fruit fly," *San Jose Mercury News*, January 1981, page B1

16. "People working doggone hard," Charles Overmiller, *Medfly Project Chronology*, page 48

17. "No, no, a thousand times no." Susan Yoachum, *San Jose Mercury*, February 6, 1981,
"We are repaying California for the privilege of living here." Ibid.

18. "You have exceeded our expectations." *Peninsula Time Tribune*, January 23, 1981, B13

19. Ed Pope, "Glowing report on Medfly fight," *San Jose News*, January 23, 2981, B1

20. "I don't care about you," Gary E. Swan, "No one has ever called B.T. Collins Subtle," *San Jose Mercury*, February 6, 1981, B1.

21. "Is this any way to run a railroad," Gary E. Swan, "Medfly chief explains how pesticide was found ineffective," *San Jose Mercury*, February 4, 1981, B3

22. "Useless Spray deplored by medfly project chief." Ibid

23. "If it were killing the medfly, we'd still be using it." Swan, "Medfly chief explains."

24. Senator Okeefe. Bob Schmidt, "Medfly fight officials asked to explain choice of pesticides," *San Jose News*, February 4, 1981, B4

25. "chances are excellent there never will be a need to aerial spray with the pesticide Malathion," "Editorial," *San Jose Mercury*, February 10, 1981, B6

26. Contingency plans, Susan Yoachum, "Contingency Plans proceed for aerial medfly spraying," *San Jose Mercury*, February 10, 1981. 1A
27. "We cannot lock the door and throw away the key." Ibid

Chapter 7 (My Mother is Hospitalized)

1.. *Memo on Criteria for Recommending the Aerial Application of Malathion Bait Spray*. Author's files
2. Letter from Governor Brown (Author's files)

Chapter 8 (Cautiously Optimistic)

1. "a suit," Roderick E. Walston, "The Great Medfly War: A short Memoir on the Legal Battle," *Stanford Lawyer* Fall/Winter 1981, P 13
2. Richard D. Hall, "California Asks High Court to Ban Texas Quarantine", *Sacramento Bee*, February 25th, 1981.
3. "The program is going well." Armando Acuna, Conditions set down for aerial fruit-fly spraying" *San Jose News*, February 20, 1981, page B1.
4. Senator O'Keefe. Chuck Buxton, "Fruit fly probe stalled, Sen. Dan O'Keefe bows to farm interests' fears," *San Jose Mercury*, March 3, 1981, A1
5. Cari Beauchamp, "Press Release #55," A Copy of Governor Brown's letter to Attorney General Deukmejian requesting his assistance in obtaining a judicial determination that the Texas quarantine proposed for March 1 was legally unjustified. February 19, 1981.
6. aerial spraying would pose a "life-threatening risk," Bernard Bauer, "Malathion threatens hundreds, doctors warn," *San Jose Mercury, March 8, 1981, A1*
7. "nonsense and absolutely naïve,", Ibid."
8. "Kahn is all wet." Bauer, "Malathion threatens hundreds."
9. Malathion quote, "Unfounded fear of spraying," "Editorial," *San Jose Mercury*, March 11, 1981
10. Full Page Ad, "YOUR HELP IS NEEDED," *San Jose Mercury*, January 5, 1981, B8

11. Full Page Ad "Report To The South Bay Community On The Progress of The Mediterranean Fruit Fly Eradication Project, *San Jose Mercury*, March 15, 1981, page A9

12. TO KILL A MEDFLY, George Farnham, The *Daily Medfly*, February 13, 1981

13. "WILD FLY FOUND," George Farnham, The *Daily Medfly*, March 18, 1981

14. "dumping an estimated 80 tons," "D-Day Approached in the War on Fruit Flies," Rick Carroll*, San Francisco Chronicle*, April 22, 1981, A4

15 "Malathion is 'recognized as a nerve poison,' Ibid,

16. "probably...an exercise in futility." "Editorial," *San Jose Mercury*, April 7

17. "To be concerned," "Editorial," Ibid

18. "Judge Evades Medfly Spray Issue." Rick Carroll, *San Francisco Chronicle*, April 11, 1981

19. "California Gets Flies from New Oahu Lab", Harry Whitten, Star-bulletin Writer, *Honolulu Star-Bulletin,* April 17, 1981, B-4

20. Preliminary Injunction denied, and suit dismissed. John Paulding, "Judge refuses injunction against aerial spraying," *San Jose Mercury* April 28, 1981, 1B

21. "Nothing is less important than the score at Halftime," Linda Goldston, "Project Chief rates battle as 'total failure', "*San Jose Mercury*, July 14, 1981, page 5A.

22. Dr. Nadel of the IEAE visits the project and attends the TRC meeting, Charles Overmiller, "Medfly Project Chronology", page 61, *Minutes of the TRC meeting,* April 23, 1981

23. Korean War, Hampton Sides, *On Desperate Ground*, pages 134-135, Anchor Books, NY

24. Helicopters, *Gypsy Moth Report*. Marjory A. Hoy [Marjorie A. Hoy, Associate Professor, Department of Entomological Sciences, and Associate Entomologist in the Experiment Station, University of California, Berkeley] *California Agriculture* July 1982 page 4-6

25. Tracy Wood, "Medfly War Opens New Frontiers in Pest Control," *Los Angeles Times*, September 28, 1981

26. See Operating on Tiny Carcasses" by John Balzar, *San Francisco Chronicle*, April 22, 1981), A4.

27. Technical Review Committee recommends continued ground program, Charles Overmiller, *Medfly Project Chronology,* April 23, 1981, Page 62-62.

28. Bruce Keppel, "Medfly Infestation Appears to be on Verge of Ending," *Los Angeles Times*, April 26, 1981, A3,22

29. "cautiously optimistic," *Oakland Tribune*, April 28, 1981,

30. Armando Acuna, County on verge of medfly victory, *San Jose Mercury*, May 27, 1981, A1,20

31. War against Medfly Appears Successful," Walt Wiley, *Sacramento Bee, June 2, 1981,*

32. "Likeable Yet Detested, *Sacramento Bee*

33. Editorial, "Medfly: The Good Fight," *Sacramento Bee*, June 20, 1981

34. Quotes by Shannon Wilson of USDA, Harry Jaffee, "Lack of male Medflies has the experts stumped," *Sun Star, (Merced, CA)*, June 24, 1981.

BOOK THREE - JULY 1981

Chapter 9 (Aerial Spraying Becomes Unavoidable)

1. Leigh Weimers "One speck of evidence and fame flies away," *San Jose Mercury*, July 8, 1981,

2. Tom Harris, "Maggot find reactivates medfly fight," *San Jose News*, June 27, 1981, Page A1

Medfly Maggot Discovery Spawns New Concerns, *Sacramento Bee*, June 28, 1981, A8

3. "Aerial spraying a step closer" Tom Harris, *San Jose Mercury*, July 1, 1981, page A1

4. "Does seem like an emergency," Tom Harris, *San Jose Mercury*, July 3, 1981, page A1,16

5. "It's a very significant possibility." John Johnson, "Medfly Invasion Area Expanded," *Sacramento Bee*, July 1, 1981, A1,24

6. Press Release #81-110 Jerry Scribner's testimony before the Senate and Assembly Rural Caucus on July 1, 1981, regarding aerial spraying

including a four-page attachment titled "Health Information for the Public Relative to Aerial Application of Malathion Bait"

7. "a substantial possibility," Harris, "Medfly spraying chances are good", *San Jose News*, July 1, 1981, A1

8. "We simply must succeed in our eradication, and we must succeed now." Tom Harris and John Spalding, "State gearing up to spray medfly, Target date of July 13 is set after more larvae discovered," *San Jose News*, July 1, 1981, Page A1

9. Rick Dower and John Flinn, "State Sues to allow aerial Medfly Spraying," *San Francisco Examiner*," July 2, 1981

10. "I'm afraid it is uncontrollable…now," Tom Harris and Chuck Buxton, *San Jose News*, July 2, 1981, Page B1,4

11. "At stake may be the economic viability of our largest industry," Harris, July 2,

12. John Johnson, "Aerial Spraying is Only Way to Halt Medfly, Official Says" *Sacramento Bee*, July 4, 1981, Page 1

13. Chris Thompson, *Sacramento Union* July 2nd.

14. "I know what it took just to mobilize the 2,000 people," Tom Harris, "Medflies spread north," *San Jose Mercury*, July 4, 1981

15. Eisenhower quote, Stephen E. Ambrose, *Supreme Commander: The War Years of Dwight D. Eisenhower*. Doubleday & Company, Garden City New York, 1970, page 418

16. John Johnson, "Aerial Spraying Is Only Way to Halt Medfly, Official Says," *Sacramento Bee*, July 3, 1981, A1

17. "easy choice, "John Johnson, *Sacramento Bee, July 1st*

18. "health effects," John Johnson, *Sacramento Bee*

19. "does seem like an emergency." Tom Harris, *San Jose Mercury*, July 3, 1981, page A1,16

20. Jerry Scribner, *"Remarks" to City Councils*, July 6, 1981

21. Susan Sward, "Roadside Sale Ban in Medfly War" *San Francisco Chronicle*

22. "Even pregnant women," Tom Harris, State closes all fruit stands in medfly fight, *San Jose Mercury*, July 6, 1981, B1

23. "Do I look like a fruit fly"? "Bernard Bauer, "Citizens lash out at medfly review panel," *San Jose Mercury*, July 8, 1981, Page A1,16

24. "Don't spray on me." John Johnson, "Emotions Heat Up as Brown Nears Medfly Decision" *Sacramento Bee*, July 8, 1981, Page A,6

25. "Stop the Cancer Mist," Bauer, "Citizens lash out…"

26. "Better Med than Dead," "They Said Thalidomide Was Safe," Ellen Goodwin, "Aerial spraying proposal draws praise and blasts," *San Jose News*, July 8, 1981, page 8A

27. "holocaust," Bauer, "Citizens lash out."

28. "We must and will fight you in court," Goodwin, "Aerial spraying,"

29. "what does it do to a baby's skin?" Goodwin, "Aerial spraying"

30. May 6th speech, "Outline and Text of my remarks to the Mountain View City Council, July 6th, 1981.

31. Governor's secret planning, Steven Capps, "Brown's hectic fight against aerial spraying," *San Francisco Examiner*, July 12, 1981

32. "The state is simply in a position where it has no choice." Tom Harris," Brown delays a decision by medfly panel," *San Jose Mercury* Wednesday, July 8, 1981, page A1,16

33. "If the State doesn't opt for spraying," John Spalding," Brown gets deadline on aerial spraying," *San Jose News*, Wednesday, July 8, 1981, A1.

34. *"Editorial," San Jose Mercury*, "Aerial Spraying: Not Yet" July 8, 1981, page 8B

35. "pharmacologists," Editorial, Ibid

36. Abby Cohn and George Estrada, "Some may evacuate to avoid spray," *Oakland Tribune* July 12, 1981

37. Tom Harris, "Brown delays a decision by medfly panel", *San Jose Mercury*, July 8, 1981, page A1

38. "The Medfly Technical Review Committee unanimously recommends," *TRC Minutes* July 7, 1981, Charles Overmiller, *Chronology of Events*, July 1980-September 1982, Page 76

38. Governor Brown turns down the unanimous recommendation," Jackie Montague-Wynne, The Daily Medfly, July 8, 1981

39. "There are human beings out there." "Brown Bars Aerial Medfly Spraying" *Sacramento Bee* July 9, 1981, A-1.

40 1.'I believe ground application would work, if we have the kind of cooperation, I think we're going to get,' Chris Thompson Business

Writer "Brown rejects aerial fly spray" *Sacramento Union*. page A 1 and A-2.

42. "a hero's welcome from local officials hailing his decision." Steve Wiegand, "Big Land Campaign Instead", *San Francisco Chronicle* July 9, 1981.

43. "hearty congratulations," Steve Wiegand, Ibid

44. "A courageous action," Steve Wiegand, Ibid

45. "Are we a self-governing people," Steve Wiegand, Ibid

46. "Decision is Roundly Criticized." John Johnson, "Brown Bars Aerial Medfly Spraying," *The Sacramento Bee*, July 9, 1981, A1,14

47. "playing Russian roulette" Chris Thomson, "Brown rejects aerial fly spray" The *Sacramento Union*, July 9, 1981, A1,2.

48. Jim Dufer "Senate Vote Defies Spraying Decision; Assembly May Act," *Sacramento Bee*, July 9, 1981.

49. "We're talking about an insect that is a threat to the food supply," Johnson, "Brown Bars Aerial."

50. "the most crass (sic) political move," Johnson, "Brown Bars Aerial"

51. Tom Harris, "All-out attack launched today" *San Jose Mercury News*, July 9, 1981, A1

52. Cartoon, Lou Grant, "WAITER, there's A FLY In My Soup!" *Oakland Tribune*, 7-21-1981

53. Cartoon of Brown crouching in a tent-shaped Medfly trap hanging in a tree, Dennis Renault, *Sacramento Bee*,

54. Larry Liebert, "Medfly—Brown's Toughest Decision," *San Francisco Chronicle*, July 8, 1981

55. "terrible and very disquieting," John Spaulding and Ellen Goodman, "Federal government 'forced his hand.'" *San Jose News*, July 10, 1981

56. "A federal go-ahead for spraying," Ibid

Chapter 10 (Brown Orders Aerial Spraying)

1. Headline, "MEDFLY CRISIS—THE FULL STORY," *San Francisco Chronicle* July 10, 1981, page 1

2. Rick Carroll, "Huge Battle Begins –New Calls for Aerial Spraying", *San Francisco Chronicle*, July 10, 1981, A1,4.

3. Photo of ground spray personnel, Fred Larson, *San Francisco Chronicle*, July 10, 1981, A1

4. John Johnson, "State Produce Faces New US Quarantine," *Sacramento Bee*, July 10, 1981, A1,24.

5. John D. Cox, "Quarantine Would Peril Economy," *Sacramento Bee,* July 10, 1981, A1,24

6. David Perlman, "The Medical Debate Over Malathion's Effects," *San Francisco Chronicle*, July 10, 1981, A1, 20

7. "We've got two infestations" Rick Carroll, "Huge Battle Begins" *San Francisco Chronicle*, July 10, 1981, A1,4

8. "Photo of pickets with signs reading," "We oppose "Death from the Sky" and "Malathion from the Air is Chemical War," *Sacramento Bee,* July 11, 1981. A3

9. "My God, they've got guards everywhere." John D. Cox, "Special Security Alerted in Medfly Program, Sacramento Bee, *Sacramento Bee*, July 11, 1981, A3"

10. John Johnson and Richard D. Hall, "Angry Brown Orders Spraying, Governor's Medfly Stand Yields to Federal Pressure," *Sacramento Bee*, July 11, 1981, A1, 12.

11. Richard O'Reilly, "Brown Bows to U.S. on Aerial Spraying. Governor Says Action Was Forced on Him by Threat of Quarantine", *Los Angeles Times*, July 11, 1981

12. "Some of my pregnant friends are leaving," Steve Johnson, "Spraying Areas Chosen today 36-hour warning guaranteed by project chief", *San Jose Mercury News*, July 11, 1981, A1

13. H.C. Reza, "Road checks Seize 5,000 Pounds of Produce," *San Francisco Chronicle*, July 10, 1981, A 3.

14. Photo, Eric Luse, "The Commander," *San Francisco Chronicle*, July 10, 1981, A3

15. Jim Dufer, "Assembly Meets in Crisis but Flies Away in Minutes," *Sacramento Bee*, July 11, 1981, A3.

16. Tom Harris, "The agony of medfly choice," *San Jose Mercury*, July 10, 1981, Page 1,6A

17. Carol Benfell, "Easy Answers don't exist over spraying," *Tribune*, July 13, 1981

18. Steven Capps, "Brown's hectic fight against aerial spraying," *San Francisco Examiner*, July 12, 1981

19. John Spalding, "Preliminary plan being developed if aerial medfly spraying is needed," *San Jose News,* April 30, 1981

20. Gypsy Moth Program, CDFA, *Final Report on 1977 Gypsy Moth Eradication*

21. Tracy Wood, "Medfly War Opens New Frontiers in Pest Control," *Los Angeles Times*, September 28, 1981

22."The quarantine would require a massive fumigation program," John Johnson, "State Produce Faces New U.S. Quarantine," *Sacramento Bee*, July 10, 1981, Page A1,24

23."The action of the Reagan administration in threatening a quarantine is sabotage," John Spalding and Ellen Goodwin, "Federal Government 'forced his hand'," *San Jose Mercury News*, July 10, 1981, A1

24. "this critically important decision," Tom Harris, "All-Out attack launched today," *San Jose Mercury News*, July 9 Page A1.

25. "Subjecting that many people, including pregnant women," Harris, "All-Out attack"

26. "Brown's decision." Harris, "All-Out attack"

27. "It was more of a deep, personal thing for him." Harris, "All-Out attack"

28. Robert Van Den Bosch, *The Pesticide Conspiracy*, Anchor Books, Doubleday, Garden City, New York, 1980 (Paperback)

29. Brown "Not impressed, Ronald W. Powell, "Medfly Swarmed into Political Arenas," *Sacramento Bee*, April 4, 1982, A8

30. "Wherever the trucks are, we're going to be there," Leah Halper, "Aerial-spraying opponents vow to disrupt program," *San Jose Mercury*, July 13, 1981, A4

31. "malathion-laden helicopters," Bernard Bauer," Unused highway will be base for the malathion Helicopters", *San Jose Mercury News*, July 11, 1981, A3

32. "he didn't want people to be storming Moffett Field," Bauer, "Unused highway"

33. Political Cartoon of Brown in a Medfly Trap, "Never mind the medfly, did you get Jerry Brown?" Bill Mauldin, *Chicago Sun-Times*, July 1981, Pritzker Military Museum & Library, Chicago, Illinois

34. "he didn't want people to be storming Moffett Field," Marjorie Miller, "Moffett barred to copters, *San Jose Mercury*," July 13, 1981, B1

35. "We're getting caught in a political battle," Steve Johnson and Tom Harris, "Quarantine area widened by U.S." *San Jose Mercury*, July 14, 1981, A1

36. "The police force in San Jose would bear the brunt." Ibid

37. "We possibly won't go at 12:01 Tuesday," John Spalding and Marjorie Miller, "Spraying may be delayed 24 hours," *San Jose News*, July 13, 1981. A1

38. "People don't leave because of smog," John Flinn," Spray area widened as flies spread," *San Francisco Examiner*, July 12, 1981

39."deciding jointly if there is a need to expand the quarantine area," "Spraying may be delayed,"

40. "There's not going to be any aerial spraying until I am satisfied," John Spalding and Joanne Grant, "Aerial Spraying area is expanded," *San Jose News*, July 13, 1981, A1

Chapter 11 (Aerial Spraying—The Legal Battle)

1. Photo of Tents, Fred Larson, *San Francisco Chronicle*, July 13, 1981, A1

2. "Copters at Secret Base," Rick Carroll and H.G. Reza, Medfly Spraying Set, Copters at Secret Base, Final Legal Try Today," *San Francisco Chronicle*, July 13, 1981, A1,18

3. "a very strict...very conservative," Ron Gonzales, "Judge hearing Malathion suit known as tough-minded juris," *San Jose Mercury*, July 13, 1981, A6

4. "there is no rush, "John Spalding and Joanne Grant, "Aerial Spraying area is expanded," *San Jose News*, July 13, 1981, A1

5. "I wish I could say something else," Ronald W. Powell, "Judge Upholds Brown's Authority Refuses to Block Medfly Spraying," *Sacramento Bee*, July 14, 1981.

6. "spreading like a prairie fire, William Endicott and Tracy Wood, *Los Angeles Times*, July 14, 81, A1

7. "the only effective means" Ibid

8. "We possibly won't go at 12:01 Tuesday." John Spaulding and Majorie Miller, Spraying may be delayed 24 hours," *San Jose News*, July 13, 1981. A1

9. "You can't even take your hand off the phone," Gary E. Swan, "D-day in medfly project headquarters," *San Jose Mercury*, July 14, 1981, 1A

10 "There's your answer," Swan, "D-Day."

11. "The application is herewith denied," Don DeMain, "Spraying gets legal approval," *Oakland Tribune*, July 14, 1981.

12. Wayne King, "California Courts Won't Bar Spraying to Kill Fruit Flies," *New York Times*, July 13, 1981. accessed 12/12.2013

13. "total chaos," Swan, "D-Day"

14. "We've had cooperation," Swan, "D-Day."

15. "Scribner keeps ducking into his office," Jim Dickey, Jeff Kaye, Dick Egner, Cathie Calvert, Bernard Bauer, and Joel Achenbach, "Day One: Chop-chop-chop in the skies as war begins," *San Jose News*, July 14, 1981, P 1A

16. "can't someone else help you," Dickey, et al, "Day One."

17. "the phones continue to ring," Swan, D-day

18. "I've been on the phone," Jim Dickey, and others, "Day One: Chop-Chop-Chop

19. It's 9:37," Ibid

20. "If we see some muzzle flashes," Bernard Bauer, "Tight security keeps medfly base secret," *San Jose Mercury*, July 15, 1981, page 1A

21. "I've flown these things back with 50 holes in them," John Johnson and Ronald W. Powell "Solo Copter Poised to Begin Spraying" *Sacramento Bee*, July 14, 1981, A1

22. "You son-of-a-bitch" Copters at Secret Base" *San Francisco Chronicle*, 14 July 1981

23. "I may just come here and be with you," Wayne King, "Californians Set to Shun Spraying," *New York Times*, July 13, 1981

24. "I'm part of the mess, so I guess I'll share in the experience." Wayne King, "Californians Set to Shun Spraying," *New York Times*, July 14, 1981

25. Walt Wiley, "Brown Beds Down in Spray Area Home," *Sacramento Bee*, July 14, 1981

26. "[residents are] the people that have to take the burden of this, while the rest of the State gets the benefit." Ibid

Chapter 32 (Another Night in the Cemetery)

1. Photo of Judge Allen, Mike Maloney, *San Francisco Chronicle*, July 14, 1981, A1
2. "Public Health, not emergency powers, is the issue, he says." John Flinn and Caroline Yung, *San Francisco Examiner*, July 14, 1981
3. "a lot of hysteria" John Johnson and Ronald W. Powell, "Aerial Offensive on Medfly Begins," *Sacramento Bee*, July 14, 1981, A1,12
4. "ground spraying not going to control the medfly," Don DeMain, "Spraying gets legal approval," Oakland Tribune, July 14, 1981.
5. "like a cup of coffee," Johnson and Powell, Aerial
6. "can buy it in any grocery store" Steve Johnson and Ron Gonzales, "Quarantine Area widened by U.S." *San Jose Mercury*, July 14, 1981, A1
7.. "I've personally used it for years." Johnson and Gonzales, "Quarantine Area"
8. "if one person gets ill," Ronald W. Powell, "Judge Upholds Brown's Authority. Refuses to Block Medfly Spraying," *Sacramento Bee*, July 14, 1981, A1
9. Red Cross, William Endicott, and Tracy Wood, "Courts OK Spraying of Medfly Pest," *Los Angeles Times*, July 14, 1981, A1,3
10. Arthur Golden, "Spraying Exodus fails to Develop," *San Diego Union*, July 14, 1981,
11. Aleta Watson and Bill Strobel, "Few refugees seek shelter in medfly war", *San Jose Mercury*, July 15, 1981, A8
12. "if there is any adverse effect," Tracy Wood, and Claudia Luther, "120 Mile Area is Target of Anti-Medfly Serial Spraying," *Los Angeles Times*, July 15, 1981, A3,21,22
13. Steve Johnson and Ed Pope, "Fruit-stripping order is eased," *San Jose Mercury*, July 15, 1981, A1,8
14. coverage painted an embarrassing picture, Rick Carroll, "2ND Night of Aerial Spraying," *San Francisco Chronicle*, July 15, 1981,

15 "Their guesses," Bernard Bauer," Tight security keeps medfly base secret," *San Jose Mercury*, July 15, 1981, A1,8

16. Did a pregnant woman die in an auto accident fleeing spraying? I vividly remember being informed of this at the time, but I have not been able to document that such a death, in fact, occurred.

17. "The infestation constitutes a disaster," Steve Johnson and Tom Harris, "Medfly disaster aid requested for the area, Low-interest loans sought for residents," *San Jose Mercury* July 16, 1981, A1,7

18. Tony Bizjax and Ted Thomas, "Brown Asks Reagan to declare disaster in Medfly area," *Sacramento Union*, July 16, 1981, A1

19. Walt Wiley, "Governor Asks President Reagan for Disaster Aid, Medfly Spreads North Fueling Worst Fears," The *Sacramento Bee*, July 16, 1981, A1,18

20. More Southern States Restrict California Crops, Ibid.

21. Bruce Koon and Rick Carroll, "Major Disaster Area, 'Medfly Called Out of Control," *San Francisco Chronicle*, July 16, 1981, A1,28

22. Bruce Koon and Rick Carroll, "Brown Letter on 'Disaster' Criticized," *San Francisco Chronicle*, July 17, 1981

23. Tracy Wood and Richard O'Reilly, "Brown Asks U.S. to help on Medfly Request," *Los Angeles Times*, July 16, 1981, A1,3,16

24. Jay Mathews, "Gov. Brown Seeks U.S. Help in Air War Against Medfly,", *Wahington Post*, July 16, 1981

25. "now beyond the control of the state." Steve Johnson and Tom Harris, "Low-interest loans sought for residents," *San Jose Mercury*,

26. "I wish he had worked more closely with his people at the (state) department of agriculture," Tracy Wood, "Fight Medfly and Be Quiet," *Los Angeles Times*, July 17, 1981, A1,3

27. Steve Johnson and Ed Pope, "Fruit-stripping order is eased," *San Jose Mercury*, July 15, 1981, A1

28. "I don't feel as a taxpayer I got a fair shake," Steve Johnson and Tom Harris, "Low-interest Loans sought for residents," *San Jose Mercury* July 16, 1981. A1

29. John Spaulding," Switch raises; new furor, confuses medfly warriors," *San Jose News,* July 15, 1981, A1

30. Editorial, "The Great Fruit Strip Tease: Take it off…no, Leave it on" *San Jose News*, July 16, 1981, B10

31. Jack Lynch, "Weary, Frustrating Struggle to Strip the Trees," *San Francisco Chronicle*, July 14, 1981

32. Steve Johnson and Tom Harris, "U.S. Allows Spray Base at Moffett," San Jose Mercury, July 17, 1981, A1,6

33. "as long as they get the bait on," Tracy Wood and Richard O'Reilly, "Brown asks U.S. to Help, *Los Angeles Times*, July 16, 1981, A1,3,16

34. "Everyone is sort of ducking these days," Susan Sward, "Environmental Groups Keeping a Low Profile," *San Francisco Chronicle*, A4

35. "We are between a rock and a hard place," Sward, Environmental Groups

36. "our vision is so clouded by the sterile flies," Sward, Environmental Groups

37. "by Saturday morning," Bruce Koon and Rick Carroll, "Brown Letter on 'Disaster' Criticized," *San Francisco Chronicle*, July 17, 1981

38. Jeanie Borba and Rob Goble, "5 Southern States Demand Fumigation," *Sacramento Bee*, July 17, 1981, A1,22

39. Texas Quarantine, Rick Carroll, and Ann Bancroft, "Surprise Move, State Hit by Ban on All Fruit," *San Francisco Chronicle*, July 18, 1981, A1, 14

40. "just about half the area covered" Brown on ABC, Ibid

41. "It's not the way to do it," Koon and Carroll, Brown Letter

42. Steve Johnson and Rebecca Salner, "Town gets apology for tardy spraying." *San Jose Mercury,* July 21, 1981. A1, 7

Chapter 13 (The Man Who Drank the Malathion)

1. "Five CCC fruit strippers hospitalized," Rick Carroll and H.C. Reza, "Medfly Spraying Set, Copters at Secret base," *San Francisco Chronicle*, July 13, 1981, A1,18

2. "It tasted horrible., like kerosene" "State Official Says He Drank Malathion and 'Feels Fine', *San Francisco Chronicle*, July 16, 1981, A3

3. "I drank it because you don't ask your troops to do anything you wouldn't do," Susan Sward, "A Toast to Malathion," San Francisco *Chronicle*, July 16th, 1981, A3

4. "Residents have been needlessly terrified," Steve Johnson and Tom Harris, "Low-Interest loans sought for residents," *San Jose Mercury*, July 16, 1981, 1A

5. July 20, Rebecca Salner, "Police not eager to enforce tree-stripping requirement," *San Jose Mercury*, July 14, 1981, A4

6. "comb neighborhoods and report violators," Editorial, *San Jose Mercury*, July 16, 1981

7. July 20 meeting with Brown and the police chief,

8. "we don't see why California Highway patrolmen," Editorial. "Enforce the fruit-striping law—and slap on the fines," *San Jose Mercury*, July 15, 1981

9. Susan Sward and Rick Carroll, "Florida Embargo Overruled," *San Francisco Chronicle*, A1,24

10. "You'll have to speak up son, I don't hear Yankees too well," Roderick E. Walston, "The Great Medfly War: A short Memoir on the Legal Battle," *Stanford Lawyer* Fall/Winter 1981, P 13

11. "the governor was saying one thing and you [meaning me] another." Johnson, Steve, and Rebecca Salner, "Town gets apology for tardy spraying." *San Jose Mercury*. July 21, 1981. Page A1, 7

12. "California officials block Texas quarantine of state's fruit." Ibid

13. Rominger flies to Texas, Paul Shinoff, "Medfly quarantine fight moves into courts," *San Francisco Examiner*, July 20, 1983

14. remind the public," John Spaulding, "Growers looking to high court, State joins fight to overturn embargoes on California fruit," *San Jose Mercury News*, July 21, 1981

15. "met with lawyers from California," Rick Carroll, and Paul Liberatore, "Court Bars Texas Quarantine on Produce from California," *San Francisco Chronicle*, 21 July 1981, A1,18.

16. John Flinn, "Governor warns that stripping of fruit trees must continue," *San Francisco Examiner*, July 23, 1981

17. "Nobody recommended I approve aerial spraying before the technical committee met two weeks ago," John Spaulding, "Growers looking to high court "

18. Susan Sward, "Quarantines Confuse State," *San Francisco Chronicle*, 21 July. 1981, A2.

19. Pope, Ed. "California wants Supreme Court to end blockade." *San Jose Mercury* July 22, 1981. 6A.

20. "The Supreme Court gave the defendants until Friday to file their responses." Koon, Bruce and Carroll, Rick. "State Fights the Embargoes." *San Francisco Chronicle*. July 22, 1981. A1,28

21. "Only one percent of California's produce comes from the three infested counties." Susan Sward and Rick Carroll, "Florida Embargo Overruled." *San Francisco Chronicle* July 24, 1981, A1,24

22. John Johnson, "Florida Judge Dissolves Tough Crop Quarantine", *Sacramento Bee*, Friday, July 24, 1981, A11

23. Hayakawa, Ira R. Allen, Hayakawa May Scrap 2nd Run If He Doesn't Perk Up in The Polls, *Sacramento Bee*, July 30, 1981, A 21 "convinced right now that we're on schedule,"

24. "The chaos of Day 1 had given way to simple busy-ness," Claudia Luther, "Frenzy Finished at Medfly Center." *Los Angeles Times*, July 23, 1981,

25. 'the mood has really shifted." Ed Pope, "California wants Supreme Court to end blockade," *San Jose Mercury*, July 22, 1981, A6

26. "The general feeling on the project and off is that eradication is inevitable," Ibid

27. Supreme Court, Richard D. Hall, "Good News from Two Fronts in War on Medfly, State Wins Support in Court, *Sacramento Bee*, July 25, 1981, A3

28. Jasper Ridge accidentally sprayed Colleen Fitzpatrick, "Part of Stanford's scientific preserve sprayed." *San Jose Mercury*, July 22, 1981. P 6A.).

29. "their last night of operations will be Wednesday," Bruce Koon and Rick Carroll, "State Fights the Embargoes," *San Francisco Chronicle*, July 22, 1981, A1,28.

30. FEMA denial, "the situation has stabilized," Ellen Hume and Jerry Belcher, "Brown's Medfly Plea Rejected," *Los Angeles Times*, July 23, 1981. Page A1,23].

31. Rick Carroll and Susan Sward, "U.S. Won't Give State Medfly Disaster Aid Brown Smells Politics," *San Francisco Chronicle*, July 23, 1981, A1, 28.

32. The situation "should have been solved a long time ago on a state level," Ibid

33. Rotary club speech, Johnson, John, Bee Staff Writer, "Weary 'Mr. Medfly' Shows His Battle Scars," *Sacramento Bee*, Friday, July 24, 1981, page A 11.

34. A new stripping enforcement unit, Richard Hall, "Good News, "*Sacramento Bee*, A3

35. Bernard Bauer, "Daytime spraying area is broadened." *San Jose Mercury* July 27, 1981. Page A1,7.

36. Rick Carroll, "Medfly Street Battle Begins," *San Francisco Chronicle*, July 28, 1981, 5.

37. Colleen Fitzpatrick, "Ground-spray pesticide diazinon is far more potent than malathion." *San Jose Mercury*, July 28, 1981. Page A7.

38. the "constant flow of confiscations" Claudia Luther, "Frenzy Finished."

39. quotes by inspectors Lewis and Stegmiller "Do you have any fruit?" Ed Pope, "Inspectors get tough on forbidden fruit," *San Jose Mercury*, July 22, 1981, A1,6. Also, in the *San Jose News*, July 22, 1981, A1, 20.

40. Ed Pope and Steve Johnson, "Kidney unit closed after patient mysteriously dies," *San Jose Mercury News*, July 30, 1981, A1,2.2

41. Stephen Gruber, "Malathion didn't cause dialysis death," *San Jose Mercury*, July 31, 1981, B1,8.

42. Tom Harris, and Bill Romano, "Bullet hole found in malathion copter," *San Jose Mercury*, July 28.1981, A1,6.

43. John Spaulding, "Bullet hole found in medfly 'copter—security tightened", *San Jose News*, July 29, 1981. Medfly: A3

44. Susan Sward, "Bullet Hole Found in Medfly Helicopter," *San Francisco Chronicle*, July 28, A1,28.

45. John Spaulding, "After a ragged start, medfly war smoothing out," *San Jose News*, July 30, 1981, A1,6

BOOK FOUR - AUGUST 1981

Chapter 14 (A New Fight Looms)

1. Stephen Magagnini, "New Plans for Ground, Air Medfly Battle," *San Francisco Chronicle*, 27 July 1981, A1,16.
2. Erica Goode, "Growers in San Joaquin Valley Praying Extra Hard," *The San Francisco Chronicle*, July 27, 1981.
3. "California Finds Fruit Embargo Is 2-Way Street," *San Francisco Chronicle*, 27 July 1981, A2,
4. Ed Pope, "Eradication effort will be tested in next two weeks," *San Jose Mercury*, July 31, 1981, 6A.
5. "Provided the current infestation does not change before then, the U.S. Department of Agriculture will not propose any changes in the current quarantine." Susan Sward, "Hopeful Report, Two big Advances on Medfly Front," *San Francisco Chronicle,* July 31, 1981, A2.
6. "A new fight looms in the Medfly war," Rick Carroll, "Medfly Pits State Against Scientists," *San Francisco Chronicle*, August 1, 1981, A5.
7. Ed Pope, "Aerial Spraying may be doubled," *San Jose Mercury*, August 1, 1981. A1,10.
8. Tom Harris, "The Great Malathion Dosage Dispute," *San Jose Mercury News*, August 2, 1981, A1,7
9. Bill Workman, "Spray Zone People Allegedly Feel Better," *San Francisco Chronicle*. August 5, 1981, A4
10. Kent Demaret, "Politics and Pests Don't Mix, The Medfly Is a Case in Point, Experts Say," *People Magazine*, August 3, 1981, 37-39
11. Demaret, *People Magazine*.
12. Tom Harris, "Fertile fly survives the spraying," *San Jose Mercury*, A1, 6.
13. "Scientists' brace for medfly abuse," Bernard Bauer, *San Jose Mercury*, August 6, 1981, 4A
14. Tom Harris, "Five fertile medflies discovered, *San Jose Mercury*, August 6, 1981. Page A1,4.
15. Susan, Susan, and Bill Workman, "3 Medflies Found in Florida Tree," *San Francisco Chronicle*, August 6, 1981, 3.
16. John Johnson, "Medfly Find May Extend South Bay Aerial Spraying," *Sacramento Bee*, August 7, 1981, A1,18.
17. new scientific members, *Minutes of TRC Medfly Technical Review Committee*, August 6, 1981

18. "What data had been gathered," Dr. James Brazzel, John Pozzi, Gary Agosta, and Mert Price, "USDA Program Evaluation of Aerial Spray Program", August 22, 1981 (Scribner file)

19. "I'm not going to play that down," Susan Sward and Bill Workman, "Medflies Found Outside the Zone of Aerial Spraying," *San Francisco Chronicle*, August 7, 1981, A1,16.

20. "I'm not going to play that down." Tom Harris and Ed Pope, "Aerial spraying ordered for section of San Martin*," San Jose Mercury*, August 7, 1981.A 20

21. Quote "a program of minimals (sic) from the beginning almost to the lack of regard of biology," John Johnson, "Medfly Find May Extend South Bay Aerial Spraying", *Sacramento Bee*, August 7, 1981, A1,18.

22. I was "not very happy," Ibid

23. adding 179 square miles to the spraying, Susan Sward, "Medfly Fighters Widen Spray Zone," *San Francisco Chronicle*, August 8, 1981, A1,12.

24. "It is in a difficult area. Bear Creek runs through the town," Marjarie Miller, "Medfly infestation feared in Santa Cruz County," *San Jose Mercury News*, August 9, 1981, A1, 12.

25. "We haven't lost the war. It's just a bigger battlefield." Ed Pope, "Medfly threatening farming's heartland," *San Jose Mercury News*, August 11, 1981, A1,4.

26. Ed Pope, "New medfly find poses threat to Central Valley," *San Jose Mercury*, August 11, 1981, A1, 10.

27. "as the fruit fly marches steadily toward their fields," John Johnson, "Medfly Found at Livermore," *Sacramento Bee*, August 11, 1981, A1,10.

28. We signed a tentative contract (for fixed-wing aircraft), Tom Harris, "Planes eyed if spray zone is expanded," *San Jose Mercury*, August 12, 1981, B 1,4.

29. (Milpitas) "sprayed immediately without much notice to the residents," Bill Workman, and Stephen Magagnini, "Medfly Spraying Widens", *San Francisco Chronicle*, August 14, 1981, 1,6

30. John Johnson, Claire Cooper "Final Try to Block Medfly from Valley." *Sacramento Bee*, August 13, 1981, A1, 24.

31. Tom Harris, "Medfly fight follows bugs east, west," *San Jose Mercury*, August 14, 1981, A1,20.

32. "Florida Finds Medfly Outside Spray Area; Tampa Quarantined," *Sacramento Bee*, August 15, 1981, A2.

33. "Florida Attacks Medfly," Florida Department of Agriculture, *Plant Industry News*, September 1981 Vol 23, No. 1.

34. "To farmers, Brown is the other pest." Armando Acuna, "To farmers, Brown is the other pest" *San Jose Mercury*, August 14, 1981, A1,10].
See also "Farmers Blame A 2nd 'Pest," *Los Angeles Times*, printed August 16th in the *Sacramento Bee*, A1,32.

Chapter 15 (Medflies Reach the Central Valley)

1."Initiate articles of impeachment," Jim Dufer and Ted Bell "Medfly Battle Plan Under
Fire," *Sacramento Bee*, August 15, 1981, A1,14 at page 14

2. Scribner "reacting," Dufer and Bell, Medfly Battle Plan, A1

3. "Disaster has struck," Dufer and Bell, Medfly Battle Plan, A1
"ignored every recommendation," Dufer and Bell, Medfly Battle Plan, A14

4. Hilary Lorraine, "The California 1980 Medfly Crisis: An Analysis of Uncertainty Management under Conditions of Non-routine Problem Solving, "*Ph.D.* Thesis University of California. Nov. 1984, 59-62

5. "What Thurman did," *Capitol Newscope*, Sacramento Bee, August 23, 1981, A3.

6. "When in Westley, do as the Westlians Do," *Capitol Newscope*,

7. "Scribner should not be the fall guy," John Johnson, "Valley Readies Its Defenses," *Sacramento Bee*, August 15, 1981. Page A1,14

8. "too many people to answer to," Ibid

9. "If that isn't corrected, Jerry's got to get out of there," ibid.

10."very, very, bad," Larry Liebert, "Medflies Reach Valley; Brown stays Home," *San Francisco Chronicle*, August 15, 1981. 4,5.

11. [not] "much bigger than any other day," Larry Liebert, Medflies Reach Valley

12. "pure political posturing," Dufer and Bell, Medfly Battle Plan, A14

13. "We have a great deal of confidence," Dufer and Bell, Medfly Battle Plan, A14

14. "Hallett knows full well," Dufer and Bell, Medfly Battle Plan, A14

15. "We weren't lucky," Johnson, "Valley Readies is defenses, A14.

16. "We have a problem," "Medflies Hit the Valley," Rick Carroll and Bill Workman, *San Francisco Chronicle*, August 15, 1981, 1,12.

17. Armando Acuna, *San Jose Mercury*, August 15,1981, A4

18. "I make no apologies for the effort we have made," Ed Pope, "Copters spray Central Valley," *San Jose Mercury News*, August 15, 1981, A1,3,4,5,

19. "testy" "Medfly Crisis 'Out of Control'", Rick Carroll, *San Francisco Chronicle*, August 15, 1981, 1,12.

20. A bin not thoroughly cleaned as cause, "Ed Pope, "Canners want medfly out of the business," *San Jose Mercury*, August 15, 1981, A4

21. "It's out of control now. They'll have to spray the whole state," Rick Carroll, *San Francisco Chronicle*, August 15, 1981, 1,12.

22. "not out of hand", "Medfly bombers over Valley, Stanislau invaded, Brown blamed," Chris Thompson, *Sacramento Union*, August 15, 1981, pages 1,2].

23. Pope, Ed, "Copters spray Central Valley Response to new finds immediate," *San Jose Mercury News*, August 15, 1981, A1,4

24. John Johnson, "50 Medflies Found; Quarantine in Valley," *Sacramento Bee*, August 16, 1981, A1,32

25. Tom Harris, and Jack Foley, "Fumigation may be avoided," *San Jose Mercury*, August 15, 1981, A3.

26. Thom Akeman, Stanislaus Find Raises Hopes in Medfly War," *Sacramento Bee* August 17, 1981, A1,11.

27. John Johnson, "Medfly Invasion Not Expected to Hurt Consumers This Year," *Sacramento Bee*, August 18, 1981, A12.

28. Bruce Obbink and table grapes, McClatchy Newspaper Service, "State Crops Embargoed by Japanese," *Sacramento Bee*, August 18, 1981, A1,12.

29. Erica Goode, and Susan Sword, "Arrest in Threats to Medfly Copter," *San Francisco Chronicle*, August 18, 1981

30. "basest form of political demagoguery," Jim Dufur, "GOP Plan: Impeach Governor," *Sacramento Bee*, August 18, 1981, A1,12.

31. "playing on the fears," Dufer, Ibid

32. "a full partner," Dufer, Ibid

33. 'We stand by Scribner," Dufer, Ibid

34. "co-manager type of supervision, Dufer, Ibid

35." the Governor's personal staff to get out," Dufer, Ibid. Ed Pope, "Japan slaps embargo on state's crops," *San Jose Mercury*, August 19, 1981, A1,15A.

36. Rudyard Kipling's poem "IF." (I found it in the Los Gatos City Library in a collection of Poems. I no longer recollect the title of the collection. However, the poem is widely available.

37. Larry Martz, "Lord of the Flies," *Sacramento Magazine*, October 1981, 59-60

Chapter 16 (Cooler Heads Prevail)

1. "no decision has been made yet," Erica Goode, and Susan Sward, "Arrest in Threats to Medfly Copter," *San Francisco Chronicle*, August 18, 1981, 2.

2. Statewide embargo impact, "State Crops Embargoed by Japanese", *Sacramento Bee*, August 18, 1981, A1,12.

3. On impact, see also Thom Akeman, "Stanislaus Find Raises Hopes in Medfly War" *Sacramento Bee*, August 17, 1981, A1,11.

4. Hallet's campaign, Jim Dufer, "GOP Plan: Impeach Governor," *Sacramento Bee*, August 18, 1981, A1, 12.

5. Heringer quoted Susan Sward, "Japan Stands Firm on State Fruit Quarantine," *San Francisco Chronicle*, August 19, 1981, A1,18.

6. "Japan Stands Firm," Sward, "Japan Stands Firm," A1

7. Not to "unfairly quarantine California," Ed Pope, "Japan slaps embargo on State's Crops," *San Jose Mercury*, August 1981, A1,15.

8. Texas, Sward, Japan Stands Firm

9. Brown breakfasts with legislators, Sward, Japan Stands Firm

10. Eisenhower and divided leadership, Stephen P. Ambrose, *The Supreme Commander 1970*

11. Brown fought back, Buxton, Chuck, "Brown has harsh reply for critics" *San Jose Mercury*, August 20, 1981, A1, 20.

12. GOP 'Win' Ends Plans to Impeach, *Sacramento Bee*, August 20, 1981, A1,30,

13. Barbara Serrano and Bill Lindelof, "Japanese Relent, Will Ease Embargo," *Sacramento Bee*, A1,30

14. Tom Harris, "State Juggles Medfly Staff," *San Jose Mercury*. August 20, 1981. Page A1,20

15. Tracy Wood, LA Times "Medfly Moves South, Invades Hollister Area," *The Sacramento Bee*, August 23, 1981, A1,4.

16. Susan Sward and Allyn Stone, "Fertile Medfly Found in Oakland," *San Francisco Chronicle*, August 27, A 1, 20.

17. Bill Lindelof and John Johnson, "Medfly in Oakland; Spray Zone Widens," The *Sacramento Bee*, A1,24

18. Jackie Montague-Wynne, *The Daily Medfly*, August 26, 1981.

19. *Minutes of TAC*, August 25-26.

20. Brown interview in Washington Post, Katharine Macdonald, *Washington Post,* "THE 1982 ELECTIONS: THE CALIFORNIA SENATE RACE," November 1, 1982,

21. "ask me Nov. 2", Macdonald, "1982 ELECTIONS."

22. Armando Acuna, "Additional Spraying Suggested," *San Jose Mercury*, August 28, 1981, B1,3.

23. Quote by Darryl Ward, Joe Stein, *Lift*, published by Zig Zag Papers, March 1985, page 50

24. John, Johnson, "Tough Times for Medfly War Leader" *Sacramento Bee*, September 4, 1981, 1,24

25. Ted Koppel, "The Mediterranean Fruit" *ABC Nightline*, August 26, 1981 (Videotape available at Syracuse University Libraries Special Use Collections Research Center)

26. Sacramento Bee Staff, "More Medflies in LA; Funding Worries Grow," *Sacramento Bee*, August 28, 1981, 1,20.

27. Erica Goode, "L.A. County Quick to Act Against Medfly," *San Francisco Chronicle*, August 28, 1981, 4.

28. Erica Goode and Allyn Stone, "L.A. Draws Medfly War Zone," *San Francisco Chronicle*, August 28, 1981, 1,18.

29. Gary E. Swan, "L.A. heat, smog upstage aerial spraying," *San Jose Mercury*, August 28, 1981, A1,24.

30. John Johnson, "Medfly Experts Are Encouraged," *Sacramento Bee*, August 30, 1981, A1,28

31. Jerry Scribner, *The Cause of the 1981 Medfly Infestation*, August 31, 1981. (Scribner files)

32. the minimum release had to be at least fifty thousand fertile flies. *Medfly Technical Review Committee Transcript*, August 6. 1981 cited in "Hilary Lorraine, The California 1980 Medfly Crisis: An Analysis of Uncertainty Management under Conditions of non-routine Problem Solving," *Ph.D. Thesis* University of California. Nov. 1984.

33. Joe Vargo, "Scribner Blames Fertile Peruvian Medflies for 3Outbreak," *Sacramento Bee*, September 2, 1981, A13.

4. Karen Corwin, *Comments on the 1981 Medfly Infestation*, September 2, 1981. (Scribner files)

35. Dr. Nadel's visit in April. *Medfly TRC Minutes*, April 23, 1981

36. John Johnson, and Mike Castro, "Lab official In Peru Denies Shipping Batch of Fertile Flies," *Sacramento Bee*, September 3, 1981, A3

37. Chuck Buxton and Tom Harris, "Early alarm was sounded on Peru flies," *San Jose Mercury*, September 4, 1981

38. John Fogerty, "U.S. Finds State Goof on Medfly," *San Francisco Chronicle*, September 9, 1981, A1,20.

39. "Hawaiian fly now blamed for fruit infestation," *San Jose News*, September 9, 1981, B1,3.

40. Hilary Lorraine, "The California 1980 Medfly Crisis: An Analysis of Uncertainty Management under Conditions of Non-routine Problem Solving," *Ph.D. Thesis* University of California. Nov. 1984.

41. Editorial, "The Peruvian medfly caper," *San Jose Mercury*, September 9, 1981, 10B.

42. Editorial, "Medfly: Pointing the Finger," *LA Times*, September 7, Page II 6.

BOOK FIVE   FALL 1981 - December 1982

Chapter 17 (The Beginning of the End)

1. Technical Advisory Committee -Medfly *Minutes* September 9-10

2. Ed Pope, Medfly spraying may persist, *San Jose Mercury*, September 10, 1981, page B1,3.

3. Peter H. King and Richard Saltus, A hard look/Big winter Medfly fight looms. *San Francisco Examiner*, September 6, 1981

4. Richard Hall, "Congress Approves Medfly Aid, *Sacramento Bee*, September 12, 1981, A22.

5. Snipers Hit Medfly Copters Over Santa Clara Valley, *Sacramento Bee*, September 16, 1981. A3.

6. Bee News Service, "Senate Passes Farm Bill Medfly Rider Attached. *Sacramento Bee*, September 19, 1981

7. [Staleys] "Spray Operation Skipped Over Medfly Find Area," *Sacramento Bee*, September 15, 1981, A1,32

8. Tom Harris, "Medfly spray missions call for precision flying," *San Jose Mercury News*, September 6, 1981, B1,2

9. Ed Pope, "Weekly spraying ends in parts of 2 counties," *San Jose Mercury*, A1,22

10. John Flinn, "Some Medfly Spray to end, headline in *San Francisco Examiner*, "Stops this weekend despite a new find," San Francisco Examiner, October 9, A1,22

11. Technical Advisory Committee- *Minutes* October 7th and 8th,

12. Medfly Pilot's Last Words above picture of crash scene, Mike Mahoney, Photographer, *San Francisco Chronicle*, A1

13. Ann Bancroft, "I'm Losing It---Then Static," *San Francisco Chronicle*, October 23, 1981, A1

14. John Johnson, "Fatal Copter Crash Won't Halt Medfly Spraying," *Sacramento Bee*, October 23, 1981, A20

15 Front page photo of flames by Dave Floyd *Mercury News*, October 23, 1981, A1

16. Front page photo of Fremont house and medfly copter in daylight after fatal crash taken by John R. Fulton Jr. of the *Mercury*, October 23, 1981, A1

17. Ed Pope, "Copters return despite crash," *San Jose Mercury*, October 23, 1981, A1,20

18. 'one night…The whole valley was a blanket of fog', Harris, Medfly spray missions.

19. Ed Pope, "Spraying delayed by bad weather," *San Jose Mercury*, October 28, 1981, B1

20. Leon Lindsay, "Medfly: Down but not out in California," *Christian Science Monitor*, November 2, 1981

21. "Unusual Incident at Medfly Station – S.R. 152 and Pacheco Pass" *Highway Patrolman*, January 1982, page 22

22. Ed Pope, "Spraying winds down, Last week of malathion drops for 27 cities," San Jose Mercury November 10, 1981.

23. "Optimism," Ed Pope, "Medfly optimism, 'We'll win,' eradication project official says," *San Jose Mercury*, November 19, 1981, 4B.

24. Jose Stell, "Medfly headquarters draws buzz of complaints," *San Jose Mercury* October 9, 1981, B1

25. Joe Stell, "Los Gatos fed up with medfly office", *San Jose Mercury*, October 30, 1981, B9

26. Isi Siddiqui, "The Fruit Fly Workshop at U.C. Davis," *Memorandum to R.E. Rominger*,
November 5, 1981

27. Tracy Wood, "State Cutting Back Medfly Spraying Will Trim Effort in North but Continue in L.A. County," *Los Angeles Times*, A3, 22

28. *Minutes* of Medfly TAC, January 12-13, 1982

29. Bill Mandel, "Secret report: Medflies will be back stronger in '82," *San Francisco Chronicle-Examiner*, November 22, 1981, page A2.

30. Ed Pope, "Ex-medfly worker suing state for harassment," *San Jose Mercury News*, November 20, 1981

31. Jim Dickey, "Medfly 'dooms' state agriculture." *San Jose News*, July 17, 1981

32. Knipling quote "discovered" too late, "Stephen Ferris, "Medfly Crisis: Who's to blame," *Fresno B*ee, November 22, 1981, A1,3

33. "Looking back...the first and fundamental mistake was failing to recognize the fly had [already] become widespread and entrenched" Susan Sword, "The Man at the core of the Medfly Battle," San *Francisco Chronicle,* July 18, 1981, page 4A

34. Stephen Ferris, "Sterile fly strategy a matchmaking flop," *Fresno Bee*, November 23, A1,8

35. "the brains of the outfit," Stephen Ferris, "Critics say aerial attack was delayed too long," *Fresno Bee*, November 24, 1981, A1,10

36. "no evidence to indicate they were part of a spring breeding population," Stephen Ferris, "Criteria not pursued," *Fresno Bee*, November 26, 1981
37. John Johnson, "Fruit fly Disputes Rage On," *Sacramento Bee*, December 12, 1981, Page A3
38. Mark Saylor and Carl Cannon, "It's 'our agricultural Vietnam,'" *Sunday Mercury News*, July 12, 1981, A1,42.
39. "egg to egg" lab tests, Ronald W. Powell," "Ag Panel Wants Secret Medfly Lab Closed," *Sacramento Bee*, August 22, 1981, page A3
40. Carl M. Cannon, "Medfly Workers pull the shades, bust some heads," *San Jose Mercury*, July 22, 1981, A7
41. Hilary Lorraine, "The California 1980 Medfly Crisis: An Analysis of Uncertainty Management under Conditions of Non-routine Problem Solving," *Ph.D. Thesis* University of California. Nov. 1984,
42. Lorraine, "1980 Medfly Crisis, "pages 133,165 (switch to green dye)
43. Lorraine, "1980 Medfly Crisis, "page 137 (switch to visual sort)
44. Lorraine, "1980 Medfly Crisis, "page 141 (salted traps I.D. test)
45. Lorraine, "1980 Medfly Crisis, "page 146 (Cunningham quote on head punching)
46. Lorraine, "1980 Medfly Crisis, "page179-180 (lack of a list of fly finds)
47. Lorraine, "1980 Medfly Crisis," Page 180. (Ability to withstand the chill-down process)
48. Lorraine, "1980 Medfly Crisis "page 177 (small size of Mexican flies) Interview with Cherryl Denny,
49. "George, they don't hold them down." (Scribner Recollection)
50. Charlie Overmiller, Medfly Eradication Project *Chronology of Events* 1980-82
51. *TRC minutes* July 30, 1980

Chapter 18 (Mission to Japan)

1. Spraying to continue in Los Angeles until April 28, 1982, *TAC minutes* January 12-13, 1982
2. "Planted," Ed Pope, "Suspicious find of fly probed," *San Jose Mercury*, November 27, 1981

3. "incredible revenant" Dugald Stermer, "Medfly Back to Bug US Again?" *San Francisco Sunday Examiner Chronicle,* April 4, 1982, P 8

4. "most claims ever filed," Steven A. Capps, "A hard look/$28 million in Medfly lawsuits," San Francisco Examiner, March 21, 1982, A1,24

5. George Deukmejian, "Letter to Edmund. G. Brown" regarding state exposure to medfly claims, November 25, 1981. (Scribner files)

6. Alice A. Lytle, Secretary State and Consumer Services Agency, "Memorandum to B.T. Collins, Chief of Staff, Governor's Office" on Medfly Spraying Liability, January 26, 1982, (Scribner files)

7. Ed Pope, "All quiet on the medfly front—for now," *San Jose Mercury,* April 26, 1982, B 1,2,3

8. Jerry Scribner, *Memo to Hans Van Nes,* (Details Japanese Tour of California farms), April 27, 1982, (Scribner files)

9. "The medfly eradication project has been conducted with exemplary regard for the protection of public health. David Discher, M.D*., Report of the Governor's Health Advisory Committee, Medfly Eradication Program,* April 15, 1982, page 22.

10. "On May 19[th,] Rominger and I depart for Japan." Jerry Scribner, *Memo on Itinerary for meetings in Japan* (Scribner files)

11. Ronald W. Powell, "Japan Lifts Ban on Fruit," *Sacramento Bee,* May 26, 1982, A1,24

12. Tina Taggart, Editor *CDFA News*, pictures on the front cover of meetings captioned, "Negotiations with Japan," July 1982,

13. Trip to Japan, Jerry Scribner, *Memorandum to Files Trip to Japan,* June 1982, (Scribner files)

15. "No new Medfly life stages," *Dick Jackson, Detection Up-date to TRC Meeting June 10-11, 1982*

16. Suan Yoachum, "State declares victory in two-year medfly War," *San Jose Mercury,* September 22, 1982, B1

17. Richard Hanner, "Carmichael man hero of Medfly campaign," *Sacramento Bee,* Neighbors section, B,4

18. John Spaulding, "State's spirits soar as battle to save fruit industry ends," *San Jose Mercury,* September 21, 1982. B2

19. Richard E. Rominger, Director CDFA, and Mary Anne Graves, Director California Department of the Finance, *Preliminary Report of Medfly Eradication Project Expenditures*, October 15, 1982, page 2.

20. Richard E. Rominger, Director CDFA and Mary Anne Graves, *Preliminary Report, Attachment 1*, page 9
21. Richard E. Rominger, *Final Report of Medfly Eradication Project Expenditures*, December 15, 1982
22. Symposium, "Medfly and the Aftermath" *Entomological Society of America, Annual Meeting*, Toronto, Canada December 1982, APHIS 81-60

Epilogue

1. Symposium, "The Medfly in California: The Threat, Defense Strategies, and Public Policy," *HortScience 18(1)* February 1983
2. D.S. Jackson and B.G. Lee, "Medfly in California 1980-82" *Bulletin of the Environmental Society of America*, Winter 1985
3. Ephraim Kahn, MD, MPH, Richard J Jackson, MD, MPH, Donald O. Lyman, MD, MPH, and Arthur James W. Stratton, MD, MPH, "A Crisis of Community Anxiety and Mistrust: The Medfly Eradication Project in Santa Clara County, California," 1981-82," *Am J Public Health*, November 1990, Vol 80. No. 11
4. Steve Lyle, "Sterile Medfly Release Set for San Jose," *CDFA News Release #07-082* (2007), with a two-page description of the Medfly Preventive Release Program and a picture of the facility in Los Alamitos.
5. "There is absolutely no danger to anyone from this spray" (quote by NY City Mayor Rudolf Guiliani), Andrew C. Rivkin, "As Mosquito Spraying Continues, Officials Stress Its Safety," *New York Times*, September 14, 1999, Downloaded 10/30/2017
6. "This is a very safe chemical," Ibid.

Medfly Bibliography and Source Material

Abbott, Denise, "California Bureaucracy vs. The Medfly and The Winner Is?", *Big Valley*, January 1982, P 56-63 (Scribner file)

Ambrose, Stephen E. *The Supreme Commander, The War Years of General Dwight D. Eisenhower*, Doubleday 1979 page 25

Ayers, Ed L., "The Two Medfly Eradication Programs in Florida," Florida State Horticultural Society, 1957

Bates, Tom, "The Malathion Mystery," *California Reporter*, Jan. 1982, 43-44

Block, John R., "Letter dated May 4, 1982, to the Japanese Minister of Agriculture, following up on the April 6-9 Japanese Ministry of Agriculture Forestry and Fisheries (MAFF) Technical Review of the Medfly Project" with attached Agenda. (Scribner file)

Brazzel, James, Pozzi, John, Agosta, Gary, Price, Mert, "USDA Program Evaluation of Aerial Spray Program", August 22, 1981(Scribner file)

California Crop and Livestock Reporting Service, "Exports of Agricultural Commodities Produced in California, Calendar Year 1980," (Scribner Reports file)

California Department of Food and Agriculture, "California Agriculture 1981" (Scribner Reports file)

Cairns, Kathleen A. "The Case of Rose Bird: Gender, Politics, and the California Supreme Court," *University of Nebraska Press*, Published 2016

Carey, James R., "Demography and Population Dynamics of the Mediterranean Fruit Fly, Ecological Modelling, 16 (1982) 125-150

Carey, James R., "The Mediterranean fruit fly in California: Taking Stock," California Agriculture, January-February 1992, p, 13-17

Churchill-Stanland, Cherryl, Stanland, Russ, Wong, Tim, Tanaka, Norimitsu, McInnis, Donald, Dowell Robert, Size as a Factor in Mating Propensity of Mediterranean Fruit Flies, in the Laboratory, *Journal of Entomology 79*, 1986 p614-619

Clingston, Bert, "The Quiet Man," California Business, April 1977, Page 36-51

Conley, Kathryn L.," Field Guide to Medfly Infestation," Medfly Project 1981

Corwin, Karen, "Comments on the 1981 Medfly Infestation," September 2, 1981.

Cox, Haywood, Memorandum to Dick Jackson, "Chronology of Project Trap Density and Adult Fly Collections, December 10, 1981, (Scribner files—Trapping and Fruit Collection)

Dahlsten, Donald L. and Garcia, Richard, Editors, Hillary Lorraine Associate Editor *Eradication of Exotic Pests*, (Chapter 6 "Public Policy Considerations: The Medfly Case History," pp74-86 by Jerry Scribner), Publisher, Yale University Press 1989.

Demaret, Kent, "Politics and Pests Don't Mix, The Medfly Is a Case in Point, Experts Say," *People Magazine*, August 3, 1981, 37-39

Deukmejian, George, "Letter from Department of Justice to Governor Brown, related to potential state liability arising from the Medfly Eradication Program," November 25, 1981. (Scribner file)

Dilley, Don, "Letter to Senator Vuich, and Assemblyman John Thurman," August 18, 1981 (Scribner Dilley file)

Dilley, Don, et. al. "Minutes of the Technical Review Committee 1980-82" (unpublished) (Scribner files)

Discher, David, M.D., "Report of the Governor's Health Advisory Committee, Medfly Eradication Program, April 15, 1982," (Scribner Health file)

Dowell, Robert V., "Mediterranean Fruit Fly in California, The Threat," (unpublished paper by CDFA Medfly Research Manager) (Scribner file)

Dowell, Robert, Memorandum to Jerry Scribner, "Medfly Research," Feb 11, 1982 (Scribner Research File)

Doyle, Michael, and Strauss, David, *How to Make Meetings Work*, Publisher Playboy
Paperbacks, Publication Date January 1, 1976.

E.F. Knipling, "Technology for the Eradication of Mediterranean Fruitfly by Introductions", March 1981 (Scribner file)

Farmers Ins. Exchange v. State of California, [175 Cal. App. 3d 499] decided Dec.10, 1985, (Scribner files)

Farnham, George, Montague-Wynne, Jackie, Blake, Roger, Zeller, Annie, *The Daily Medfly*, -1981-82 (Rominger collection U.C. Davis Archives)

Florida Department of Agriculture and Consumer Services "Florida Attacks Medfly,", Plant Industry News, Vol 23, No. 1. September 1981 (15-page pamphlet)

Galante, Mary Ann, "Medfly Leaving a Legal Trail," *The Western Law Journal*, Sept-Oct 1981.

Gjullin, C.M., Probable Distribution of the Mediterranean Fruit Fly (Ceratitis Capitata Weid.) In The United States, Ecology Volume XII, 1931.

"Gypsy Moth Eradication," Final Report, CDFA, 1977

Hagen, K.S., W.W. Allen, and R.L. Tassan, "Mediterranean fruit fly: The worst may be yet to come," *California Agriculture*, 1981, 35:5-7.

Harris, Ernest J., "The Threat of the Mediterranean Fruit Fly to American Agriculture and Efforts Being Made to Counter this Threat," Presidential Address, presented at the December 1975 meeting of the *Hawaiian Entomological Society*

Hastie, William, Undersecretary of the California State and Consumer Services Agency,
"Citizens' Claims and State Liability Concerning Medfly Spraying (Scribner Damage Claims file)

Hawkes, Glenn R., Stiles, Martha C., "Final Report, Gypsy Moth/Medfly Follow-Up Study," *University of California, Davis Department of Applied Behavioral Sciences*, September 1983 (Scribner, Report file)

Hayden, Tom, "Jerry Brown, "The Mystic and the Machine," *Rolling Stone Magazine*, Dec. 19, 1974

Helms, William F., "Letter to Richard Rominger, August 13, 1981," (Scribner file)

Jackson, D.S., and Lee B.G., "Medfly in California 1980-82," *Bulletin of the ESA*, (The Ecological Society of America) Winter 1985

Jordan, William, "A Fruitless Pursuit, *Science 82, April 1982*, p 62-68

Kahn, Ephraim, MD, MPH, Jackson, Richard J, MD, MPH, Lyman, Donald O, MD, MPH, and Stratton, James W Stratton, MD, MPH, "A

Crisis of Community Anxiety and Mistrust: The Medfly Eradication Project in Santa Clara County, California, 1981-82," *Am J Public Health*, November 1990, Vol 80. No. 11

Kipling, Rudyard, "IF" (I found it in the Los Gatos City Library in a collection of Poems, the title of which collection I have no longer recollect. However, the poem is widely available.

King, Frank and Gillmore, Rod, "1981 Florida Medfly Invasion," *Florida Department of Agriculture Plant Industry News* Sept. 1981, Vol 23, No. 1

King, Wayne, "California Courts Won't Bar Spraying Kill Fruit Flies," *New York Times*, July 14, 1981, accessed 12/12/2013.

Lorraine, Hilary, "The California 1980 Medfly Crisis: An Analysis of Uncertainty Management under Conditions of Non-routine Problem Solving," *Ph.D. Thesis* University of California, Berkeley. Nov. 1984.

Martz, Larry, "Lord of the Flies," *Sacramento Magazine*, Oct. 1981, p59-60

Mitchell, Daniel J. B., "The Governor vs. the Fly: The Insect that Bugged Jerry Brown in 1981," Chapter 1 of California Policy Options 2021, *UCLA Luskin School of Public Affairs*, pp5-26.

Lyons, James M., "A History of the University of California Statewide IPM Program" (Scribner file)

Matthews, Jay, "Gov. Brown Seeks U.S. Help in Air War Against Medfly," *Washington Post,* July 16, 1981

"Medfly Continues to Bug California," *Science*, Vol 214, 11 Dec. 1981, p 1221-1224

Medfly Project, "Medfly Fact Sheet and Chronology (Scribner files—History}

Medfly Project, "Report to the South Bay Community on the Progress of The Mediterranean Fruit Fly Eradication Project, March 15, 1981 (Scribner files—History)

Messenger, P.S., Flitters, N. E., "Effect of Variable Temperature Environments on Egg Development of Three Species of Fruit Flies," *Annals of the Entomological Society of America,* Volume 52, Issue 2, 1 March 1959, Pages 191–204, https://doi.org/10.1093/aesa/52.2.191, Published: 01 March 1959

Mitchell, Daniel J., "The Governor vs. the Fly: The Insect That Bugged Jerry Brown in 1981," California Policy Option 2021, UCLA Luskin School of Public Policy, 2021, p 5-26

Myers, Beverlee A., Memorandum, "Health Hazard Assessment of Aerial Application of Malathion in Santa Clara County," December 16, 1980, (Rominger Collection U.C. Davis Archives, and Scribner Health file)

Overmiller, Charlie, "Medfly Eradication Project Chronology of Events" 1980-82, (Scribner file-Chronology). Note this file also includes an original draft Chronology prepared by State personnel that included political events and observations scrubbed by Overmiller. On the other hand, the Official Chronology tracks in greater detail the detection of wild flies and larvae and other official actions.

Palo Alto History.Com "Palo Alto Pests: The 1981 Medfly Invasion," http//www.paloaltohistory.com/palo-alto-medfly-invasion.php. accessed 8/12/2013.

Patrusky, Ben, "Stalking the Medfly," *Science Year 1983*, World Book Inc, p 70-85

Pease, Howard, *Heart of Danger: A Tale of Adventure on Land and Sea with Tod Moran, Third Mate of the Tramp Steamer "Araby"* Published by Doubleday, Doran & Company, Garden City, New York, 1946.

Pawel, Miriam, *The Browns of California*, Bloomsbury Publishing 2018

Raglin, Dennis E, "Rain of Controversy: The 1981 California Medfly Crisis," *The Center for California Studies California State University*, Sacramento May 1996 (Scribner files—History)

Roe, Emery M. "Narrative Analysis for the Policy Analyst: A Case Study of the 1980-1982 Medfly Controversy in California," *Journal of Policy Analysis and Management*, Vol 8, No, 2 (Spring 1989) pp 251-273
Rominger, Richard E. "The Medfly Eradication Project, A Status Report, December 15, 1981

Rominger, Richard E. "Pest Response Task Force Report," December 31, 1981. 96 pages

Rominger, Richard Elmer," Papers D-087, "Archives and Special Collections," *UC Davis Library*, University of California, Davis.

Rominger, Richard E. Director CDFA and Grave, Mary Anne, Director California Department of the Finance, "Preliminary Report of Medfly Eradication Project Expenditures," October 15, 1982 (Rominger Collection U.C. Davis Archives, Scribner file)

Rominger, Richard E. "Letter Richard Rominger to Walter V. Hays May 21, 1981 (Scribner files)
Saul, Stephen, "Letter to James Brazzel," Dec. 21, 1981, enclosing the manuscript described below that was being submitted to the J. *Economic Entomology*.

Rohwer, G. G., "The Mediterranean Fruit Fly In Florida—Past, Present, and Future," Presented at the 40th Annual Meeting of the *Florida Entomological Society*, September 11, 1957.

Saul, Stephen, Tsuda, Dick, Wong, Tim, "Manuscript: Laboratory and Field Trials of Soil Applications of Methoprene and Other Insecticides for Control of Mediterranean Fruit Fly, Ceratitis Capitata." (Scribner Research File)

Schrag, Peter, "The California Fruit Fly Wars," *The Nation*, October 10, 1981, P 339-340

Scribner, Jerry, "State Work Plan: Santa Clara County Medfly Eradication Project -December 18 through January 31, "December 22, 1980 (Rominger Archives at U.C. Davis)

Scribner, Jerry, "Outline and Text of Remarks to Mt. View City Council, July 6, 1981 (Scribner files—Speeches)

Scribner, Jerry, "Statement, Jerry Scribner, Medfly Project Director, Presented to the Santa Clara County Board of Supervisors on February 9, 1981, (Scribner files—Speeches)

Scribner, Jerry, Memorandum to Scot Campbell, "Criteria for Recommending the Aerial Application of Malathion Bait Spray to Eradicate Mediterranean Fruit Fly in Santa Clara County, California." February 18, 1981. (Scribner files)

Scribner, Jerry, Memorandum to Jerry Thomas, "The adoption of criteria for recommending the aerial application of Malathion Bait", March 16, 1981 (Scribner files)

Scribner, Jerry, Medfly Cartoon Collection and Text: "Sociopolitical Impact: State and County Levels" (Scribner files—Speeches)

Scribner, Jerry, Remarks to the Mountain View City Council July 6, 1981 (Scribner files)

Scribner, Jerry, Memo, "The Cause of the 1981 Medfly Infestation," August 31, 1981 (Scribner files

Scribner, Jerry, Memorandum to Richard Rominger, "Status of the Medfly Eradication Project," December 2, 1981, (Scribner files—History)

Scribner, Jerry, Memorandum to Hans Van Nes, "The Status of the Medfly Eradication Project," April 27, 1982 (Scribner files—History)

Scribner, Jerry, Text of the Slide Presentation of the Northern California Medfly Project History,
undated, (Scribner files—History)

Scribner, Jerry, "Trip to Japan", May 19, 1982 (unpublished manuscript) (Scribner files—Japan)

Scribner, Jerry, Memo to Files, "Trip to Japan May 22-26, 1982." (Scribner files—Japan)

Scribner, Jerry, Talk to the Rotary Club of Yuba City, October 22, 1982, (Scribner files—Speeches)

Scribner, Jerry, "Medfly and the Aftermath, A Review of the California Action Program," Remarks at the Dec 2, 1982, Meeting of the Entomological Society of America Meeting in Toronto, Canada," (Scribner files—Speeches) (also published in APHIS 81-60)

Scribner, Jerry, Miscellaneous speeches (Author's copies unpublished) Scribner files

Scribner, Jerry, "The Medfly in California: The Threat, Defense Strategies, and Public Policy," Hort Science 18(1), February 1983, pp 47-52

Scribner, J, "The Medfly in California: Organization of the Eradication Program and Public Policy," Hort Science 18(1), February 1983 pp 47-52.

Siddiqui, Isi, "The Fruit Fly Workshop at U.C. Davis," Memorandum to R.E. Rominger, November 5, 1981 (Scribner files)

Stein, Joe *Lift,* Chapter 4 "The Great Bug War" published by Zig Zag Papers (1985)

Symposium, The Medfly in California: The Threat. Defense Strategies, and Public Policy, HortScience 18(1), February 1983

Symposium, "Medfly and the Aftermath" Entomological Society of America, Annual Meeting, Toronto, Canada December 1982, *APHIS 81-60*

Tassan, Richard L., Letter to Jerry Scribner on Medfly Life Cycles, September 22, 1981, (Scribner files—Medfly Life Cycles)

Uelmen, Gerald F., "The Tragedy of Rose Bird," accessed via Google search 2/6/22, at https://*www.dailyjournal.com/articles* 368409-

USDA publication, Plant Protection, and Quarantine: "Helping U.S. Agriculture Thrive—Across the Country and Around the World", 2016, page 23. (https://*www.aphis.usda.gov/publications/plant_health/report-ppq-2016.pdf*) accessed 3/12/2023.

Van Den Bosch, Robert, *The Pesticide Conspiracy*, Anchor Books, Doubleday, Garden City, New York, 1980 (Paperback)

Walston, Roderick E., "The Great Medfly War: A short Memoir on the Legal Battle, *Stanford Lawyer*, Fall/Winter 1981, P 13

Weinland, Henry, *The Flying Invaders*, (Naturegraph Publishers), date? 25-26

Wong, Tim T.Y., Whitehand, Linda C, Kobayashi, Richard M., Ohinata, Kuchi, Tanaka, Norimitsu, and Harris, Ernest J., "Mediterranean Fruit Fly: Dispersal of Wild and Irradiated and untreated Laboratory-Reared Males." *Environmental Entomology* Vol. 11, No. 2, 1982

Wong, Tim T. Y., Kobayashi, Richard M., Linda C. Whitehand, Henry, Donald G., Zadig, Dorthea A. and Denny, Cherryl L., "Mediterranean Fruit Fly (Diptera: Tephritidae): Mating Choices of Irradiated Laboratory-Reared and Untreated Wild Flies of California in Laboratory Cages, Journal of Economic Entomology, 77:38-62 (1984)

Wong, Tim, Nishimoto, Jon, Couey, Melvin, Mediterranean Fruit Fly (Diptera: Tephritidae): Further Studies on Selective Mating Response of Wild and of Unirradiated and Irradiated, Laboratory-Reared Flies in Field Cages, *Annals of the Entomological Society of America* Jan 1983

Index

A
advisory committee meetings, 83, 90, 139, 193, 230, 241
aerial malathion spraying, 32, 88, 103, 264
agricultural commissioner, 11, 25, 102, 188, 203
Agricultural Council, 38, 123
Agricultural Research Service (ARS), 19, 82, 205
Agosta, Gary, 180, 199
airports, 11, 52, 101, 124, 161, 175, 187, 194
Alameda County, 64, 115, 210, 221, 246
Apricots, 10, 28, 37, 112, 120, 145, 218, 234
April emergence, 109, 116
Assemblymember John Thurman, 36, 53, 84, 102, 215, 226
Attorney General's Office, 89, 121, 142, 172, 186, 255, 267

B
Bay Area, 34, 37, 70, 84, 126, 135, 156, 193, 242, 261

Beilenson, Senator Anthony C, 17, 20, 38, 270
biological control, 35, 95, 128, 134, 203, 365, 271
Bird, Rose, See Secretary Rose Bird, 21, 26, 262
birth defects, 35, 104, 133, 256b
Block, See Secretary John Block
blockade, 93, 172, 185, 190, 202
Boulder Creek, 210, 221, 246
Bowman, Don, 147
Brown, former Governor, Pat, 140
Brown Speaker Willie, 141, 215, 227
bullet hole, 195, 290

C
California
        birth defects monitoring program, 256.
        Farm Bureau, 36, 134, 141, 211, 225
        Highway Patrol (CHP), 97, 138, 143, 148, 185, 244
        Legislature, 10. 15, 36, 38, 54, 100, 122, 204, 260
        Resources Agency, 123, 132, 143, 190, 221

Caltrans, 55, 62 ,66, 72, 143, 149, 166, 174
California Grape and Tree Fruit League, 38, 172
Campbell, Scot 92

314

315

professionals, 174, 188, 202

programs, 14, 123, 246, 264

errors, 125, 204, 250-252

Evergreen Helicopters, 114, 173, 179, 191, 243, 244

F

farm workers, 15, 22, 24, 34, 214, 264

Farnham, George, 105-6, 266

FAA 30, 148

FDA (Food and Drug Administration), 104, 190

Federal Emergency Management Agency (FEMA), 192

Fertile, release, 234

fixed-wing planes, 89, 101, 113, 1190, 211, 214, 216, 217, 221, 232, 244,

Florida, 9, 12, 14, 21, 30, 37, 39, 74, 79, 84, 95, 104, 113, 131 149, 177, 185, 205, 210,213

foothills, 166, 191, 208

Ford, Harvey, 33, 121, 198, 212, 217, 219, 225, 230, 257

fruit collection, 59, 71, 83, 97, 120, 153

fruit-stripping, 31, 48, 52, 55, 65, 75, 78, 124, 132, 134, 140, 142, 149, 154, 180, 184, 187, 193, 196, 208, 212, 250

G

Getz, Charlie, 160, 163

Gilstrap, Dr. Frank, 101,141, 151, 202, 206, 248

Governor Jerry Brown
Inauguration 1975, 15
Brown's decision, 132, 140, 152, 204
Declarations of Emergency, 137, 150
Impeachment threat, 215, 221, 226, 229

Gray Davis, 123, 126, 132, 216, 221, 226, 229

ground temperatures, 95, 241, 246

growers, 10., 38, 81, 87, 93, 146, 186, 188, 198, 220, 224, 254

Gypsy Moth, 29, 113, 114,149

H

Hallett, Carol, Assemblymember and Minority Leader, 141, 190, 209, 212-217, 221, 224-229

Hammond, Rich, 143-144, 181, 210

Hawaii, 9, 18, 23, 27, 35, 73, 78, 85, 90, 94, 110, 204, 233, 250, 257, 271

Made in the USA
Las Vegas, NV
20 September 2024

eb2c5806-6f0e-470a-8943-92cf77d9b09bR01

.